W9-ABG-391

Talking Difference

Gender and Psychology
Feminist and Critical Perspectives

Series editor: Sue Wilkinson

This international series provides a forum for research focused on gender issues in – and beyond – psychology, with a particular emphasis on feminist and critical analyses. It encourages contributions which explore psychological topics where gender is central; which critically interrogate psychology as a discipline and as a professional base; and which develop feminist interventions in theory and practice. The series objective is to present innovative research on gender in the context of the broader implications for developing both critical psychology and feminism.

Sue Wilkinson teaches social psychology and women's studies at Loughborough University. She is also Editor of *Feminism and Psychology: An International Journal*.

Also in this series

Subjectivity and Method in Psychology
Wendy Hollway

Feminists and Psychological Practice
edited by Erica Burman

Feminist Groupwork
Sandra Butler and Claire Wintram

Motherhood: Meanings, Practices and Ideologies
edited by Ann Phoenix, Anne Woollett and Eva Lloyd

Emotion and Gender: Constructing Meaning from Memory
June Crawford, Susan Kippax, Jenny Onyx, Una Gault and Pam Benton

Women and AIDS: Psychological Perspectives
edited by Corinne Squire

Attitudes toward Rape: Feminist and Social Psychological Perspectives
Colleen A. Ward

Feminism and Discourse: Psychological Perspectives
edited by Sue Wilkinson and Celia Kitzinger

Talking Difference

On Gender and Language

Mary Crawford

SAGE Publications
London • Thousand Oaks • New Delhi

First published 1995
Reprinted 1996

SAGE Publications Ltd
6 Bonhill Street
London EC2A 4PU

SAGE Publications Inc
2455 Teller Road
Thousand Oaks, California 91320

SAGE Publications India Pvt Ltd
32, M-Block Market
Greater Kailash – I
New Delhi 110 048

British Library Cataloguing in Publication data

A catalogue record for this book is
available from the British Library

   ISBN 0-8039-8827-3
   ISBN 0-8039-8828-1 (pbk)

Library of Congress catalog card number 95-69396

Typeset by M Rules
Printed and bound in Great Britain by
Biddles Ltd, Guildford and King's Lynn

To Roger

Contents

Preface

Like music, talk is a set of skills and a performing art. Its rich and subtle nuances are open to many interpretations. It unfolds in 'real time,' and written representations can capture only a small part of its meaning. People use talk to persuade, assert, harass, and harangue; to make love and to arouse hatred; to delight and to dominate.

Do women and men use talk differently? With the re-emergence of the women's movement in the 1970s, scholars in psychology, linguistics, speech communication, anthropology, and other disciplines began to search for relationships between language and sex, and to think about how cultural gender roles influence speech style. Is the talk of women deficient or devalued? Are women unassertive? Is speech style fixed in the gendered experiences of childhood? Why does it seem that cross-sex communication is fraught with ambiguity and danger? All these questions have been the subject of research scrutiny and a continuing source of mass media interest.

This book is not a disinterested survey of research in which studies are amassed and tallied in an attempt to pin down the 'true' sex differences in language use. Instead, I critique the emphasis on essential sex differences that has characterized research on gender and language. I explore what I believe are more fruitful ways to think about women, men, and talk. The book is aimed primarily at researchers and students in gender and language, whatever their disciplinary background. My involvement in interdisciplinary Women's Studies programs over the past sixteen years has taught me that gender – what culture makes of the (perceived) dichotomy of sex – is a complex system of classification and social control operating at social structural, interactional, and individual levels. To understand it, and to effect social change, we must speak and theorize across the traditional boundaries of our academic disciplines. My greatest hope for *Talking Difference* is that by stimulating transdisciplinary thought and dialogue, it will foster more sophisticated research and theory.

Although the subtitle of this book, 'On Gender and Language,' is a general one, my focus is quite specifically on conversation – talk as an interpersonal event. There are, of course, many other topics that could be subsumed under 'gender and language:' the representation of women, including 'linguistic sexism;' relationships between language

xii   *Talking difference*

and thought; and language change, such as the move toward 'nonsex-ist' usage. Each of these has been a fascinating area of exploration for feminist thinkers about language, and I have participated in those explorations in some of my other writings. But the topic of talk – language as social action – deserves an analysis of its own, especially in light of claims that have been made about fundamental differences in speech style between women and men.

This book builds on my earlier published work, some of which was collaborative. My interest in the assertiveness training movement is longstanding. The employment of speech act theory and the analysis of the implied philosophy of assertiveness training originated in work done with Amy H. Gervasio. The overall emphasis on gender as a complex social system rather than just an attribute of individuals, and my belief in the importance of situational determinants of behavior, have been developed in ongoing collaboration with Rhoda K. Unger. My critical approach to the history and rhetoric of psychology, including feminist psychology, has been shaped in working with Jeanne Marecek.

Talking Difference was conceived in one feminist community and brought to birth in another, as I moved from West Chester University of Pennsylvania to the University of South Carolina during its gestation. People from both communities, as well as others more geographically scattered, helped me throughout the process. My analysis of the 'date rape' talk show transcript in Chapter 4 was enriched by discussions with Mary McCullough. Jeanne Marecek, Marjorie Harness (Candy) Goodwin, Deborah Cameron, and Janis Bohan generously offered helpful suggestions on various early drafts of chapters. Series editor Sue Wilkinson provided constructive feedback and an abundance of patience. Jeri Barber transcribed the date rape text from audio tape, and Kathleen Anderson helped to annotate it. Mary McCullough, Judith James, and Gabriela Imreh offered whatever I needed to keep me going, from cups of tea to an afternoon of roller blading to a serious shopping trip. The graduate students in women's studies at the University of South Carolina have been a constant source of energy and insight. Stopping my writing to go to class usually turned out to have surprising bonuses. Lori Fitton, graduate assistant *extraordinaire*, assisted me daily, always with calm competence, humor, and a 'can-do' attitude. In the process I suspect she learned more than she ever wanted to know about inter-library loan, APA format, oddball word-processing programs, and the demands of a professor's life.

This work was also supported by a special sabbatical for the purpose (1991–92) from West Chester University. Psychology department chairs at both my academic homes have facilitated my efforts to combine research, teaching and service: Edward Pollak, Lester Lefton, and Keith Davis.

The person most central to the development of this book – and all my work – is my life partner Roger Chaffin. Because he is an accomplished cognitive psychologist and a generous colleague, his critiques of my arguments and evidence have been informed and constructive. Because he is committed to an egalitarian relationship, his equal participation in parenting and domestic life have provided me with that most precious gift, time to do my work. At this moment in history, there are no easy paths for women and men who want to be colleagues, friends, parents, and partners to each other, no ready scripts for how to do it all. Instead, there is constant negotiation leading to difficult decisions and very real sacrifices. Roger has done all that and managed to find time for love, laughter, music, and adventure as well. For his sacrifices, his support, and the joy he brings to my life I am grateful to Roger.

To all who have supported my work and believed in its value, I offer my thanks.

Columbia, South Carolina
February 3, 1995

1

Talking across the Gender Gap

People believe in sex differences. As one best-selling book puts it, when it comes to communication, *Men are from Mars, Women are from Venus* (Gray, 1992). Social scientists have helped to create and confirm that belief by conducting innumerable studies of every conceivable linguistic and stylistic variation between the sexes and by developing theories that stress differences rather than similarities and overlap (West and Zimmerman, 1985). In *Language and Woman's Place* (1975) the linguist Robin Lakoff proposed that women use a speech style that is ineffectual because it is overly polite, hesitant, and deferent. The assertiveness training movement of the 1970s and 1980s – a therapeutic fad led by psychologists whose clients were largely women – engaged perhaps hundreds of thousands of people in attempts to change their way of communicating. A rationale for the movement was that some people (especially women) suffer from poor communication skills and irrational beliefs that prevent them from expressing themselves clearly and directly. More recently, linguists and communication experts have created another conceptual bandwagon by applying theories of cross-cultural communication to women and men. According to this view, 'men from Mars' and 'women from Venus' are fated to misunderstand each other unless they recognize their deeply socialized differences.

The view of gender and language encoded in these writings and therapies is that fundamental differences between women and men shape the way they talk. The differences are conceived as located within individuals and prior to the talk – as differences in personality traits, skills, beliefs, attitudes, or goals. For the millions of people who have become acquainted with issues of gender and language through reading best-selling books telling women how to be more assertive or how to understand the 'opposite' sex, or through watching television talk shows featuring communication experts who claim that talk between women and men is cross-cultural communication, a powerful narrative frame is provided and validated: that gender is difference, and difference is static, bipolar, and categorical. Absorbing such messages, it would be very difficult *not* to believe that women and men are indeed opposite sexes when it comes to talk.

As a feminist researcher/teacher in women's studies and the

psychology of women, I have found such gender-and-language research and theory both interesting and unsatisfying. I have often felt frustrated and disappointed after reading the latest journal article or book on sex differences in (fill in the variable): question intonation, talk time, tag questions, conversational topic, joke-telling. Like many people, I love to eavesdrop. Waiting on line at the bookstore, reading a bulletin board in the hallway while a couple of colleagues chat nearby, or sitting on a park bench where mothers talk while their children play, I listen to people's talk with a little thrill of voyeuristic joy. In people's casual, everyday talk we have a tantalizing glimpse into how they negotiate the terrains of their social worlds. As I listened, and later as I recalled such talk, I tried to fit it into the theories and conceptual categories of gender-and-language research. The difficulty of this task fed my frustration with the research. Increasingly, I began to feel that research on gender and talk needed to be reframed and reformulated.

Consider for a moment how people use humor and wit to interact with their friends and co-workers. An eavesdropper will quickly see that in unstructured settings there is considerable laughter and banter. Occasionally, someone might repeat a joke they have heard. But most of the humor that people encounter in mundane interaction consists of spontaneous conversational witticisms and joviality (Graeven and Morris, 1975; Kambouropoulou, 1930). This kind of humor emerges from ongoing interaction, and much of it is a form of social play, expressed in ways as varied as kidding, punning, and story-telling. People can also use humor toward more serious goals. They can introduce forbidden topics and meanings in a safely indirect way. They can even ridicule, insult, and harass others with relative impunity ('Can't you take a joke?').

Although this sort of interactional humor seems embedded in its immediate social context, psychologists have acted as though the best way to understand humor is to bring it into the laboratory, and folklorists have behaved as though collecting jokes captures it. In the prototypical psychology experiment on humor, 'subjects' sit down alone in a room, are shown a series of written jokes or cartoons, and are asked to rate how funny they are on seven-point scales. Females and males are routinely compared and when statistically significant differences are found they are discussed and explained. When similarities are found they are considered unremarkable and not in need of explanation. In folklore studies, observers often collect formulaic jokes or observe joke-telling in everyday public settings. Much of this research presents the typical female as a person who lacks both the ability to appreciate others' humor and the desire or ability to create humor herself. It reinforces and maintains the widely held belief that women lack a sense of humor.

There are interesting questions which cannot be asked from within this framework. How do people use humor to attain conversational goals? What do ordinary people mean when they say that someone has 'a good sense of humor?' Do women (and men, and members of other social categories) have characteristic forms or styles of humor, and, if so, what functions do they serve? How is the expression of humor and wit constrained by social context and social hierarchy? Conversational humor is just one example of the dynamic nature of language use. What I want to suggest with this example is the possibility that much of what appear to be 'natural' differences (for example, men creating humor, women applauding their efforts) are created in ongoing interaction and given further reality by social science research practices. This idea may seem revolutionary to some. After all, sex differences are 'there.' If they didn't exist, we couldn't measure and record them. Yet despite many hundreds of research studies, there is little agreement on the 'real' sex differences in speech style.

In this book I will critically examine research on the question of whether women and men speak differently. This research originated from many disciplines and subdisciplines, including communication studies, anthropology, sociolinguistics, linguistics, and cognitive and social psychology. Much of it is feminist in conception: its origins in the most general sense are in the rebirth of a feminist social movement starting in the late 1960s (Thorne et al., 1983). However, for the most part research on gender and language use has failed to develop a social critique that would serve feminist ends of understanding and ending sexism, racism, heterosexism, and other forms of discrimination. In large part, I believe, this failure is the result of how the questions have been framed. Instead of trying to delineate the real or essential sex differences in speech style, I will show why that question is the wrong one to ask. I will then reframe questions about men's and women's talk, asking: How are gender relations enacted and maintained in talk? How is this enactment connected to power and status? How is it intertwined with the enactment of racism, heterosexism, and other forms of discrimination? And how have feminists appropriated talk for political change?

Gender as Difference

Should social scientists study sex differences? The question is a matter of considerable debate (Kitzinger, 1994). Some researchers maintain that scientific data can dispel myths and stereotypes about women (Halpern, 1994; Hyde, 1994) and offer corrections to both feminist and antifeminist dogma (Eagly, 1994). Others maintain that the hope of such 'truths' is naive, because 'sex differences' have no real existence outside particular knowledge frameworks. These critics maintain that rather than a neutral and objective tool for uncovering the fundamental natures of women and men, science is a social enterprise embedded in relationships of power (Hare-Mustin and Marecek, 1994; Hollway, 1994). This is a debate in which I have not been neutral (Crawford, 1989a; Crawford and Marecek, 1989; Crawford and Unger, 1990; Unger and Crawford, 1989, 1992). Each researcher's epistemological starting point affects the kinds of questions she or he believes are interesting and important (Unger, 1992). My own epistemological stance has developed over many years of thinking and writing about women and gender. Increasingly, I have come to believe that we should be asking different, more profound questions (cf. Kitzinger, 1994). What is the social and political context of sex difference research? What functions are served by various accounts of fundamental differences? What questions remain unasked because of social scientists' preoccupations with sex differences? And what are the relationships between academic research on women and the mass culture, especially the self-help industry?

Though many have questioned it (cf. Thorne and Henley, 1975; Thorne et al., 1983; Torres, 1992), sex difference has remained a dominant framework for research and theory on gender and language. I view this framework as invalid, not only on epistemological grounds, but because it has had particular, demonstrable negative consequences. I will discuss the consequences of a sex difference approach more generally before shifting the focus to a new perspective.

Gender Dichotomized and Decontextualized
Research on sex differences in language use has proceeded on the assumption that if the variables under study were clearly enough defined and accurately enough measured, the difference could be stated as fact and its meaning understood. However, difference is fluctuating and variable. Often, highly publicized sex differences turn out to be limited to particular subgroups, or not replicable in further studies. They have a 'now-you-see-them, now-you-don't' quality that seems inconsistent with using them as fundamentals of human nature (Unger, 1992; Unger and Crawford, 1992). And, even when a sex difference is defined in ways that are quite specific and quantifiable, its meaning is not socially neutral. Rather, the meaning of a sex difference is the product of social negotiation; it is culturally produced. And it is produced in the context of a pre-existing system of meanings in which difference is polarized.

Even if we accept the search for sex differences as a valid question, and the differences obtained in research as veridical, the 'truth' about their meaning is elusive, and ideologically influenced. Consider one highly publicized sex difference: mathematics performance on standardized tests. Janet Hyde and her colleagues (Hyde et al., 1990) have provided a compelling example of how the meaning of this difference is distorted as a result of treating it as absolute and interpreting it outside its social context. On average, white males do slightly better than white females on standardized mathematics ability tests. However, among African–Americans and Asian–Americans, the sex difference is smaller. Age is an important variable, too: girls outperform boys until adolescence. When odd samples (such as specially selected mathematically precocious adolescents) are removed from the overall calculations, the difference shifts in the other direction – girls slightly outperform boys. Like other sex differences, the similarity is much greater than the difference, and the difference itself may be an artifact of sampling. Yet popular media continue to dichotomize the sexes, reporting that the difference is a dualism. Headlines and cover stories stress that girls can't do mathematics, announce that estrogen destroys spatial ability, and trumpet the supposed innate superiority of boys: 'The Gender Factor in Math: a New Study shows Males may be Naturally Abler than Females;' 'Do Males have a Math Gene?;' 'Male Superiority;' 'Boys have Superior Math Ability, Study says.' One would never suspect from the headlines that there is much more overlap than difference in boys' and girls' performance or that other factors besides sex are related to test scores (Beckwith, 1984; Eccles and Jacobs, 1986; Hyde, 1992; Hyde et al., 1990). And the focus on sex as an explanation impedes the recognition that ability testing is itself a social construct:

> Excluded are whole areas of human achievement that contribute to success in school and work . . . Such characteristics and skills as intuition, motivation, self-understanding, conscientiousness, creativity, cooperativeness, supportiveness of others, sensitivity, nurturance, ability to create a pleasant environment, and ability to communicate verbally and nonverbally are excluded from standardized tests. By accepting and reflecting the androcentric model of knowledge, standardized tests reinforce value judgments that consider this model of knowledge more valid and important than other ways of viewing the world. (Teitelbaum, 1989: 330)

Consider the polarization of sex differences with respect to conversational style. Suppose a study demonstrates (for example) that women use more adverbs than men. How large does that difference have to be before we are justified in labelling men and women more different than similar? Should its importance be judged in terms of a hypothetical average woman/man, in terms of the extremes of difference, or in terms of overlap? And what does that tell us about 'human nature?' The answers to these questions involve value judgments about the meaning of difference. Value judgments are also involved when researchers attempt to see 'the big picture' by comparing the results of several studies of the same behavior. How many studies are sufficient to settle a question? How consistent must the results be? Is it important to study people of different age groups, social classes, ethnic groups, and cultures – or is it safe to assume that what is true for North American college students is true for all?

One of the most persistent methodological problems is the difficulty of separating sex from all the other factors it is related to in our society. The number of variables that interact with sex has been called the most pervasive problem in sex and gender research (Jacklin, 1981). These interactions lead to *confounding*, in which the effects of two or more variables are mixed and it becomes impossible to decide which variable is causing effects. Because sex is related to many differences in background and status, researchers can rarely know whether their female and male samples are really comparable.

Suppose we were trying to determine whether women or men use more polite speech styles. Doing a naturalistic study, in which we simply eavesdropped on people in public places, we would be faced with the problem that women and men in public spaces may be pre-sorted into categories other than sex that are relevant. Food servers, secretaries, and bank tellers are more likely to be women; head waiters, office managers, and bank supervisors are more likely to be men. It would be very difficult to avoid confounding sex with status – and social demands for politeness vary greatly with speakers' status. Suppose we decided to conduct instead an experimental study. We would certainly not compare, say, 55–60-year-old male physicians with their homemaker wives. Such a comparison would obviously be unfair because the different backgrounds, life opportunities and experience of the two groups, rather than their being male or female, could account for differences in speech style. But even when a researcher attempts to measure comparable men and women (or boys and girls) it is often unclear what characteristics should be matched and which are irrelevant. And even the most careful matching cannot circumvent the objection that women and men who are in 'identical' situations may be functioning in different social worlds *because of others' social reactions to them as women or men*. Moreover, others react not only to a person's sex as a cue for how to behave toward them, but to race, (dis)ability, attractiveness, age, and other salient dimensions of social classification.

Feminist objections to sex difference research originated in efforts to rid it of sex bias (Grady, 1981). But as the feminist critique developed, it became apparent to many that such research, even when it met requirements for being 'nonsexist,' generated more problems and paradoxes than it resolved (Crawford and Marecek, 1989; Hare-Mustin and Marecek, 1990, 1994).

Gender and Power: Erasures

Understanding of gender in the social sciences has been so thoroughly shaped by the idea of difference that it frequently seems that the only alternative available to maximizing difference has been to minimize it by focusing on evidence that women and men do not differ. Yet neither strategy confronts underlying issues of power, status, and domination (Hare-Mustin and Marecek, 1988, 1990, 1994; Kitzinger, 1994).

Power has been a very difficult concept to theorize for psychologists (Griscom, 1992; Yoder and Kahn, 1992). While power is a word we all use in everyday meanings, it is often left undefined and implicit in psychological research. When it does feature in research, the concept is often used naively 'as something directly observable and measurable, a property possessed by discrete individuals, an internalized "motive" which can be measured and then correlated with other variables' (Kitzinger, 1991: 112). The concept of social and political power is absent even in much feminist psychological research, or, if mentioned, it is in passing, as a sort of generic explanation of research results. Power is not investigated in its own right – it is used as a 'rhetorical flourish' rather than an explanatory concept (Kitzinger, 1991).

Within gender-and-language research, power has been conceptualized by contrasting a *dominance* framework with the prevailing *difference* framework. Theorists have argued that language is man-made: men control meanings and women's realities remain unarticulated and perhaps even un-thinkable (Ardener, 1975; Kramarae, 1981; Spender, 1980). Empirical researchers have analyzed how verbal and nonverbal communication expresses and maintains male dominance (cf. Henley, 1977; Thorne and Henley, 1975; Thorne et al., 1983; Zimmerman and West, 1975). As a counterpoint to the neutralizing of power relations that takes place in a sex difference framework, the naming and study of dominance in communication has been very important. However, the conceptualization of how power and status are expressed and reproduced in talk has retained much of the dualistic nature of the sex difference approach: men use talk to dominate, and women are dominated by talk. In much of this work, it is unclear whether women lack control of language because they lack social power, or whether they must gain control of language before they can gain social power (Cameron, 1985). There is a need for a more textured conception of power in gender-and-language research, one that recognizes power 'not as a monolithic, all-encompassing strategy, but as shifting terrain of professional and everyday discourses' (Kitzinger, 1991: 124).

Generic Woman

The sex difference approach treats women as a global category. But women (and men) are located along other socially salient dimensions, too – such as race, (dis)ability, sexuality, class, and age. Foregrounding sex as the only or most important difference moves these other dimensions to the background and contributes to the tendency to rely on simplistic explanations for observed differences.

Researchers on sex differences often have not considered the diversity of women as they chose samples for study or offered interpretations of their findings (Fine, 1985; Reid, 1993). It is a mistake to assume that all women necessarily have much in common with each other simply because they are women. A woman of wealth and privilege may have more in common with men of her own social class than with poor women. Women of color share with men of color – and not with white women – the lived experience of racism. Lesbians share the experiences of social invisibility, heterosexism, and homophobia with gay men and bisexual people of both sexes, not with heterosexual women. The social positions of older and disabled women are not comparable to those of young, able-bodied women. When a research study concludes that women are different from men, it is important to ask: 'Which women do we mean?' (Bohan, 1993).

Incorporating the diversity of women into gender-and-language research is a complex process. Feminist scholars realized early on that simply adding women to old male-centered paradigms is not sufficient (McIntosh, 1983; Spelman, 1988). Similarly, simply adding a sample of African–American women or lesbians, without reconceptualizing the questions and methods of our research, is not sufficient to create a feminist social science for all women.

Essential Woman
The sex difference approach is an *essentialist* approach. That is, it views gender as a fundamental, essential part of the individual. Essentialism conceptualizes gender as a set of properties residing in one's personality, self-concept, or traits. Gender is something women and men *have* or *are*; it is a noun (Bohan, 1993). The claims that women as a group lack the skills to speak assertively, suffer from irrational beliefs that prevent them from speaking effectively on their own behalf, or universally value cooperative, intimacy-enhancing speech styles are all based on an essentialist stance. They portray women's speech as relatively uniform across situations and determined by early socialization; women speak in particular ways *because they are women*.

Essentialism does not necessarily imply biological determinism, or even necessarily stress the importance of biological underpinnings for gender-specific characteristics (although historically this has been a prevalent form of essentialism with respect to gender). Rather, it is the location of characteristics within the individual and not their origins (socialized or biological) that defines essentialism. Essentialist models 'portray gender in terms of fundamental attributes which are conceived as internal, persistent, and generally separate from the ongoing experience of interaction with the daily socio-political contexts of one's life' (Bohan, 1993: 7). These fundamental attributes (comprising 'masculinity' and 'femininity') are believed to determine gendered roles and actions.

The distinction between the terms *sex* and *gender*, developed early in the contemporary wave of feminist research (cf. Unger, 1979) was a significant attempt to separate the biological (sex) from the social (gender) and thus to open ways to critique the social. However, the cultural force of essentialism is such that this distinction has not been maintained. Instead, it has degenerated into confusion, inconsistency, and terminological squabbles (Deaux, 1993; Gentile, 1993; Unger and Crawford, 1993). Instead of defining socially constructed modes of being and behaving, *gender* has collapsed into *sex*. 'The semantics of dualism spin a subtle but deadly web, one that entraps both concepts' (Putnam, 1982: 1).

The (re)conflation of sex and gender has become ludicrous. New sex difference studies, virtually identical to those published two decades ago, are now labelled studies of 'gender differences.' A lengthy report on National Public Radio discusses selective abortion based on the *gender* of the fetus; a psychological experimenter refers to the *gender* of the rats in his maze; the packaging for a man's sweater is labelled *gender: male*. As headlines on mathematics performance remind us ('The Gender Factor in Math: a New Study shows Males may be Naturally Abler than Females'), such 'gender differences' are the old differences dressed up in a new label. They are still seen as fundamentally residing within the individual and divorced from their social contexts, and they are as readily biologized as ever. Ironically, a feminist usage intended to theorize the social construction of masculinity and femininity is now enlisted to obscure it.

Woman as Problem and Therapeutic Solutions
In the interpretation and application of social science research, the processes by which difference becomes a rationale for oppression can be observed (Crawford, 1989a). When women's ways of talking (or any other behaviors) are labelled as deficient, they become problems to be remedied. Unfortunately, one of the predominant frameworks within feminist psychology has been 'woman-as-problem,' in which women are seen as acting against their own best interests through gender-influenced deficiencies or irrational beliefs (Crawford and Marecek, 1989). Explanatory concepts, such as fear of success (Horner, 1970), the Cinderella complex (Dowling, 1981), role conflicts (cf. Crawford, 1982),

and co-dependency (Beattie, 1987), frequently stop short of social critique and encourage women to find personal, individual solutions through psychotherapy. Even if they are not in a formal therapeutic setting, women are told by experts that they should be working on improving themselves and their relationships through unremitting self-scrutiny and self-analysis.

Self-help books about heterosexual relationships – *Smart Women, Foolish Choices; Women who Love too Much* (Cowan and Kinder, 1986; Norwood, 1985) – are written as though women are both ignorant and incompetent. Women are portrayed as not knowing what they need or want to be happy and lacking the skills or techniques that would allow them to have satisfying relationships with men. These books foster gender illusions by dichotomizing women and men, portraying them as fundamentally different and opposed in personality and needs. Each of the popular psychology books on relationships 'recognizes a valid relationship issue for women, and then places the blame on the woman for having allowed herself to become involved in this painful situation' (Worell, 1988: 480). In this analysis, Judith Worell could equally well have been writing about the plethora of books on communication that tell women how to interpret the talk and behavior of men (*Why Can't Men Open Up?*, Naifeh and Smith, 1984), and how to improve their own ways of talking (*The New Assertive Woman*, Bloom et al., 1975).

Within the prevailing individualistic discourse of psychology, responsibility for change is placed within the individual, a stance which fosters victim-blaming and discourages collective action. Consider, for example, the consequences of construing date and acquaintance rape as the result of miscommunication, a topic I will explore in Chapter 4. Women are encouraged to work on their communication style, victimization becomes little more than a personal problem, and attention is diverted from societal norms that condone the ownership of women and violence against them. Or consider the consequences of encouraging women to remedy inequities of pay, status, and ghettoization in the workforce through assertiveness training, a trend documented in Chapter 3. The possibility that an assertive speech style may be evaluated differently when used by a woman than by a man is not readily articulated. In the essentialist discourse of self-improvement, powerlessness is conceptualized as a skills deficit or an attitude problem. Collective action based on group discrimination seems irrelevant.

But what about sex difference research that does *not* proceed from an assumption of female inferiority? There are several lines of research within feminism that assert women's ways of thinking and reasoning to be different from men's but equally competent, perhaps even superior (Belenky et al., 1986; Gilligan, 1982). In gender-and-language research, women have often been characterized as having a more cooperative speech style than men, within a framework that stresses that cooperative and competitive styles are equally valid (Maltz and Borker, 1982; Tannen, 1990). Though these characterizations of difference may be appealing to some researchers, they may become 'conceptual bandwagons,' enlisted to maintain existing power relations (Crawford, 1989a; Mednick, 1989). Often, the 'feminine' qualities they extol are ones that benefit men (Hare-Mustin and Marecek, 1994). The dangers of extolling feminine virtues were apparent to many of the pioneers of modern feminist psychology (Rosenberg, 1982). Difference – even though originally conceptualized as evaluatively neutral or in terms of women's strength, superiority, or virtue – is almost always transformed into 'deficiency' for women. Because Western culture has long evaluated masculinity as inherently superior to femininity, claims of women's difference are likely to be assimilated into that framework (Crawford, 1989a; Hare-Mustin and Marecek, 1988).

Deborah Tannen, whose best-seller *You just don't Understand* (1990) presents a scrupulously non-judgmental model of difference, has provided an interesting example of the process of 'rendering-woman-into-problem'. In a newspaper article, she had related an anecdote about a conversation between a heterosexual married couple in their car in which the woman asked her husband if he would like to stop for a drink. He replied 'No,' and they did not stop. However, the woman was annoyed because her husband did not realize from her question that she wanted to stop for a drink. He, in turn, was frustrated because she had not stated her preference directly:

> My analysis emphasized that the husband and wife in this example had different *but equally valid* styles. This point was lost in a heavily edited version of my article that appeared in *The Toronto Star*, which had me advising: 'The woman must realize that when he answers "yes" or "no" he is not making a non-negotiable demand.' The *Star* editor had deleted the immediately preceding text, which read: 'In understanding what went wrong, the man must realize that when she asks what he would like, she is not asking an information question but rather starting a negotiation about what both would like. For her part, however, the woman must realize that . . .' Deft wielding of the editorial knife had transformed my claim that women and men should *both* make adjustments into a claim that women must make a unilateral effort to understand men. Informing women of what they alone must 'realize' implies that the man's way is right and the woman's wrong. This edited version was reprinted in a textbook, and the error proliferated. (Tannen, 1990: 15)

Framing gender as difference has produced a body of empirical research, analysis, and popularization that has reflected categorical notions of gender and has recreated those oppositional categories. Moreover, it has too often located the cause of social problems, including communication problems, in women. It is difficult to criticize or change this paradigm from within it. Calls for 'nonsexist research' too often maintain the parameters of a science that treats sex as a subject variable, decontextualizes behavior, obscures issues of power and provides the prevailing discourse with 'evidence' of women's limitations.

If exhortations to move beyond difference models are to be useful, they have to include two important kinds of analysis. First, they must show particular, concrete, social consequences of the difference formulation. Secondly, they must reframe the issues in ways that are useful and congenial to researchers. In other words, critics have the responsibility of showing what is wrong with a sex difference approach and how to improve upon it. I plan to accomplish those tasks in the following chapters using a social constructionist approach. While my approach owes much to theories originating outside feminism about the social construction of knowledge (Berger and Luckmann, 1966; Gergen, 1985), I hope to develop it in ways that are specifically feminist and that address some of the feminist criticisms of these postmodernist-influenced psychologies (Burman, 1990; Gavey, 1989).

Reframing Gender and Language: a Social Constructionist Approach

In contrast to an essentialist stance, the social constructionist views gender as a social construct: a system of meaning that organizes interactions and governs access to power and resources. From this view, gender is not an attribute of individuals but a way of making sense of transactions. Gender exists not in persons but in transactions; it is conceptualized as a verb, not a noun. Feminist sociologists, starting with Candace West and Don Zimmerman (1987), speak of 'doing gender,' and feminist psychologists are adopting the term to designate how sex is a salient social and cognitive category through which information is filtered, selectively processed, and differentially acted upon to produce self-fulfilling prophecies about women and men (Unger and Crawford, 1992).

Janis Bohan (1993: 7) illustrates the difference between essentialist and social constructionist modes of thought:

[C]onsider the difference between describing an individual as friendly and describing a conversation as friendly. In the former case, 'friendly' is construed as a trait of the person, an 'essential' component to her or his personality. In the latter, 'friendly' describes the nature of the interaction occurring between or among people. Friendly here has a particular meaning that is agreed upon by the participants, that is compatible with its meaning to their social reference groups, and that is reaffirmed by the process of engaging in this interaction. Although the essentialist view of gender sees it as analogous to the friendly person, the constructionist sees gender as analogous to the friendly conversation.

If 'friendly' were gendered, an essentialist position might argue that women are more friendly than men. Whether this quality came from biological imperatives, from socialization, or from a combination of both, it is now a trait of women. A constructionist position would argue that the gendering of friendly transactions is the product of social agreements about the appropriateness of certain behavior. The differential exposure of men and women to those contexts that elicit friendly behavior results in a linkage between sex and friendliness, and friendliness becomes gendered.

Gender-related processes influence behavior, thoughts and feelings in individuals; they affect interactions among individuals; and they help determine the structure of social institutions. When gender is regarded not as an attribute of individuals but as a system of meanings, the processes by which differences are created and power is allocated can be understood by considering how gender is played out at three levels: societal, interpersonal, and individual.

The Gender System
All known societies recognize biological differentiation and use it as the basis for social distinctions. Although there is considerable variability in the genetic, hormonal, and anatomical factors that form the basis for the label 'male' or 'female,' they are treated for social purposes as dichotomous categories (Unger and Crawford, 1992). Gender is what culture makes out of the 'raw material' of (already socially constructed) biological sex. The process of creating gendered human beings starts at birth. The newborn infant's vagina or penis represents sex – and, in middle-class Western society, if the genitals should be ambiguous medical science is recruited to surgically eliminate the troublesome variability. The pink or blue blanket that soon enfolds the baby represents gender. The blanket serves as a cue that this infant is to be treated as boy or girl, not as a 'generic human,' from the start.

Because gender is a governing ideology within which narratives or scripts are created, gender distinctions occur pervasively in society. Most broadly, the discourse of gender involves the construction of masculinity and femininity as polar opposites and the essentializing of the resulting differences. The texts of gender that have been deconstructed by feminist theorists include the narrative of romance (Radway, 1984; Unger and Crawford, 1992), the liberal humanist view of lesbianism (Kitzinger, 1987) and the rhetoric of difference and deficiency discussed above (Shields, 1975, 1982; Weisstein, 1968).

The Social Structural Level: Gender as a System of Power Relations
Men have more public power in most societies, controlling government, law, public discourse, and academics. Alternative views of gender

relations are culturally muted, and ideologies of gender can be represented and reproduced as 'objective facts' (Fine, 1985). Conceptualizing women as a culturally muted group (cf. Kramarae, 1981) implies that researchers must make special efforts to uncover and understand their systems of meanings. Understanding gender at the structural level involves this sort of searching for suppressed meanings. It can also involve analyzing how the academic disciplines participate in the social construction of gender and the muting of alternative perspectives through their rhetorical practices, their gate-keeping with respect to publication, and their theoretical biases. Far from being socially neutral, scientific disciplines are actively involved in the maintenance and reproduction of power relationships in ways that are not made explicit (Kitzinger, 1991). Finally, understanding gendered social structures involves analyzing the representation of 'scientific knowledge' in mediated communication (mass media).

The Interpersonal Level: Gender as a Cue   Gender cues are used to tell us how to behave toward others in social interactions, although much of this sex-differential treatment happens outside awareness. For example, observations in elementary school classrooms show that, although teachers believe that they are treating boys and girls the same, boys receive more attention, both positive and negative, than girls do. Boys are yelled at and criticized more in front of their classmates. Moreover, in some classes a few boys are allowed to dominate class time by interacting constantly with the teacher, while most students remain silent (Eccles, 1989; Sadker and Sadker, 1994; Spender, 1982).

The behavior of men and boys is often evaluated more positively than the behavior of women and girls. Even when a woman and a man behave in identical ways, their behavior may be interpreted differently (Crawford, 1988; Porter and Geis, 1981; Wallston and O'Leary, 1981; Wiley and Eskilson, 1982; Yarkin et al., 1982). Moreover, sexual categorization is not simply a way of seeing differences, but a way of creating differences. When men and women are treated differently in ordinary daily interactions, they may come to behave differently in return. Thus, gender can be conceived as a self-fulfilling prophecy – a set of processes by which gender difference is created, the observed differences are conflated with sex, and belief in sex difference is confirmed.

An example of self-fulfilling prophecies in conversational interaction comes from a laboratory social psychology experiment (Snyder et al., 1977). Male college students were shown a photograph of a woman who was either conventionally attractive or unattractive, and then had a short telephone conversation with her. However, the men were unaware that there was no relationship between the photograph they saw and the woman they talked to. The women, in turn, were unaware that their conversational partners had received any information about their heterosexual attractiveness. Nevertheless, judges who later heard only the women's part of the conversations rated those women who had been talked to *as though they were attractive* as more friendly, sociable, and likable than those who had been talked to as though they were unattractive.

Feminists are critical of the construct of attractiveness as it has been used in social psychological research. It objectifies women and privileges heterosexuality. This study certainly exemplifies those limitations, as well as demonstrating the manipulation and deception of research participants. Yet, by abstracting some features of social interaction from their normal context, the study shows how social actors can create their own social reality even in brief encounters. Presumably, men who thought they were interacting with attractive women spoke in ways that cued more socially engaged and 'friendly' behaviors from their conversational partners, perhaps because they shared the widespread belief that 'What is beautiful is good' (Dion et al., 1972). The men produced the behaviors they expected through their talk and probably confirmed their belief in a link between attractiveness and positive personality traits in women. Yet the 'traits' they believed in were produced by their own modes of social interaction.

The Individual Level: Gender as Masculinity and Femininity   Within the discourse of gender, certain traits, behaviors, and interests are associated with each sex and assumed to be appropriate for people of that sex. Gender is assumed to be dichotomous – a person can be classified as either 'masculine' or 'feminine' but not both – and to reside within the individual. Moreover, the masculine pole of this constructed dichotomy is the more valued.

One of the more direct ways that mainstream psychology has participated in the social construction of gendered identities has been by developing scales to measure masculinity–femininity in which the masculine/feminine roles of 'instrumental' and 'expressive' traits 'are in large part euphemisms for male dominance and female subordination' and using the scales as instruments of social control (Lewin, 1984: 198). More recently, some researchers have used the term *androgynous* to describe people who combine traits traditionally assigned to one or the other sex. A man or woman who is both self-reliant (a masculine trait) and affectionate (a feminine trait) could be characterized as androgynous (Bem, 1974). The concept of androgyny, while seemingly a progressive step beyond conceiving masculinity and femininity as polar opposites, still situates gender as a set of individual traits, and, in conceptualizing androgyny as a combination of opposites, reifies the very dichotomy its advocates attempted to challenge (Lott, 1981).

People develop their sense of self within prevailing discourses, including the discourse of gender (Shotter and Gergen, 1989). To a greater or lesser extent, women and men come to accept gender distinctions visible at the structural level and enacted at the interpersonal level as part of the self-concept. They become gender-typed, ascribing to themselves the traits, behaviors, and roles normative for people of their sex in their culture. Women, moreover, internalize their devaluation and subordination. Feminist theories of personality development (for example, Miller, 1976/86) stress that 'feminine' characteristics such as passivity, excessive concern with pleasing others, lack of initiative, and dependency are psychological consequences of subordination. Members of subordinate social groups who adopt such characteristics are considered well adjusted, even though the characteristics would not be considered healthy for adult men. Those who do not are controlled by psychiatric diagnosis, violence or the threat of violence, and social ostracism.

Much of the psychology of women and gender has consisted of documenting the effects of internalized subordination. Laboratory and field research, as well as clinical experience, attest that, compared to boys and men, girls and women lack a sense of personal entitlement (Major et al., 1984), pay themselves less for comparable work (Major and Deaux, 1982), are equally satisfied with their employment even though they are paid significantly less than men (Crosby, 1982), lose self-esteem and confidence in their academic ability as they progress through the educational system (Chipman and Wilson, 1985; Eccles et al., 1985; Sadker and Sadker, 1994), and are more likely to suffer from disturbances of body image, eating disorders, and depression (Hesse-Biber, 1989; McCaulay et al., 1988; McGrath et al., 1990).

Gender, then, is a self-fulfilling prophecy (Unger and Crawford, 1992). Women *are* different from men. Yet, paradoxically, this is not because they are women (Bohan, 1993). Each of us behaves in gendered ways because we are placed in gendered social contexts. Women encounter different social contexts from men. Women and men face different expectations and norms even for what look like identical situations. Therefore, if women try *not* to 'do gender,' they will confront the social consequences of violating these norms and expectations.

In explaining observable differences, people often make what psychologists call the *fundamental attribution error*: they overemphasize the internal, individual causes of behavior and underestimate the importance of the situation. Although psychologists' labelling of this tendency as 'fundamental' suggests that it is a universal feature of human cognition, it is culturally and historically specific (J.G. Miller,

1984). From a social constructionist perspective, we can ask how errors of attribution are socially fostered and how they contribute to essentializing women's behavior.

Keeping Sight of the System
I have conceptualized gender as a system operating at three levels in order to provide a heuristic for examining gender effects on language use. I hope that it will foster thinking across disciplinary boundaries. Gender at the social structural level has traditionally been the province of sociolinguistics, sociology, anthropology and mass communication studies, while the interactional level has been encompassed by social psychology and interpersonal communication studies and the individual level by clinical, developmental and personality psychology. In studying women and language each researcher must focus on one level, but it is best to keep sight of the system as a whole. Moreover, I hope that conceptualizing gender as a social system will help researchers in gender and language recognize that they share conceptual and methodological concerns with those attempting to understand other systems of social classification such as age, 'race,' sexuality, and class.

A Social Constructionist View of Language

From a social constructionist perspective, language is viewed as a set of strategies for negotiating the social landscape – an action-oriented medium in its own right (Potter and Wetherell, 1987). In contrast, researchers using a sex difference perspective have sometimes assumed that speech features are static in meaning. If interrupting, using excessively polite language, or telling a joke is assumed always to have the same conversational function, examples can be counted with little ambiguity, and men and women compared. Conceptualizing language as dynamic and fluctuating in response to speakers' goals and intentions in particular social circumstances makes counting sex differences more complicated and suggests the use of interpretive research strategies such as ethnomethodology (Garfinkel, 1967), speech act analysis (Gervasio, 1987; Gervasio and Crawford, 1989), and discourse analysis (Potter and Wetherell, 1987; Todd and Fisher, 1988).

A social constructionist view of language emphasizes that talk is a powerful resource that is brought to bear in influencing other people, enlisting their help, offering them companionship, protecting ourselves from their demands, saving face, justifying our behavior, establishing important relationships, and presenting ourselves as having the qualities that they (and we) admire. Whether we are operating in informal talk among friends, or in more formal or task-oriented interaction, such as a job interview or a dialogue between social worker and client, we use the same system of conversational interaction, adapted for the situation (Nofsinger, 1991). As researchers in ethnomethodology and discourse analysis have pointed out, the reality constructed through language forms the basis of social organization (Heritage, 1984; Potter and Wetherell, 1987).

When 'gender' and 'language' are thus placed in a social constructionist framework, different questions emerge than those that proceeded from a sex difference perspective. At the structural level, we can ask questions about gender along with those of 'race,' class and age. We can examine how the academic disciplines construct and justify an individualistic understanding of gender. The texts of a discipline, such as research reports and public presentations, and their representations in the mass media, become objects of analysis. Analyzing the ways that social scientists choose to represent themselves and their research in their publications is currently a lively area of study in which research literature is taken as an archive of cultural assumptions and self-presentational strategies, a resource that can be deconstructed. I will focus such a lens on various research examples, including assertion, humor and wit, and the search for sex differences in speech features.

At the interactional level, we can ask questions about how conversational dynamics are influenced through status cues conveyed by sex, and about how interactions of sex, status, and power affect speakers' options and credibility. Because the social positions of speakers differ, and language is a flexible tool, similar strategies may have different meanings. Finally, the individual can be viewed as reflecting the internalization of the discourses of gender. Here we can ask how people come to have beliefs about sex differences in speech style and about what constitutes 'appropriate' speech for women and men, and how those beliefs are encoded and enacted in one's self-presentation.

Organization of the Book

In the chapters that follow, I will give a critical history of each of four sites in gender-and-language research. I will attempt to deconstruct the assumptions about human nature, sex and gender, and the proper ways of going about scientific research that underlie the development of these lines of inquiry. I will then reframe each topic in ways that I believe are congenial to a feminist social constructionist inquiry.

Among the earliest feminist conceptualizations of gender and language is the work of Robin Lakoff (1973, 1975), who proposed that women characteristically use a speech style that is hesitant, ingratiating, and weak. Spurred by her claim, and seeing a vacuum to be filled by quantitative data, researchers began to count sex differences in the use of tag questions, empty adjectives, fillers, qualifiers, and other features of 'women's language.' In Chapter 2, I analyze Lakoff's theory and the research stemming from it. Though conducted by women/feminist researchers, much of this research was aimed at documenting the inferiority and limitations of women's speech. In conceptualizing women's speech as problematic, its implicit goal was to help women change. But imposing a masculine/feminine, strong/weak dichotomy on speech style helped obscure structural and situational influences. The approach underestimated the flexibility and nuance of usage and failed to recognize speech as a socially situated performance. Rather than resolving questions about what are the real or essential differences between men's and women's speech, 'women's language' research illustrates the paradoxes of a sex difference approach.

Partly as a result of liberal feminist and behaviorist influences in North American psychology, assertiveness training became a focus of much scholarly research and popular attention at about the same time. Between 1970 and the mid-1980s in the US, dozens of books were published on how to speak assertively; many became best-sellers. The majority of these books were directed specifically at women. However, very little research explored the actual effectiveness of the prescribed behavior in everyday settings. Researchers asked, 'What is wrong with women's talk?', but rarely, 'What happens when women change their ways of talking?' or 'How might gender expectations affect the evaluation of women's and men's speech style?' In Chapter 3, I document the influence of the assertiveness training movement and examine research on the social outcomes of assertion. Such analysis has relevance both to those who provide therapies to women and as an example of how a body of research can reflect hidden assumptions and values with respect to women, gender, 'race,' and class.

While feminists have analyzed in depth the hidden assumptions of research and therapies grounded in social learning, cognitive developmental, and psychoanalytic theories, the gendered assumptions of behaviorally based therapies, such as assertiveness training for women, have generally gone unquestioned. By analyzing speech acts outside their social contexts and prescribing an invented form of speech that violates conversational maxims, behaviorists imposed an unexamined ideology on clinicians, researchers, and the general public. Following a social constructionist line of inquiry, I conceptualize assertion as a speech act. This approach encompasses an understanding of the gender and status relationships that are created and maintained in conversational interaction.

The most recent incarnation of the 'different languages' approach proposes that women and men have different conversational styles because they have different conversational goals, which they learn in the play groups of their childhood. This 'two-cultures' (Maltz and

Borker, 1982) or 'miscommunication' model (Henley and Kramarae, 1988, 1991) is the focus of Chapter 4. It proposes that communication failures and (what appears to be) male dominance in conversation arise because men view conversation as a way to negotiate status, while women view it as a way to establish intimacy. In contrast to earlier approaches, which were based on the assumption that women's styles are deficient, the two-cultures model stresses that difference need carry no judgment of relative worth. In best-selling books that have made the approach a part of popular culture (e.g., *You just don't Understand*), researchers such as Deborah Tannen (1990) urge mutual understanding rather than attempting to change the communication style of either sex.

The two-cultures model would seem to have great potential for encouraging investigation of the ways in which subjectivities are constructed in ongoing interaction. Researchers could explore implications of relegating boys and girls to different social groupings and statuses. From a social constructionist perspective, it is because girls and boys are relegated to different social groupings that different parts of their identities/subjectivities become salient and they construct explanations of their behavior in terms of masculine/feminine dichotomies such as status and intimacy. Yet, like the deficiency models before it, the two-cultures model has collapsed differences of social identity into sex differences. The result is an approach which implies that gender inequalities would fade away if only women and men learned to understand that they are fundamentally different.

I will explore the implications of this popular approach to male–female communication by analyzing the discourse of acquaintance rape. In analyzing talk about this form of violence against women and the educational attempts to eliminate it, I will show that the miscommunication model leads to victim-blaming, deflection of accountability from violent men, and a focus on monitoring and restricting women's, but not men's, behavior.

What people do with humor in mundane interaction sheds new light on questions of how power, status, dominance, and group identity are created and manifested in talk. Research on humor, mentioned earlier in this chapter, is analyzed more closely in Chapter 5. As an alternative to the study of sex differences, I turn to recent social constructionist work on the social conditions in which people create humor and the interactional functions of spontaneous humor. Using studies of women's humor as a starting point, I analyze the social and political functions of feminist humor. The interactions among levels of the gender system are particularly salient in this chapter as I examine how humor can function to create group consciousness and then be enlisted as a means of political action on behalf of a subordinated group.

Throughout this book, the processes and consequences of framing gender as sex differences are analyzed. This process is not socially and politically neutral (Crawford, 1989a; Crawford and Unger, 1990). In a social context of unequal structural and social power, differences become deficiencies of women, possibilities for social change are dissipated into limited efforts on the part of individual women, and women are encouraged to believe that in recreating themselves they can resolve problems of inequality. As the final paragraph of a popular book on assertiveness puts it, the woman who has trained herself to be assertive is 'a new woman, a complete human being. And only this new woman has the power to stop discriminating against herself' (Butler, 1981: 320).

Research on 'women's language' framed language as a set of static linguistic features to be counted. Research on assertiveness framed it as verbal behavior to be modified. Research on humor had little to say about conversation or about humor as a strategy for social change. Even when research has been conducted in naturalistic and interactive contexts, and grounded in a model that does not hierarchize difference, as is true of much of the 'two-cultures' research, it may not transcend the limits of a sex difference approach, especially in its popularized versions. This history shows that the use of context-sensitive methods (discourse analysis, participant observation, ethnography) is not in itself sufficient to guarantee that language will be conceptualized as a socially strategic process and women as active agents. It is also necessary to study and analyze the rhetorical/textual practices of the discipline and to use all methods reflexively. Moreover, it is necessary to recognize the effects of structural inequality on language and the role of language practices in maintaining – and disrupting – that inequality.

2
The Search for a Women's Language

Early in the 1970s, the idea that women and men speak different languages began to gain increased attention among linguists, psychologists, and communication researchers. Virtually every possible source of linguistic variation – pronunciation, grammar, vocabulary, syntax – was regarded as a possible locus of sex differences. Stylistic differences, too – politeness, hesitancy, nonassertion – were seen as potentially gender-linked, and studies comparing female and male speakers surged (West and Zimmerman, 1985).

On first hearing, the notion of a 'women's language' seems odd. A person's linguistic identity is usually anchored in a language that has been conventionally named, often in close alliance with national boundaries. If I am asked what language I speak, it is acceptable to say 'English' or 'Spanish,' but bizarre to say 'Women' or even 'Women's Spanish.' Conventions about the naming of languages are so strong that it is difficult to consider varieties that do not have recognized proper names as 'legitimate' languages (Scult, 1986). Yet, heightened interest in women's issues and the need to delineate sex differences made it seem not only legitimate but imperative to categorize and label women's and men's language.

None of the researchers involved maintained that the speech of women was categorically different from that of men. In fact, they frequently cited early work by anthropologists in 'exotic' cultures to illustrate that, whatever the conventions of Carib, Chukchi, or Koasati – such as requiring women and men to use different words for the same concept – there were no such limitations in English. Instead, what was meant by 'women's language' in English was a system of sex-linked linguistic signals, a set of features used by both sexes but more by women than men. Researchers coined several new terms: 'women's language' (Lakoff, 1973); 'the female register' (Crosby and Nyquist, 1977); 'genderlect' (as in dialect) (Kramer, 1974b); and, more recently, 'gender-linked language' (Mulac et al., 1986). Whatever the term adopted by individual researchers, sex differences in language use burgeoned into an active site of research.

Language and Woman's Place: the Influence of Robin Lakoff

It was the work of linguist Robin Lakoff that began the search for the definitive features of women's speech. She introduced the term 'women's language' in a 1973 article in *Language in Society*, and made it the title of a 1978 book chapter. Her 1975 book *Language and Woman's Place* has been enormously influential, as Figure 2.1 illustrates. Virtually every empirical study of sex differences in language use for the next two decades would cite her works:

> Despite criticisms . . . her book has stood the test of time. *Language and Woman's Place* is still in print, and it is the most cited work in the field. It is virtually impossible to pick up a book dealing with women and language without finding a reference to Lakoff. Whether the author agrees or disagrees with her thesis, Lakoff is mentioned. She is often given credit as the spring-board for an author's work. Even when not cited, she is clearly the source for many who have taken up one or another of her ideas. (Hill, 1986: 18)

Language and Woman's Place was widely reviewed and discussed in both scholarly journals and mass media (for example, *Psychology Today* magazine). An interview with Lakoff appeared even in the notorious US tabloid *National Enquirer*. As one critic noted, 'When an issue is discussed in the *National Enquirer*, one may safely assume that it has penetrated the public consciousness!' (Hill, 1986: 17).

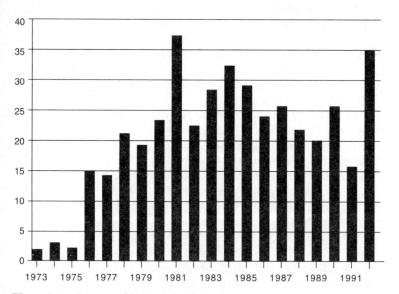

Figure 2.1   *Citation of Robin Lakoff's* Language and Woman's Place *(1975) and Lakoff (1973) (Social Science Citation Index)*

Lakoff (1975: 4–5) wrote that her goals in assessing women's language were threefold: to 'provide diagnostic evidence from language use' on gender inequity; to discuss whether anything can be done about gender inequity 'from the linguistic end of the problem;' and to provide, not the final word on sexism and language, but a 'goad to further research.' She expressed the belief that linguistic behavior reflects hidden feelings and attitudes, and is especially useful in revealing them because 'linguistic data are there, in black and white, or on tape, unambiguous and unavoidable.'

What were the arguments and claims that had such a large and lasting impact? Using introspection and linguistic intuition as her method, Lakoff (1975) suggested that a distinct group of features – lexical, syntactic, and pragmatic – distinguishes the speech of women:

1 *Specialized vocabulary*   Women are likely to use more precise terms for colors (*mauve*, *plum*) and to have richer vocabularies in areas that are traditionally female specialties, such as cooking (*sauté*, *knead*) and sewing (*whipstitch*). (Of course, men would be expected to have correspondingly larger vocabularies in masculine areas such as sports and auto mechanics.)

2 *Expletives*   Women use milder forms ('*Oh, dear!*' or '*Darn!*') while men use stronger ones ('*Dammit!*' or '*Oh, shit!*').

3 *'Empty' adjectives*   Those that convey only an emotional reaction rather than specific information. Lakoff gives both gender-neutral examples (*great*, *terrific*) and examples of those that are largely restricted to use by women (*divine*, *adorable*). Contemporary examples of the latter might include *gorgeous*, *sweet*, and *cute*.

4 *Tag questions*   In syntax as well as usage, a tag question is 'midway between a statement and an outright question':

> (a) *The way prices are rising is horrendous, isn't it?*

Lakoff proposed that tags are used when a speaker is stating a claim but has less than full confidence in the truth of the claim. In some situations, then, a tag question would be a perfectly legitimate sentence form:

> (b) *I had my glasses off. He was out at third, wasn't he?*

She proposed that women used one particular type of tag question more than men: the type in which the speaker's own opinions are being expressed, as in the first example above. The effect is to convey uncertainty and lack of conviction.

5 *Intonation*   Women use a wider range of pitch and intonation

generally. They also use exaggerated expressiveness, which Lakoff called 'speaking in italics.' Further, they are prone to use a rising intonation in what would otherwise be a declarative statement:

(c) *Excuse me, you're standing on my foot?*

The effect is to convey indecisiveness and uncertainty.

6 *'Superpolite' forms*   Women use compounded and indirect request forms,

(d) *I wonder if you would mind handing me that book.*

as well as other excessively polite and euphemistic language.

7 *Hedges*   'Well,' 'You know,' 'Kinda,' 'Sort of' and other constructions which appear to be 'an apology for making an assertion at all' (1975: 54).

8 *Hypercorrect grammar*   This involves an avoidance of terms considered vulgar or coarse, such as '*ain't*,' and use of precise pronunciation, such as sounding the final g in words such as '*going*' instead of the more casual '*goin'*.' This characteristic is related to 'superpolite' language.

9 *Joke-telling and humor*
   '[I]t is axiomatic in middle-class American society that, first, women can't tell jokes – they are bound to ruin the punchline, they mix up the order of things, and so on. Moreover, they don't "get" jokes. In short, women have no sense of humor.' (1975: 56)

   Lakoff believed that these speech features form a cluster that constitutes a recognizable *style* of speaking. Elaborating on the concept of style, she argued that the smaller units (hedges, tag questions) that make up a style function to create a unified general effect. The effect of women's style is largely negative. It is perceived as deferential, uncertain, and a reflection of 'girlish confusion' (1978: 147). It is a powerless style. Lakoff wonders why women persist in using it, since modern women are not lacking in power: 'We could shuck off deferential style just as we did hoop skirts and girdles' (1978: 149). She concludes that it functions to achieve and maintain 'non-responsibility' for one's actions, and that this goal is characteristic of women because of early socialization:

[N]on-responsibility is a form of learned helplessness . . . We could account for women's continued adoption of this style by pointing out that little girls are still frequently brought up in ways that subtly instill in them a sense of incompetence: they are discouraged from being daring, and encouraged to be docile, well-mannered, and passive. It is of course true that anyone raised this way will display these traits, and non-responsibility is by no means confined to women. But it is a characteristic feminine style, rather than a characteristic masculine style, because little girls are generally rewarded for displaying this sort of incompetence and punished if they don't . . . (1978: 150)

The Quest for Difference: Empirical Research on Women's Language

With Lakoff's call for attention to sex as a variable, the women's movement arrived in linguistic research. Her claim that women characteristically use a speech style that is hesitant, ingratiating, and weak was based on her intuitions as a speaker rather than on more systematic observation. The effect was to spark a quest for confirming empirical evidence. One of the most frequent – and indignant – criticisms of her work was that it was 'not empirical.' Hill (1986) notes that Lakoff was wildly successful in her goal of providing a goad to further research; however, she accomplished it by goading others into irritation. Similarly, Frank (1978) points out that studies of sex difference in syntax were 'inspired by indignation over the absence of empirical evidence' in Lakoff's work. Researchers began to count sex differences in the use of tag questions, empty adjectives, fillers, qualifiers, and so on.

This search for the facts, the 'real' differences in women's and men's speech, was conducted with a naive faith in the infallibility of quantitative methods for revealing the truth about communication. Researchers often wrote of dispelling falsehoods and discovering truth. After noting that 'myths' about sex-based differences are 'very much alive,' Frank (1978: 57) continues:

> In the search for the reality, we find islands of facts in a sea of speculation. Some of the facts corroborate the myth, while others refute it; some indicate little or no sex-based difference where one was expected, others turn up unexpected differences, and some suggest behavioral differences diametrically opposed to expectations. In brief, we do not yet know enough to be able to describe accurately the features of women's language in America, or even to say whether the sex-based differences found do pattern into systems which can fairly be termed 'genderlects' . . . We can say, however, that sex has been shown to be a variable which should no longer be ignored in sociolinguistic work.

Although the impetus was feminism, in the sense that the new interest in women's language occurred in tandem with the resurgent US women's movement, and the researchers were usually women and often self-identified feminists, the emphasis on discovering specific features that distinguish the speech of women and men was, paradoxically, a conservative one. Researchers were responding to a history of negative claims about women's speech. In challenging a sexist tradition, they assumed a reactive, rather than proactive, stance. By focusing on sex differences – by adding sex of subject as another variable in quantitative studies – they pursued research that remained within the accepted procedures and traditions of their disciplines (Rakow, 1986). They responded to the general sociocultural influence of feminism on the one hand and to the pressure to remain within disciplinary boundaries on the other. An important specific influence was that Lakoff framed the study of gender and language in terms of difference. Because *Language and Woman's Place* was written with wit, verve, and conviction, and because it fit pre-existing stereotypes of women's speech, it formed a powerful template for conceptualizing the issues for decades to come.

I will not attempt to draw conclusions about what are the 'real' sex differences in various speech features based on research. The limitations of such a 'box score' approach to literature review are touched on in Chapter 1, and excellent bibliographies detailing individual studies are available (Thorne et al., 1983). The search for sex differences in speech style may be a classic example of the validity of the proverb, 'If they can get you to ask the wrong questions, they don't need to worry about your answers.' To illustrate the complexities and limitations of assessing speech features and reaching conclusions about sex difference, I will briefly assess studies of one particular feature, the tag question.

As described earlier, Lakoff identified tag questions (those attached to the end of declarative statements) as a women's language feature. She proposed that tags are used when a speaker is stating a claim but has less than full confidence in the truth of the claim. Thus, the speaker can take a stance midway between a statement and a direct question:

(e) *She's really a good pianist, isn't she?*

In some situations a tag question would be acceptable from a person of either sex; for example, when the speaker legitimately does not have certainty about the truth of her/his assertion:

(f) *He's been drinking again, hasn't he?*

Lakoff proposed that women use one particular type of tag question more than men, the type in which the speaker's own opinions are being expressed. The effect is to convey uncertainty and lack of conviction about one's own beliefs or opinions.

The tag question may have seemed the ideal women's language feature to investigate empirically. Easier to operationally define than euphemisms or speaking in italics, easier to tabulate than intonation patterns, less subject to interpretation than empty adjectives or hypercorrect grammar, tag questions formed what must have seemed the perfect feature to count in a straightforward test of Lakoff's hypothesis.

Is there a sex difference in the use of tag questions? Sometimes the answer is that women use them more, as in studies of heterosexual married couples' conversations with each other (Fishman, 1980), college students in problem-solving groups (McMillan et al., 1977) and a sample of elderly people (Hartmann, 1976). Sometimes the answer is that men use them more, as in studies of professional employees in a corporate setting (Johnson, 1980), participants at an academic conference (Dubois and Crouch, 1975), and students in informal conversations (Lapadat and Seesahal, 1978). In other studies, women and men used tag questions in about equal proportions (Baumann, 1976). When tag questions were counted as part of a composite of speech features (the 'female register'), women used the style more in two out of three situations studied (Crosby and Nyquist, 1977). Occasionally one finds the same study cited as evidence for both sex difference and similarity. For example, Zahn (1989: 60) cites a study by Mulac and Lundell (1986) as showing 'no sex-related differences'; Pearson et al. (1991) cite the same study as showing that 'tag questions are more common in women's language than men's' (p. 115).

What can we conclude from this grab-bag? It becomes obvious that Lakoff's claim was oversimplified. 'The study of isolated variables almost invariably leads to further questions about the effect of setting, topic, roles, and other social factors that may interact with gender. It also raises questions about language function and use . . .' (Thorne et al., 1983: 13). I will have more to say below on how to study tag questions other than simply tallying sex differences, especially about conceptualizing tag questions as a rhetorical strategy. Here I want to emphasize the lack of closure, the *non*resolution of the sex difference question in the 20 years since Lakoff first proposed the existence of a women's language and social scientists began the search for definitive data. In the words of the researchers themselves, there is either conclusive evidence that sex differences are reliable and important:

> Not only has the language of males and females been shown to differ . . . the effect of those differences, which we call the Gender-Linked Language Effect, has been documented in a variety of settings and communicational tasks . . . (Mulac et al., 1988: 316)

Or conclusive evidence that sex differences are minimal:

> Many subsequent empirical studies have failed to substantiate [Lakoff's] claims. (Graddol and Swann, 1989: 83)

> A review of the literature shows that very few expected sex differences have been firmly substantiated by empirical studies of isolated variables. Some

popular beliefs about differences between the sexes appear to have little basis in fact, and in a few cases research findings actually invert the stereotypes. (Thorne et al., 1983: 13)

Or inconsistency of results that requires more and better research:

> [A] review of the literature suggests that this area of investigation is plagued by inconsistent findings and methodological weaknesses. Perhaps the most fundamental inconsistency is the lack of agreement about whether males and females use language differently. (Simkins-Bullock and Wildman, 1991: 149)

> In spite of all the empirical work that has been done, it is impossible to conclude with any confidence that Lakoff's nine features are the norm for most women in most situations. (Hill, 1986: 2)

> [L]ack of consistency in the studies attempting to substantiate the existence of sex-linked varieties has led some researchers to include the features described by Lakoff (1975) in the category of folklinguistic stereotypes . . . or to express some doubt as to the actual degree to which men and women differ in their speech . . . . (Zahn, 1989: 60)

Despite chronic lack of closure on the issue, few researchers have suggested that the search for sex differences may be an example of the proverbial 'wrong question' (but see Thorne et al., 1983). Even as they acknowledge that they are unlikely to find straightforward, global sex differences, many still believe that it is important to pursue the search under other names:

> [There is] a degree of 'fuzziness' of boundaries between male and female language use . . . This view, which we might think of as *fluctuating overlap*, suggests that the language differentiating male from female communicators varies with time and place. Some features that distinguish male and female speakers in one study do not distinguish them in another. In some cases, the accuracy of prediction is rather high; in others, it is relatively low . . . We believe that the *fluctuating overlap* perspective is worthy of further investigation in other communication settings. (Mulac et al., 1986: 125, emphasis in original)

Women's Language: a Research Critique

How could such a promising project lead to such inconclusive results? In 1975 it must have seemed an easy (or at least straightforward) project to test Lakoff's claims, to establish once and for all the 'real' differences between women's and men's speech styles. Twenty years later, after a great deal of research using increasingly sophisticated quantitative methods, the 'real' differences seem more elusive than ever.

A Difference is Not an Explanation

The failure stems partly from inherent limitations of framing gender issues in terms of sex difference. Simply comparing females and males on more and more variables in the absence of clear theoretical predictions is unlikely to generate useful knowledge, for reasons discussed in Chapter 1. I will illustrate some of the processes described there with examples from the 'women's language' research literature. My intent is not to criticize individual researchers, but to show limitations of even the most well-intended sex difference research.

The number of possible variables on which to test for difference is infinite. Therefore, when more and more statistically significant differences are 'found' (as they inevitably will be, given enough comparisons on enough variables, and a bias against the publication of studies reporting similarities) their meaning becomes less and less clear. Lakoff proposed nine variables for study, but researchers soon expanded the list. By 1986, Mulac et al. could list some 35 language variables that had been studied as potentially gender-linked, including such non-obvious candidates as beginning a sentence with an adverb and using present tense verbs. While Lakoff's original set of variables had a clear rationale – she believed that they clustered to form a style characterized by deference, powerlessness, and politeness – the list of variables lost theoretical coherence as it lengthened. Moreover, many comparisons gave results opposite to what was expected. Investigators had to account for more and more complex patterns of sex differences with an increasingly fragile theoretical net to cast over them.

Unfortunately, there is a readily available template for understanding sex differences when they are obtained: sex stereotypes. Stereotypes extend to nearly every aspect of human behavior (Unger and Crawford, 1992) and stereotypes of women's speech have been amply demonstrated (Kramer, 1974a, 1977). The template provided by speech stereotypes has sometimes led to what might be called empiricist revisionism, in which results counter to received beliefs about women's speech are reinterpreted to fit. A classic historical example is provided by Jesperson (1922). He argued that the speech of women – rapid, illogical, fluent – reflected a rapidity of thought and perception that were essentially shallow. As evidence that women think more rapidly but less profoundly, he cites an experiment by Romanes:

> The same paragraph was presented to various well-educated persons, who were asked to read it as rapidly as they could, ten seconds being allowed for twenty lines. As soon as the time was up the paragraph was removed, and the reader immediately wrote down all that he or she could remember of it. It was found that women were usually more successful than men in this test. *Not only were they able to read more quickly than the men, but they were able to give a better account of the paragraph as a whole.* One lady, for instance, could read exactly four times as fast as her husband, and even then give a better account than he of that small portion of the paragraph he had alone been able to read. But it was found that *this rapidity was no proof*

of intellectual power, and some of the slowest readers were highly distinguished men . . . with the quick reader it is as though every statement were
admitted immediately and without inspection to fill the vacant chambers of
the mind, while with the slow reader every statement undergoes an instinctive process of cross-examination; every new fact seems to stir up the
accumulated stores of facts among which it intrudes, and so impedes rapidity of mental action. (Jesperson, 1922: 252, emphasis added)

It is easy to imagine the interpretation that might have been constructed if the women had read more slowly or remembered less well
than their husbands!

This sort of revisionism is a historical curiosity. But the pull to
regard stereotype-consistent results as somehow more valid or legitimate remains. Consider the interpretations offered for three findings in
a recent, methodologically sophisticated study that compared male
and female speakers on 35 language features (Mulac et al., 1986). In
this study, women used more fillers or hedges, a result consistent with
Lakoff's hypothesis and with stereotypes about women as hesitant,
uncertain speakers. However, they used fewer references to people than
the male speakers, a result that is counter to stereotypes that women are
more people-oriented than men. Finally, they used more action verbs
than the men, a result that is counter to beliefs about the greater
dynamism of males and passivity of females. How do the investigators
account for these results?

The stereotype-consistent result is taken at face value: women's use
of hedges indicates 'tentativeness or uncertainty,' or perhaps 'politeness
or interpersonal sensitivity.' However, the stereotype-inconsistent
results are interpreted differently. One is not explained at all ('the fact
that the female speakers in this study used more *action verbs* than did
the males appears anomalous' – full stop). The second is dismissed on
two counts: it is probably not really an example of the variable under
study and, if it is an example, it is an unimportant one:

The comparatively large number of *references to people* is, on the face of it,
inconsistent with expectations . . . However, in the present study, many of the
references to people were indefinite in nature – 'some people,' 'anybody' – not
personalized. Furthermore, it was a comparatively weak discriminator, a fact
that attenuates our concern with its anomalous status. (Mulac et al., 1986:
124, emphasis in original)

Referring to an empirically observable difference with the term 'on
the face of it,' has the effect of setting up the reader for a discounting of
this part of the actual data of the study. The word 'comparatively,'
used twice, emphasizes the relative (not absolute) nature of the
obtained sex difference. As I noted in Chapter 1, stereotype-consistent
sex differences are often explained in ways that imply they are dichotomous. Moreover, the researchers' readiness to dismiss the unexpected

sex difference is warranted by making the 'fact' of its statistical weakness the agent of their opinions; it is the fact's doing, and not their own, that they need not be concerned with the data.

Sex difference findings never enter the scientific discourse neutrally. Rather, they are interpreted within the context of deeply held beliefs about women's natures. In accounting for their results, researchers cannot avoid being influenced by the sociocultural discourse of gender, because 'facts' about sex differences have no meaning outside that discourse. What 'counts' as an interesting or important result, and what 'makes sense' as an interpretation, are always ideological matters.

Feminists can claim no immunity to these processes. We have been leaders in analyzing the content and effects of stereotypes about women's language, with the goal of exposing patriarchal constructions of women's speech as illogical, trivial and so forth. However, attempts to characterize women's speech in opposition to cultural stereotypes may lead to an alternative set of stereotypes.

Deborah Cameron (1985) has pointed out that many feminists believe that women typically use more cooperative (and men more competitive) conversational styles. An extremely cooperative style has been expected and rewarded in all-woman feminist groups: women are expected to avoid interrupting others, to tolerate long silences as the less articulate participants formulate their thoughts, to avoid competing for the floor, to express agreement and solidarity frequently. Cameron points out that although many feminists now describe this style as 'natural' for women, it is not in fact 'natural' but has been painstakingly worked out. Often, women privately express great difficulty in adhering to the cooperative norm. Behavior achieved with much practice and limited to a specific context can come to seem an essential part of women's nature, and feminist attempts to explain it may be revised (but equally confining) versions of sex stereotyping.

Implicit Views of Language

Does Meaning Reside in Features or in their Context?   Lakoff identified specific linguistic features that she believed differentiated women and men and analyzed the social meaning of each feature, and the composite 'style,' through introspection. For the most part, she assumed a static view of language, treating each feature as having a specific function across all speakers and situations. Thus, using expletives and swear words is forceful and strong; using empty adjectives conveys triviality and lack of seriousness; using superpolite forms and hedges indicates deference and an apologetic stance, and so on. Even when Lakoff did not assume a one-to-one connection between form and function, other researchers often failed to note her distinctions and treated all examples of a feature as equivalent in testing her claims (Cameron et al., 1989; West and Zimmerman, 1985).

From a social constructionist perspective, however, the relationship between the form of an utterance and its function is not simple. In director Nancy Savoca's 1991 film *Dogfight*, four young US Marines are portrayed on the eve of their departure for Vietnam in 1963. Their constant use of strong expletives (e.g., 'fucking' as an all-purpose adjective) is used by the film-maker to convey a fragile solidarity among the four. Despite their bravado, and their attempts at predatory behavior toward women, these 19-year-old Marines are still innocents. The viewer is all too aware of what awaits them in Vietnam. Their vulnerability, rather than their power, is apparent every time one of them responds to a buddy's suggestion with '*Out-fucking-standing!*' Of course, film dialogue is not the same as naturally occurring speech. But it is interesting that the film-maker is able to convey an unconventional interpretation of men's actions through having them use a conventional feature of 'men's language.' The interpretation depends on the viewer being able to read swearing as having multiple meanings.

Multiple meanings can be assigned to all the features Lakoff proposed. In Chapter 3, I will discuss how and why people of both sexes use polite, indirect forms to make requests of others; for now, I will note that these forms have other important functions besides conveying deference. The same is true for hedges. Edwards and Potter (1992) provide an excellent analysis of a hedged speech performance from Oliver North's testimony in the Iran–Contra hearings. North, required to testify, is in the (possibly incriminating) position of having known about illegal arms shipments. Asked to describe his role and understanding of a certain transaction, North replies as follows:

> Ahm, I'm working without (.) refreshed recall, uh, let me do the best I can teh, (..) remember back teh that (.) period of time (...) I h'd had several meetings uh with Mister Ledeen?, (.) which led to a meeting (.) or two (..) with two Israeli citizens, (.) private citizens (..) an' then a subsequent meeting (.) as I recall (..) with Mister Ghobanifar (...) that in turn led to a meeting with Mister Kimche (..) an' I believe all these took place (.) prior to (..) the September shipment. (Edwards and Potter, 1992: 43)

In this brief extract we can see examples of prototypical hedges ('I believe') as well as more elaborate ones ('Let me do the best I can,' 'as I recall,' 'a meeting (.) or two'). We can also see other women's language features, such as question intonation with a declarative statement ('with Mister Ledeen?') and fillers (ahm, uh). In analyzing this extract (from Bogen and Lynch, 1989), Edwards and Potter propose that North displays himself as a cooperative, truth-telling witness, while at the same time leaving himself room to deny his own accountability should future testimony or evidence contradict his account. By hedging about his memory, North is able to leave himself room to maneuver as the hearings progress. 'North's testimony is a subtle discursive achievement, the deployment of truth and fallibility as rhetoric, . . . a hedge against the undermining of his testimony in cross-examination' (1992: 44).

Considering North's speech as an example of 'women's language' raises several very interesting questions. At the most basic level, it illustrates the practical difficulties of the feature-counting approach when applied to naturally occurring speech. What exactly counts as a 'hedge' in this extract? It also raises questions of interpretation and meaning. Can North be said to be using a 'powerless' style? He is, after all, in a difficult position, called to testify about his involvement in illegal activities and facing possibly severe sanctions. It could be argued that his power with respect to his questioners is indeed low, and that his use of prototypical women's language features is evidence that Lakoff is right; perhaps women's language is perceived as powerless because it is characteristic of powerless people. On the other hand, we can hardly argue that North, a white male of privilege and a US Marine officer, is in general a member of a powerless class of people; nor is it likely that his style is the result of early socialization. Powerlessness here is relative and situationally specific, not an essential property of an individual or class of people.

It could also be argued that North's style expresses deference and nonresponsibility, the quintessential functions of women's language. Certainly he is subtly disclaiming responsibility for the accuracy of his memory. Again, however, we could hardly argue that this is because he has been socialized to be incapable of accepting responsibility. As Edwards and Potter point out, North's nonresponsibility is a sophisticated discursive strategy that may, in the long run, serve North's interests very well. In sum, this extract shows 'women's language' being used (by a man, in this case) in ways that could not be adequately understood by counting features and assigning them to fixed categories of meaning. To understand North's testimony, we must start by viewing language as goal-directed social action (Edwards and Potter, 1992; West and Zimmerman, 1985).

Is Speech Style Inflexible and is Socialization the Culprit?   Lakoff was interested primarily in the characteristics, not the origins, of women's speech. When she attended to origins, she relied on a social learning model: women speak a hesitant, powerless, and deferential language because they have been socialized from early childhood to do so. Little girls are encouraged to be docile, well mannered, and passive; they are rewarded for displaying linguistic incompetence (Lakoff, 1978). In the next chapter, I will show how a similar explanation of women's speech was used to justify mass resocialization in the assertiveness training movement. For now, I want to note two characteristics of the social-ization explanations. First, the locus of communication difficulties is placed squarely within the individual woman – the woman-as-problem orientation described in Chapter 1. If she is not heard when she speaks, or if her words are interpreted negatively, it is her past conditioning that is to blame, and she who must change. Secondly, women's style is conceived as relatively inflexible across situations. It represents a lim-ited repertoire of communication skills that works to women's disadvantage in many or most contexts. Both these characteristics essentialize women's talk.

In a 1990 book on language and power, Lakoff continues to stress the inflexibility of the style. Although its origins are in conditions of powerlessness, she maintains that it persists even when such conditions do not prevail:

> Women's language was originally defined as a language spoken by those without access to power. But it is used by its speakers even with those over whom they do have power: with their children, for instance. And women who have achieved power in business and the professions still use it to some degree. (Lakoff, 1990: 206)

This account almost certainly underestimates the flexibility of speak-ers to adapt their language style to different situations. Work on speech accommodation theory has shown that nuances of accent change with the characteristics of one's interaction partner (Thakerar et al., 1982). Research on adults' language to children shows that (depending on cul-ture and class) speakers may adopt a special register of simplified syntax and exaggerated intonation; of course, they can readily switch registers when they turn to speak to an adult (Ochs, 1992; Ochs and Schieffelin, 1984). Even semantic meaning in the most basic sense is affected by context (Clark, 1992). For example, novel word usages emerge from the shared social context of speaker and hearer, and may remain specific to that context. To use one of Clark's examples: 'Imagine that Ed and I have a mutual friend named Max, who has the odd occasional urge to sneak up behind people and stroke the back of their legs with a teapot. One day Ed tells me, *Well, this time Max has gone too far. He tried to teapot a policeman*' (1992: 309). Here, the meaning of *teapot* depends crucially on the social context of its use. To 'get' Ed's meaning, the hearer must have exactly the right background knowledge based in shared social experience. As a flexible, skilled speaker, Clark's hypothetical Ed would not have used *teapot* in the sense he did unless he had a reasonable belief that it was likely to be interpreted in that sense. If speakers can make these sorts of decisions, we can probably expect them to make equally nuanced and sensitive decisions about using such 'women's language' features as evaluative adjectives, exact color names, and correct grammar. There is no reason to assume that women as a group are less capable than others of flexibility and nuance in speech style .

Implicit Views of Women

The notion of 'women's language' was based on considering all women as a group – the generic woman orientation discussed in Chapter 1. In setting up an opposition between women's and men's language, it also considered the language of women as an inferior variant of men's language.

Is 'Women' a Useful Category of Analysis?

Robin Lakoff was one of the pioneers of the contemporary study of gender and language. Like others writing in the early 1970s, she spoke of women as a unified group, putting aside differences *among* women and their overlapping allegiances of class, ethnicity, religious affiliation, sexual orientation, age, and (dis)ability. Sex and gender are not, of course, the only determinants of personal identity. (See, for example, the work of Kitzinger (1987) on the construction of a lesbian identity, and the work of Fine and Asch (1988) and Datan (1989) on physical stigmatization and identity.) Nor are sex and gender the only categories by which social reality is constructed in everyday interaction. While it is true that gender is a salient social and cognitive category, other markers such as 'race,' age, or social class may be equally salient depending on the interaction context (Unger and Crawford, 1992). A large part of feminist scholarship in the past two decades has been devoted to sorting out the contributions of these other factors and their interaction with gender and with each other.

Conceptualizing women as a category was an enormous contribution of 1970s feminist scholarship, and an important counterpoint to theories that had excluded women. It was probably a necessary stage in theorizing, and scholars of that era should not be blamed for failing to make finer distinctions. It is only with the benefit of hindsight that we can see the limitations of treating women as a global category.

How can researchers best encompass the multiplicity of women's identities and group memberships in studying their language? Patricia Nichols (1980, 1983) has argued that researchers should draw from both the sociolinguistic and ethnographic traditions. From the sociolinguistic tradition, we can come to appreciate group variability (for example, the realization that speakers of different social classes in the same community may have different speech styles). From the ethnographic tradition, we can gain an appreciation of the importance of local context. She maintains that ethnographic study of women *in their speech communitie*s is the best route to understanding language style and language change. 'When we ask questions about women's use of language, we must ask also, *which* women as members of *which* social groups' (1983: 54, emphasis in original).

The pitfalls of the generic woman approach can be illustrated by looking at one 'women's language' feature, the use of standard, prestige, and even hypercorrect language. It has often been claimed (by Lakoff as well as others) that women as a group use more standard language and men use more colloquialisms, regional dialect features, and so on. At least with the groups and contexts studied to date, this has been one of the more reliable sex differences observed (Thorne et al., 1983; West and Zimmerman, 1985). Its meaning has usually been explained in terms of women's linguistic insecurity or their social roles as preservers of culture. In other words, women's use of prestige forms has been seen as deficient and/or linguistically conservative.

Nichols argues that these explanations are inadequate because they assume that women behave as 'some sort of universal speech group' (1983: 64). In her own ethnographic study of speech patterns and change among African–American communities in rural South Carolina, speech style was related to age as well as gender. More importantly, speech patterns were closely related to occupational opportunities and changed in tandem with changes in those opportunities. Because opportunities differed for women and men, speech patterns diverged by sex. For men, the best available jobs were in construction and other blue-collar occupations. For women, the best jobs were in retail sales, nursing, and elementary school teaching. The men's jobs did not require or reward use of standard English; therefore, men were able to retain the Creole language variety of their childhood, which reinforced their group identity and represented a valued traditional way of life. In contrast, the women's job opportunities were heavily dependent on higher education and the ability to interact with people outside their own communities by using standard English. Nichols' study did confirm a sex difference in language use in accordance with Lakoff's hypothesis; women used standard, if not 'hypercorrect' forms more than men. More important, it shows that the meaning of a difference is best understood with reference to the speech community in which it occurs. In this case, women's adoption of standard English features is best interpreted as linguistic innovation, not conservatism. To speak of 'women's language' outside the context of a specific speech community, Nichols maintains, is 'linguistically naive' (1983: 67).

Man as Norm, Woman as Problem   The 1970s search for sex differences in language use was a resurgence of an old set of questions, though situated now in a very different social context. From the start, women's language had been perceived as not just different, but deficient. Early theorists of language attributed women's deficiency to biological or other essential causes. An oft-cited example is Jesperson's (1922) chapter 'The Woman,' from which I earlier cited his explanation of sex differences in reading comprehension. Jesperson's claims (that women have a less extensive vocabulary, less complex and logical narrative styles, and excessive volubility without sufficient prior thought) are all justified on the basis of the Darwinian notion of greater male variability, which he presents as a 'zoological fact' (Jesperson, 1922: 253).

The 1970s explanations shifted to environmental causes, particularly to gender socialization, but remained essentialist:

> Sneering at long-dead researchers like Jesperson and Sapir has become a commonplace, but a thorough feminist critique of modern sociolinguistics has been much slower to emerge . . . In general, feminists within linguistics have been more interested in furthering the study of sex difference than in criticizing it. (Cameron, 1985: 29)

Cameron suggests that feminist sex difference research has been motivated by two goals: finding an 'authentic' female mode of expression (a 'women's culture'), and identifying the power dynamics in language use to confirm that even our speech reflects and perpetuates patriarchal ideology. I would add that research in psychology and communication was motivated as well by the implicit goals of documenting the social liabilities of 'women's language' and helping women change to a more effective way of talking. Thus, much of the research was still aimed at measuring the inferiority and limitations of women's speech – not perhaps such a great move forward from Jesperson.

Lakoff (1975) clearly identifies women's language as inferior to 'neutral' (men's) language. For example, she characterizes women's syntax as 'peculiar' (p. 14), writes approvingly about women learning to switch to neutral language (pp. 6–7), and claims that women's language both denies them the means of strong self-expression and conveys triviality and uncertainty (p. 7). She characterizes women's language as contributing to or causing women's inferior social position:

> The ultimate effect . . . is that women are systematically denied access to power, on the grounds that they are not capable of holding it as demonstrated by their linguistic behavior . . .; and the irony here is that women are made to feel that they deserve such treatment, because of inadequacies in their own intelligence and/or education. But in fact it is precisely because women have learned their lessons so well that they later suffer such discrimination. (1975: 7–8)

Lakoff is certainly not the first theorist to evaluate women's communication as limited, handicapped, maladaptive, and in need of remedy (Henley and Kramarae, 1991; Thorne et al., 1983). Nor is linguistics the only discipline within which such a 'woman as problem' approach has developed. As I noted in Chapter 1, within psychology many feminist scholars have sought to explain the social position of some (or most) women in terms of social roles and learning rather than the biological factors emphasized by pre-feminist approaches (Crawford and Marecek, 1989). In psychological constructs such as fear of success, mathematics anxiety, the 'Cinderella complex,' and co-dependency, women's shortcomings are seen as arising from sex-specific (or at least gender-related) motives, fears, or self-perceptions that cause a woman to act against her own best interests. The deficit model frequently has been enlisted to explain women's low career status. Feminist approaches to women's psychological disorders often fit within this framework as well, and psychological disorders in women are linked to gender socialization in much the same way Lakoff links language deficiencies. For example, stereotypically feminine traits such as dependency, fearfulness, learned helplessness, and excessive concern about attractiveness are thought to be linked to clinical problems such as agoraphobia, depression, and eating disorders. Within this approach, feminist therapy is conceived as a kind of compensatory socialization.

Examples of *woman-as-problem* research in psychology are very easy to generate; it has been the dominant framework within the field for at least the past decade. It also feeds a thriving self-help industry in which most of the offerings are based on the premise that women are the locus of problems for themselves and others. Although many of the theories can apply to men in principle, their prototypical 'victim,' and the group to whom most self-help materials are addressed, remains female. More or less overtly, women are told that they can be 'healed' only by accepting 'total and complete responsibility' for causing their own problems, and absolving men from any accountability for their actions (Schilling and Fuehrer, 1993; Sethna, 1992).

In comparison to the biologically determinist models of the past, which explained women's problems in terms of innate inferiorities, socialization models are often seen as less limiting and more progressive. By focusing on learned, culturally transmitted patterns of behavior, the *woman-as-problem* approach opened the way to a social critique. For example, it encouraged critical evaluation of the differential experiences provided to girls and boys in early and middle childhood.

However, the *woman-as-problem* framework has serious limitations (Crawford and Marecek, 1989; Henley and Kramarae, 1991). Inherent in this approach is that men remain the norm against which women are measured. Women's behavior is seen as problematic *in comparison to men's behavior*, and the possible limitations or deficiencies of stereotypically male behavior are not considered. A focus on women's language and style functions to emphasize that women are deviant while men speak 'the' language. When Lakoff describes women's language in explicit contrast to the more forceful, decisive, and responsible style of men, which she terms neutral language, the implicit recommendation is not that the sexes should converge, or learn to understand each other, or appreciate the advantages and flexibility of each style; it is that women need to talk more like men. For example, in countering the argument that their 'polite' language gives women status as arbiters of morality and manners, she writes: 'My hope is that women will recognize that such a role is insufficient for a human being and will then realize that using this language, having it used of them, and thus being placed implicitly in this role, is degrading in that it is constraining' (1975: 52). On the other hand, Lakoff was very well aware of the double bind that is created when women adopt 'masculine' modes of behavior, and in her 1978 work she also began to critique the limitations of men's language, points that many of her critics have overlooked. I will explore her understanding of the double bind for women below.

A second limitation of the *woman-as-problem* approach is that it frequently stops short of developing the social critique that it invites. Although a generic 'society' or 'socialization' is blamed for originating women's problems, the burden of change remains with individual women, each of whom is encouraged to maximize her own adjustment or self-actualization by finding a personal solution to 'her' problems. If conditioning or sex-role socialization is responsible for women's lack of power, the implication is that women can redress power inequities by changing themselves – as though there were no real social penalties and punishments attached to stepping out of line, and no ongoing ways to enforce conformity (Kitzinger, 1991).

Blaming early socialization serves the interests of socially dominant groups. It provides the comforting assurance that change will necessarily be slow as each generation gradually and laboriously revises socialization practices. It implies that no one now in power need change his behavior, since the problems caused by socialization are deeply ingrained in its victims rather than located in current social practices. Thus, it draws attention away from how gender inequity is constituted (and continually reproduced) in those practices.

In the case of communication, women have long been encouraged by experts to tailor their communication to men's norms. Lakoff suggests that women have to be 'bilingual,' able to speak both women's and neutral language. She advocates no similar requirement for boys and men. As we will examine in detail in the next chapter, the assertiveness training movement located both the blame and the potential solution for conversational troubles within the individual (Gervasio and Crawford, 1989; Henley, 1980).

The notion that women must be competent speakers of both their own and men's language is

> more invidious than it might at first appear. We believe there is an implicit deficit theory underlying dominant US culture, which requires (and teaches, through popular magazines) females, not males, to learn to read the silence, lack of emotional expression, or brutality of the other sex as not only other than, but more benign than, it appears. From a young girl's re-framing of a boy's insults and hits as signs that he likes her, to a woman's re-framing of her husband's battering as a perverse demonstration of caring, females are encouraged to use their greater knowledge of males' communication to interpret men's assaultive behavior . . . . (Henley and Kramarae, 1991: 23)

The idea that men's violence toward women is caused by women's failure to communicate accurately or their inability to read men's true intentions from their speech is clearly encoded in the romance novel. Romance novels are read by more than 22 million US women and form a $250 million industry each year. The standard formula involves a hero who is initially cold, condescending, and brutal. However, he actually loves the heroine, and it is the power of her love that transforms him into revealing his sensitive, passionate, and caring self. Reading the romance may be one important way women learn to interpret the insensitivity of their own boyfriends and lovers as 'evidence' of love, and to take responsibility for both their partners' and their own communication (Radway, 1984; Unger and Crawford, 1992). As I will show in Chapter 4, the idea that male violence is the result of 'miscommunication' is pervasive and difficult to disrupt.

Reframing Women's Language

The search for essential differences in the speech of women and men sparked by Lakoff's work proved inconclusive, perpetuated interpretive biases, and failed to generate social critique. Like other work which frames gender as difference, it will always reach an impasse both in furthering our knowledge about gender and in bringing about political and social change (Hare-Mustin and Marecek, 1990, 1994).

Doing Gender

When research attention shifts from linguistic features of individuals' speech to the dynamics of interaction, the effects of gender become visible in new ways. When women and men are engaged in talk, certain interactional features take on characteristic patterns.

Interruption   Patterns of interruption are asymmetrical and dependent on gender and status. In conversations between women and men in public settings, 96 percent of the interruptions were by male speakers. In same-sex pairs, interruptions were about equally divided between the two participants (Zimmerman and West, 1975). The interruption effect has been found in a variety of settings and contexts: with college students in mixed-sex discussion groups, males interrupted their conversational partners three times as often as females did (West and Zimmerman, 1983). In college faculty meetings, men interrupted women more than vice versa, and speakers who had higher status in the university interrupted more (Eakins and Eakins, 1976). However, high achieved status does not necessarily protect women against being interrupted: female physicians are frequently interrupted by male patients (West, 1984).

Topic Control   In a study of heterosexual married couples, women introduced more conversational topics, but men were more likely to decide which topics would be picked up and elaborated. Women resort to more attention-seeking devices (*Know what?* or *Guess what I just heard*). Women may offer – and men withhold – conversational support in the form of assenting responses (*mm–hm, yeah*) (DeFrancisco, 1991; Fishman, 1978; Leet-Pellegrini, 1980). These patterns suggest that women do more 'interactional work:' their speech strategies function both to hold a share of conversational time and attention for themselves and to provide support to their male conversational partners.

Talking Time   Men take more than a 'fair share' of talk time in a variety of settings: classrooms from elementary school to university level (Crawford and MacLeod, 1990; Sadker and Sadker, 1994), university faculty meetings (Eakins and Eakins, 1976), college students' discussions of a social issue (Leet-Pellegrini, 1980), and so on. This is a particularly interesting finding given that being talkative is one of the strongest stereotypes of women's speech (Kramer, 1977). Dale Spender (1989) writes of the disparity between stereotype and practice in recounting her own informal attempts to analyze talk:

> Assured and reassured by countless women and men that they have a fair share of the conversation, I have remained completely unconvinced and have gone on to make my own tapes, develop my own records, and to count for myself the space allocated to women. Not terribly rigorous as research activity goes, but richly rewarding and revealing. The discrepancy between people's perceptions (my own included) and empirical reality has become a cornerstone in much of my research . . .
> I made (sixteen) tapes of academic feminists in conversation with an assortment of academic men. I set up the concealed tape recorder, and only after the conversation concluded did I introduce myself . . . and seek permission to simply count the number of minutes taken by each speaker . . . In each case, before counting the minutes taken by each sex, I asked just one question: *Do you think you had a fair share of the conversation?* All the

women said yes, one declaring that she had had more than her share; twelve men said yes, and four said no.

When I had analyzed these tapes I found that fourteen feminists who believed that they had had a *fair* share of the conversation spoke between 8% and 38% of the time. In this group were two of the men who were of the opinion that they had *not* had a fair share and they spoke for 75% and 67% of the time respectively. Two of the women did slightly better, with one achieving 40% of the conversation time and the other 42%. Both of the men in these interactions had stated that they had not enjoyed a fair share. Given that 60% and 58% do not feel like a fair share to men, the question of course arises as to what they think they are entitled to. And what do women think is their fair share of the conversational cake? The woman who thought that she had received more than her fair share spoke for 35% of the time.

. . . I was not at all surprised by these statistics. I have always used my own life as a source for research and it seems to me that in general a woman is allowed up to about one third of the conversation time in interactions with male peers. Beyond this point, *both women and men* are likely to perceive the contribution of the woman as domineering. (1989: 9–10, emphasis in original)

Spender suggests that the perception of women as the talkative sex continues because the implicit norm is silence. 'Quite simply, if a woman is expected to be quiet then any woman who opens her mouth can be accused of being talkative' (1989: 9).

Use of Silence   Silence can be used as a device for controlling interaction. For example, Fishman (1978) noted that women gave many minimal responses expressing interest (e.g., *mm–hm*) during their husbands' speaking turns, while husbands' withholding of minimal responses to their wives functioned to express lack of interest and to control topic development. In groups, the recognized expert may exert control by saying little, thus withholding approval and forcing others to attend to subtle nonverbal cues to assess the expert's position (Berger, 1985). Jack Sattel (1983) has analyzed how inexpressiveness is related to men's position of social dominance and can be used as a method of achieving and maintaining control in both male–female and male–male interactions. In Victoria Leto DeFrancisco's (1991) study, men talked less than their partners, and their most frequent turn-taking violation was *not* to respond.

The picture that emerges from studies of interaction is one of the construction and affirmation of gender inequality. Although there is some debate about how to interpret the results of studies such as these, and the pattern of results is not completely consistent (cf. Bilous and Krauss, 1988), I believe that the most sensible explanation is in terms of men's greater power and status. That is, women and men are distributed throughout the social fabric in ways that award more public, official power to men. When naturally occurring groups are studied, women

are more likely to be in lower-power positions. Even when power is arti-
ficially controlled (as in laboratory studies that assign participants to
low- and high-power positions) or when a woman has achieved status
in a relevant domain (such as female physician/male patient interactions) gender functions as a diffuse status characteristic. Males are
accorded higher status and presumed by both sexes to have more power
by virtue of their maleness.

This explanation would predict that features of interaction would be
highly variable depending on how large and how salient power differentials are in a given situation, and on how salient gender itself is in
that situation. To understand how gender relations are played out in
talk, we would need to analyze talk within its local context (i.e., the relative power and status of each participant, the salience of gender in the
situation), its larger context (the speech communities in which the
speakers function) and the cultural constructions of gender that inform
it.

As I noted in Chapter 1, most studies of social power and interpersonal communication have conceived of power as an individual
attribute rather than an attribute of a relationship. There have been
many communication studies that measure the behavior of people who
differ on power-related personality traits, but very few that study the
influences of talking style and social power in ongoing interaction.
There is a need for measurement systems and research designs that
capture the 'give and take' between people in interactions (Berger,
1985).

From Speech Style to Speech Strategy
To treat asymmetries of interaction as 'style' differences ignores social
realities. Speakers do not speak in a vacuum. They attempt to choose
language that will 'work' interactionally. Their use of language is situated and strategic. And what 'works' depends on the social status of the
speaker and the power relations between speaker and listener.
Although I believe that the study of interactional features such as interruptions and talk time is an advance over the study of linguistic
features such as tag questions, it is important that feminist researchers
do not repeat the error of simply counting features and assigning them
a unitary function such as 'dominance.'

It would be a mistake to assume that all the gendered features of
interaction described above represent *successful* conversational dominance, or indeed, always represent dominance attempts at all. The same
speech features may have different strategic functions at different times.
Not every interruption is a dominance move; not every hedge is a
weakener. While there is evidence that people who talk more are perceived as leaders, as more influential, and so forth, there are few studies

that assess whether others are actually more likely to be influenced by a more talkative person (Berger, 1985).

Tag questions, too, may be used for other conversational purposes than indicating uncertainty (Cameron et al., 1989). Consider the following example, from Edwards and Potter (1992: 117). It is taken from the court testimony of Mandy Rice-Davies, a witness during the Profumo scandal of 1963 in Britain, which involved prostitution and espionage.

> *Counsel*: Are you aware that Lord Astor denies any impropriety in his relationship with you?
> *Rice-Davies*: Well, he would, wouldn't he?
> (Prolonged laughter from jury and spectators)

Edwards and Potter analyze how this tag question undermines the counsel's allegation that Mandy Rice-Davies must be lying about having had a sexual relationship with a member of the nobility. Rice-Davies has managed to *ironize* the counsel's construction of the story, to challenge its basis in fact, by depicting Lord Astor's response as predictable and self-serving. In particular, the tag question *wouldn't he?* signals expected agreement from its hearers. It is a way of displaying confidence in one's version of the story, and of appealing to common knowledge and common sense. The audience is invited to treat the disputed claim in terms of obvious things they already know about.

Mandy Rice-Davies' rhetorical strategy is the more impressive because it draws on the sense of an ordinary person 'using ordinary language to deal effectively with the machinations of a sophisticated lawyer and the denials of a member of the aristocracy' (1992: 118). The laughter generated by her response suggests its effectiveness on that score. Moreover, undermining another person's account of events by displaying the account as a product of their own covert interests is a particularly effective strategy, since any attempt to rebut this tactic can itself be explained in terms of self-interest. The more Lord Astor denies the relationship, the more credible Rice-Davies' account seems.

However, we should not assume that rhetorical strategies are gender-neutral. The same speech features may be perceived differently due to gendered expectations – they may not 'work' the same way for women as they do for men. Lakoff was very aware of the dilemma this creates for women, describing it as a classic double bind:

> A woman is damned if she does and damned if she doesn't . . . . The command that society gives to the young of both sexes might be phrased something like: 'Gain respect by speaking like other members of your sex.' For the boy, as we have seen, that order, constraining as it is, is not paradoxical: if he speaks (and generally behaves) as men in his culture are supposed to, he generally gains people's respect. But whichever course the

woman takes – to speak women's language or not to – she will not be respected. So she cannot carry out the order, and the order is transmitted by society at large; there is no way to question it, no one even to direct the question to. (1975: 61–2)

Considerable research has supported Lakoff on this point, and this insight probably stands as the most lasting contribution of her work. An appreciation of the differential evaluation of men's and women's speech is crucial to any theory of gendered communication (Henley and Kramarae, 1991).

Beyond a Difference Model
Some theorists and researchers who originally espoused a sex difference model have since called for more nuanced approaches. For example, the influential team of Barrie Thorne, Cheris Kramarae and Nancy Henley (1983) regard the search for correspondences between linguistic features and the sex of the speaker as a (probably necessary) first stage that can now be transcended by research that is sensitive to gender in the context of setting, roles, and other social identities such as age, class, and ethnicity. Reassessing their own use of the 'genderlect' concept, they write:

> In the first phase of language/gender research, many of us were eager to piece together an overall portrayal of differences in the speech of women and men. We invented notions like 'genderlect' to provide overall characterizations of sex differences in speech (Kramer, 1974b; Thorne and Henley, 1975). The 'genderlect' portrayal now seems too abstract and overdrawn, implying that there are differences in the basic codes used by women and men, rather than variably occurring differences, and similarities . . . Genderlect' implies more homogeneity among women, and among men – and more difference between the sexes – than is, in fact, the case. (1983: 14)

Robin Lakoff's views seem to have changed somewhat less with time. The core features of 'women's language,' and her assessment of it, remain the same in her 1990 book on language and power as in 1973. Making no reference to the research of the intervening two decades, she again states that women's speech can be distinguished by particular features: diminutives and euphemisms, empty (emotional) adjectives, hedges, questioning intonation, indirect forms, and so on. New to the list are that women have a more collaborative style and are more likely to be interrupted in conversation. The idea that women are less competitive and more collaborative in conversation may reflect a feminist stereotype of women's speech (Cameron, 1985). 'Being interrupted' is an interactional construct rather than a feature of women's speech *per se*.

As in her earlier work, Lakoff (1990) notes that women must be 'bilingual,' able to switch codes from women's language to the standard language. She remains aware of the double bind for women speakers and expresses it eloquently with examples from business and politics, such as this comment on women as political candidates:

> (I)n a system of direct presidential election such as ours, a candidate must run on the basis of style, and that style must be appealing to more than 50 percent of the voters. And a woman is automatically damned on that basis, whichever option she chooses. If she talks 'like a lady,' in a deferential tone and manner, she will seem weak, unable to stand up to the Russians (or whoever the current enemy may be). We cannot 'respect' her, we say; she cannot be our commander in chief, her finger will tremble on the button. On the other hand, if she is direct and forthright, if she attacks and ripostes, that behavior doesn't make things better. If a man running for office rips into his opponent, that's politics, that's being tough. But a woman who does the same is not a woman any more, certainly not a lady. (1990: 208)

Lakoff continues to treat women as a global category, making few distinctions of class or ethnicity. The comparisons between women's and men's language still posit a male norm – the 'standard' style – and assume that women's language is relatively ineffectual, especially in hierarchical settings. It is a strategy of the powerless, adapted to coping with an inferior social position and not very useful beyond that.

Lakoff (1990) expresses considerable frustration that issues of gender and language have proved so intractable. She acknowledges that there is still 'plenty of squabbling' about what features characterize women's speech (1990: 200). Gender is the site of 'the most vexing questions about language and power', questions that 'we keep getting tangled in, finding no clear answers' (p. 199). Altogether, these questions

> bring together some of the most agonizing, complex, divisive, and ultimately insoluble issues facing our society. It is not that we have understood them and can now go on; rather, as one generation succeeds another, as some gender-related problems become ascendant and some recede, we gain new understanding. As we peel the layers of the onion of communicative difficulties between the sexes, more onion emerges: there is no core. (1990: 199)

One way out of the impasse, she suggests, is to move from analyzing overt differences to covert ones. Perhaps the use of a distinctive women's style is not so problematic after all; instead, the real problems occur when women and men use exactly the same words in the same constructions or feature, but *mean* different things. These differences in meanings lead to communication between the sexes that is potentially fraught with misunderstanding. Worse, the misunderstanding is not recognized and remedied because it is not a surface problem (one partner uses a word the other does not understand) but a deep problem (each partner uses the same utterance in the service of different conversational goals). This *miscommunication model* will be discussed in Chapter 4.

The idea that women's language is both very different from and deficient in comparison to men's was not espoused only by researchers in linguistics and speech communication. Nor did it subside as most of these researchers moved on to new conceptualizations. Psychologists, too, developed a deficiency model using their own disciplinary constructs and methods. This model of women and language was widely disseminated in the assertiveness training movement.

Women's language, in Lakoff's view, is nonassertive. She claimed that most women would use it in a wider range of environments than most men 'because women tend to feel unwilling to assert themselves in a wider range of circumstances than men do' (1975: 59). A direct connection between Lakoff's work and the assertiveness training movement has sometimes been claimed:

> One may agree or disagree with Lakoff . . . but it is more interesting to see whether people have accepted her major thesis – that such a thing as 'women's language' exists. I believe that they have, else why did so many courses in assertiveness training sprout up in the intervening decade? (Hill, 1986: 17)

As I will show in the next chapter, however, the assertiveness training movement sprang from somewhat different roots, largely those of North American psychology, and took its own distinctive course of development.

3

The Assertiveness Bandwagon

Starting in the early 1970s, mass-market books and articles began to claim that lack of assertiveness causes problems for people and to offer techniques for becoming more assertive. Figure 3.1 illustrates the trend, with titles like *Woman, Assert Yourself* and *Your Perfect Right*. At about the same time, management and consulting firms began to offer assertiveness workshops, and books aimed at therapists who wanted to train assertiveness in others also began to appear (Egidio and Pope, 1977; Lange and Jakubowski, 1976).

Research by behaviorist and cognitive-behavioral psychologists formed the background for most of these books. Indeed, assertion seems to have been something of a scholarly and therapeutic fad before it became a popular one. Reviews of the research literature on assertion enumerate literally hundreds of studies. Some discuss the definition and varieties of assertive speech. Others describe programs for assertiveness training, or evaluate their outcomes. Others devise paper-

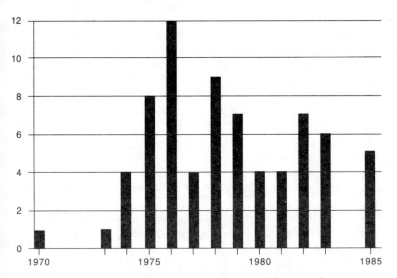

Figure 3.1   *Chronology of a self-help bandwagon: publication of assertiveness books and articles aimed at consumers*

and-pencil tests for measuring assertiveness in potential clients and report studies of reliability and validity in these tests. Still others discuss what sorts of people can benefit most from assertiveness training (Brown and Brown, 1980; Galassi and Galassi, 1978; Heimberg et al., 1977). Numerous handbooks for clinicians discuss issues of how to implement assertiveness training with people in therapy (Alberti, 1977; Lange and Jakubowski, 1976; Whiteley and Flowers, 1978).

The assertiveness training movement grew to monumental proportions. One bibliography catalogued 892 journal articles, 664 dissertations, 34 educational films and 82 (mostly mass-market) books, making a total of 1672 works devoted to becoming more assertive published from 1973 to 1983 alone (Ruben, 1985).

Professional articles were published in journals directed to practitioners (66 in *Behavior Therapy*, 36 each in *Journal of Clinical and Counseling Psychology* and *Journal of Counseling Psychology*) or researchers (59 in *Psychological Reports*) rather than in feminist journals (a total of six in *Psychology of Women Quarterly* and *Sex Roles*). Yet women were marked early on as especially in need of assertiveness training. Many of the mass-market books were aimed specifically at women buyers; some of these became best-sellers and/or were printed in more than one edition (cf. Bloom et al., 1975, 1980; Butler, 1976, 1981). In fact, women are the group to whom titles most frequently and directly appeal. There are far fewer mass-market books aimed at adolescents, old people, people of color, or other social groupings. The mass-market emphasis on women reflects the emphasis among researchers and clinical practitioners. In one volume aimed at therapists and assertion trainers, a section titled 'Applications to Special Problems and Populations' groups three chapters on women with one each on suicidal/depressed clients, group psychotherapy clients, and the elderly (Whiteley and Flowers, 1978). Another has 15 chapters on applications to various populations. These include three chapters on women and one on nurses along with four on children and adolescents and one on marital partners, divorced people, fat people, alcoholics, and phobics respectively (Alberti, 1977). The groupings suggest that women were viewed as a stigmatized population.

Because *Language and Woman's Place* (Lakoff, 1975) was widely reviewed and popularized at about the same time that the assertiveness training movement began, it is tempting to see a causal connection. However, early mass-market books aimed at women (for example, Butler, 1976) did not cite Lakoff or make explicit use of the notion of a 'woman's language.'

Why assertiveness training for women? Without exception, popular psychology books blamed gender socialization. For example, clinical psychologist Pamela Butler (1976: 6) noted that 'The acceptance of traditional femininity clearly interferes with female assertiveness.' However, authors rarely offered research evidence that women as a group have trouble asserting themselves, other than perhaps a paper-and-pencil inventory given to college students. Rather they drew heavily on stereotypes of female passivity. In the forward to Butler's book a male psychologist notes

> Raised in the deep South with the prevailing mores of the times, Dr. Butler was brought up to be 'polite,' 'ladylike,' 'passive,' and 'compliant,' even at the expense of her true feelings . . . Dr. Butler has lived through the metamorphosis from stereotyped femininity to androgyny. (Butler, 1976: 6)

A gender role conditioning rationale is articulated in volume after volume aimed at women. Women are said to carry 'early messages' in their heads

> as we tremble before employers, indirectly cajole our husbands, get hysterical with our parents, or inhibit competitive behavior. The concept of assertiveness for women is integrally linked to sex role socialization. And if women's sex role training teaches them anything, it is to be passive and dependent . . It is largely through following out the nurturant, docile 'programming' of the female role – denying their own needs and devoting themselves to winning others' love and approval – that women in particular seem to wind up with such severe deficits in assertive behavior. (Wolfe and Fodor, 1978: 141)

Another pop psychology version of the conditioning explanation was reprinted in a volume for practitioners (Alberti, 1977), thus reversing the direction of influence. In it, women are described as prone to a 'compassion trap' (i.e., too attentive to the needs of others). A quiz is provided for women to assess their weakness on this dimension. Hypothetical situations are provided: a friend arrives for a meeting an hour late, the children refuse to come in from play when dinner is ready. Responses are shown in each case for 'Doris Doormat,' 'Iris Indirect' (i.e., passive aggressive), 'Agatha Aggressive,' and the ideal, 'April Assertive' (Phelps and Austin, 1975).

A gender role conditioning model could potentially be applied symmetrically: if women need assertiveness training to counter socialized passivity, men need it to counter socialized aggressiveness and insensitivity. However, the male half of the model received little attention. This example, from a training manual's model workshop for social workers, shows how the focus on gender socialization in actuality meant a focus on women. Therapists were instructed to introduce the workshop as follows:

> Women in our society have traditionally been trained to be submissive and self-effacing. As a result of this 'training in helplessness,' many women are unable to speak up for what they feel and need. Assertiveness training can help these women act more assertively and can help aggressive persons tone

down the alienating aggressive behavior patterns they learned while growing up. (Callahan, 1980: 13–14)

Note that the client population is divided into 'women,' named three times, and 'persons,' sex unspecified, named once.

As suggested in the example above, psychologists sometimes invoked the notion of learned helplessness to explain women's self-defeating lack of assertiveness. This construct, developed in laboratory research on animals, is based on a paradigm in which animals are exposed to repeated painful electric shocks from which there is no possibility of escape. When later put in similarly painful situations in which escape is possible contingent on some relatively simple behavior, the animals fail to act (cf. Seligman, 1975). The learned helplessness analogy would seem to imply that women's supposed inability to speak up for themselves is rooted in real powerlessness which, if not current, at least existed at some time in the past. A logical inference would be to look at causes of powerlessness in women – but instead, powerlessness is treated as an attitude: '[T]he (learned helplessness) theory suggests that *when a woman's failure to act assertively has made her feel powerless* and subsequently depressed, assertiveness training would be a useful treatment for the depression' (Jakubowski, 1977: 165, emphasis added). In this account, learned helplessness is inverted; the depressed person becomes the agent of her own suffering. Assertiveness training becomes a virtual panacea for women's problems, recommended for: identity loss in newly married women, super mother syndrome, mid-life depression, depression due to loss (such as widowhood), psychological problems in job settings, psychosomatic illness, drug/alcohol abuse, and agoraphobia.

The explanatory models and rhetorical devices used by psychologists to justify assertiveness training for women are clearly grounded in mainstream (prefeminist) psychology. Robin Lakoff's linguistic analysis does not seem to have provided a direct impetus for analyzing women's speech or for a deficiency model of women's communication. Rather, linguistics and psychology seem to have arrived at the same conclusions about women's speech relatively independently. Psychologists relied on social learning theory and on learned helplessness. They assumed that women as a group are deficient in communication skills and that psychology had the answer to that deficiency. The deficiency is a relic of the past, of our misguided 'conditioning.' The implication, and the promise, is that if we do get help and are trained to speak up for ourselves, good things will happen: we will be respected and admired by others, we will get our own way more often, we will have greater personal and social power.

Assertiveness as a Psychological Construct

The Origins of a Movement

The application of behaviorism to clinical problems involving communication originated with Salter's (1949) *Conditioned Reflex Therapy*. Salter applied a conditioning model to verbal and nonverbal behaviors such as the ability to say what one feels, to contradict and disagree, and to speak directly through the frequent use of 'I' statements. In 57 case studies, he described the methods used in training verbal 'reflexes' to relieve such problems as depression, shyness, sexual problems, stuttering, and alcohol abuse. Wolpe (1958) first applied the label 'assertive' to a category of interpersonal behavior, and focused attention on the use of assertiveness training for interpersonal problems. Wolpe used systematic desensitization along with other techniques such as modeling and rehearsal in assertiveness training.

As the movement grew, it gained coherence. Behaviorally oriented therapists promoted assertiveness training as an alternative to maladaptive ways of communicating (Lange and Jakubowski, 1976; Wolpe and Lazarus, 1966). Assertiveness became more clearly conceptualized as a set of social skills amenable to training. Coming from a behaviorist orientation where techniques were viewed as value-neutral (Erwin, 1978) and language was just another behavior (Skinner, 1957), most theorists and researchers did not question the desirability of assertive speech or critically evaluate the implicit philosophy of language underlying it. Using the best tools at their disposal, they simply invented assertiveness, and began teaching this invented behavior.

Definitions of Assertiveness

Three basic definitions of assertiveness are found in the research literature. One focuses on the consequences of behavior (Rich and Schroeder, 1976). Others emphasize assertion as an expression of the self (Galassi et al., 1974; Lazarus, 1973) or as a matter of personal rights (Lange and Jakubowski, 1976). Occasionally it was noted that assertive behavior should be socially appropriate and should take into account the feelings and welfare of others (for example, Rimm and Masters, 1979). Perhaps the most succinct definition was provided by Booraem and Flowers (1978: 17): 'Assertion basically involves asking for what one wants, refusing what one doesn't want, and expressing positive and negative messages to others.'

Assertive behavior was explicitly contrasted to *passive* behavior, which was attributed to people who fail to express their true thoughts and feelings, allow themselves to be dominated or humiliated by others, and comply with the requests or demands of others even when they do not want to (Lange and Jakubowski, 1976). It was also contrasted to *aggressive* behavior, which was usually defined either in terms of its form (e.g., imperatives), its intentions (e.g., as behavior intended to dominate, humiliate or blame others), or its effects (e.g., behavior that dominates, regardless of intention) (Cheek, 1976; Rakos, 1979).

Assertion Techniques

Assertiveness training was a novel attempt to teach communication skills directly. In order to teach the rather specific ways of talking defined by trainers as assertive, talk was typically divided into types, such as 'refusals, requests, and expressions' (Booraem and Flowers, 1978). Clients were then trained in specific ways of speaking for doing each of these types of acts. The training could include coaching in non-verbal communication behaviors such as volume and emotionality of voice, eye contact, distance from other persons, body posture, and verbal fluency (Booraem and Flowers, 1978; Serber, 1977). Coaching was considered an integral part of assertiveness therapy:

> The job of the coach is to come to the asserter's aid if he or she gets stuck when practicing some situation and to give the asserter specific words to use until the individual is again able to take over the situation. . . . Coaching can be of value both in terms of teaching assertive skills and in helping to keep the anxiety level low for the individual practicing a new mode of response; consequently, its importance should not be minimized or overlooked. (Cotler, 1978: 93)

The verbal techniques used in assertiveness training contain many prescriptions and rules for constructing one's speech (Gervasio, 1987). Speech should be direct. Requests should be in the form of straight-forward questions, never indirect references or hints. Refusals should be given without excuses, justifications, or apologies. Speakers should focus on their own feelings, desires, and beliefs. To best express their feelings, they should use 'feeling verbs' and 'I–me' sentence structure; that is, they should construct sentences in which the speaker is the subject and the topic is the speaker's feelings. A few examples from readings aimed at trainers will illustrate some of the rules and the confidence with which they were promulgated.

On refusing to justify one's behavior:

> In assertiveness training clients are coached to refuse without excuses and only give reasons if they want to. Even reasons are not required. Clients are also coached to resist 'why' questions since such questions usually encourage providing excuses. (Booraem and Flowers, 1978: 32)

Other authors (for example, Cotler, 1978) teach clients that they should never say 'I'm sorry' because to do so assumes blame and guilt.

On classifying utterances into types:

> Another clear tenet of assertiveness training is that a statement is not a

request. Many clients begin assertiveness training believing that a statement such as 'I would like to go out to dinner tonight' is a request. It is not. The asserter is coached to always end such a statement with a clear request, e.g., 'I would like to go out to dinner tonight, will you accompany me?' (Booraem and Flowers, 1978: 33)

On asking for what one wants:

Assertiveness training teaches the client to ask with high frequency in order to get more of what she or he wants. . . . (Booraem and Flowers, 1978: 33)

Booraem and Flowers illustrate the usefulness of I–me statements in terminating a relationship:

The asserter is coached to say, 'The relationship is not working for me and I'm going to move on,' etc. The asserter is further coached to respond in the following ways if the partner-recipient defends or asks what she or he can do: 'It's not what you can do; the relationship isn't working for me,' 'I can't answer why; it's simply not working for me,' 'It's better for me if I move,' etc. (1978: 41–2)

Sample 'I want' and 'I feel' statements are provided by Jakubowski (1978: 159–67):

I want

I'm in a hurry and would like to get served as quickly as possible.
I'd like you to come on time for our dates.

I feel

I didn't like it just then when you told me to go on a diet.
I liked it when you helped with the dishes without being asked.

In situations where coached requests, refusals, and expressions of positive or negative feelings are not enough, clients are taught to use specific 'defensive' and 'offensive' techniques. Although many of these were more controversial than the core rules described above, they were well represented in mass-market books (for example, Smith, 1975). The following are taken from Booraem and Flowers (1978: 39); others are described in Gervasio (1987).

The Broken Record   To be used when one's assertion is responded to with criticism or a topic shift. Do not respond to anything off the point you intend to make. Keep saying, 'But the point is . . . .'

Clipping   To be used when one is being verbally attacked but the issue is unclear. Answer, but do not add information; instead, wait for the other person to make the issue clear. For example, if *A* usually makes coffee, and does not, and someone says 'The coffee is not made,' *A* is to reply 'That's right.'

The Reinforcement Sandwich   Present a positive expression of feelings along with a negative one. For example, 'I don't like what you just said and want you to know that because I want to feel comfortable with you.'

Fogging   To be used when the asserter feels that he or she is being subjected to criticism that is manipulative rather than constructive. Acknowledge that there may be some truth in the criticism – but do not explain, offer apologies, or promise to change any aspect of your behavior. A professor, in response to a student's complaints about an exam, for example, might say, 'You could be right, multiple choice exams probably *are* inherently unfair,' but offer no further encouragement to discuss or negotiate a grade change.

There was a consensus among practitioners of assertion training that, while language is a set of skills, effectively training those skills involves not only direct coaching in speech practices, but also intervention in the emotional and cognitive 'underpinnings' of speech. Thus, Alberti (1977) states that the key elements of assertiveness training are skills training, anxiety reduction, and cognitive restructuring. As part of the cognitive restructuring, clients were often told that their beliefs about assertion were irrational. For example, if a client expressed the opinion that she might lose her job if she directly refused an employer's request, she might be labelled as 'catastrophizing.' A therapeutic technique for dealing with catastrophizing was to exaggerate the client's supposedly irrational fears to the point of absurdity. 'Yes, you could lose your job, and then your apartment, and you'd be homeless and you'd starve.'

Deconstructing Assertiveness

Underlying the research literature on assertiveness was a set of values and assumptions about 'healthy' and 'adaptive' interpersonal behavior that remained implicit and unexamined. An individualistic ethic made assertion seem everyone's right. A naive belief in stereotypical sex differences guided therapy for women. The assertiveness construct disguised an implicit male norm that constructed women's speech as deficient and problematical. The social value of the new way of talking was assumed rather than examined, despite the empiricist rhetoric of the movement. Finally, the assertive speech style deviated from natural language in important ways that were not acknowledged by its proponents. I will elaborate on each of these points in turn.

Individualism versus Interdependence
The implied philosophy of social relationships in assertiveness training is one of benign self-interest (Shoemaker and Satterfield, 1977).

Individual perceptions, beliefs and feelings are valued above the maintenance and process of relationships. The ideal relationship is one of parallel self-fulfillment. Assertive techniques frequently encourage speakers to dispense with reasons or justifications for their feelings or behaviors, implying that individuals should be the sole judges of their actions. Individualism is encoded in the language of assertion techniques, as clients are directed to use 'I–me' language. The ideal of individuals taking personal stands without reasons, justifications, apologies or explanations leaves little place for a collective network of rules or values; without such a network, there is little shared basis for interpersonal negotiation when rules or norms are violated (Schur, 1976).

The individualism of the assertive philosophy may reflect the influence of the human potential movement. From this perspective, learning specific conversational techniques in order that one's own opinions and decisions should prevail is a route to self-actualization. In a larger sense, it reflects the dominant view of the self in Western culture, which is sustained by powerful ideological and structural forces (Lykes, 1985).

Feminist theorists have articulated alternatives to the notion of the autonomous self, such as self-in-relation (J. B. Miller, 1984), the self defined in terms of caring and responsibility (Gilligan, 1982), and fluidity in self-development (Kaplan and Surrey, 1984). Perhaps the most sophisticated of these alternative notions of the self is that of social individuality (Lykes, 1985), which reflects the social constructionist perspective that the self is a function of prevailing discourses. There is evidence that people who have experienced social relations of powerlessness and those who have engaged in collective social action have a notion of the self grounded in social individuality in contrast to one grounded in individual autonomy:

> Individuals from majority groups (e.g., white upper class males) whose material conditions and social relations are most likely to be consonant with individualism would be more likely to have a notion of the self as autonomous individualism. Persons in less powerful groups (e.g., women, people of color, working class people) are more likely to perceive contradictions between the assumptions of autonomous individualism and their social experiences. These individuals may also experience group solidarity or some sense of the 'givenness' of 'being-in-relation,' for their survival as a group may seem possible only in relationship. (Lykes, 1985: 364)

In the assertiveness training movement, the ethic of human interdependence and connectedness was muted by the emphasis on individual rights, and autonomy was held up as the model of mental health. Clients in therapy, as well as consumers attending assertiveness workshops and reading popular books, were urged to give up an ethic of interdependence under the guise of cognitive restructuring and relinquish a sense of self grounded in social individuality toward the illusory goal of improved mental health.

The Social Construction of a Sex Difference

Is there a sex difference in assertive skills? While there are many studies describing assertiveness training in all-women groups (which presupposes a difference), there are very few that sought to determine whether women actually behave differently from men in the situations for which assertiveness training was designed. In other words, despite adopting a sex difference framework that encouraged them to look for differences in a variety of behaviors, most investigators did not in fact look at women and men in mundane interaction.

Even from a simplistic sex difference perspective, it would seem that researchers would have recognized the necessity of conducting field studies and naturalistic observations. There are virtually no studies of behavior in the sorts of situations that appear on assertiveness inventories. The few that do exist suggest that sex differences are not prevalent. Harris (1974), for example, in a study of frustration and aggression, observed the behavior of people when someone cut into a queue in front of them. Females and males were equally likely to express displeasure to the offender. MacDonald (1982) describes similar results in a series of role-play situations.

In an interesting series of studies, Moriarty (1975) had confederates act out inappropriate behavior in increasingly blatant ways. In his first study, college students taking a verbal ability test in a laboratory were paired with a confederate who subjected them to 17 minutes of loud rock music unless they objected. Eighty percent of the students made no comment at all. Some made indirect nonverbal protests such as cupping their ears, putting down their pencils, or turning to look at the offender. According to Moriarty (1975: 45–6), most students later rationalized their passive behavior, as in the following post-experiment exchange:

> *Experimenter*: Did you tell him to turn it off?
> *Student*: No, it didn't bother me that much.
> *E*: Might it have affected your score?
> *S*: Considerably.
> *E*: Why didn't you tell him to turn it off?
> *S*: I thought about it, but I'm not that kind of person.

Reasoning that perhaps people would be more assertive in a more consequential situation, Moriarty next told students that the person who scored lower in each pair of students would then be assigned to an electric shock condition. Again, participants were subjected to the accomplice's loud rock music during the test. Again, 80 percent of students silently endured the situation. As in the first study, they denied being bothered by the music, or said they did not want to cause trouble.

Moving to a more direct confrontation between victim and violator, Moriarty then conducted an experiment in which students taking a test were confronted by a confederate who said, 'Excuse me. I was here a few minutes ago and I left my ring on the table. Did you find it?' Of course, all participants replied that they had not seen the ring. The accomplice persisted in asking whether they had seen the ring and finally asked participants to empty their pockets. Although participants offered verbal resistance ('Are you serious?') every one complied. The study was repeated in a public setting with adults who had stopped to make a call from a pay phone. Eighty percent of the unwitting participants emptied their pockets. Even when participants were graduate students in political and social science, whom the experimenters expected would be particularly aware of individual rights issues, 83 percent emptied their pockets on request.

A striking feature of this series of studies is that *all the participants were male*. While single-sex studies cannot, of course, provide evidence for sex difference or similarity, this work suggests that the notion that there is an assertive norm which only women fail to meet is spurious. As the accomplices' out-of-bounds behavior became increasingly blatant, the great majority of (educated, middle-class) males failed to assert themselves in the manner that assertiveness trainers would recommend. Instead, they relied on indirect, nonverbal means of protest, and *post hoc* rationalizations that the situation really didn't matter very much.

Studies such as these were rarely conducted within the assertiveness training movement. Rather, paper-and-pencil assertiveness inventories were developed to measure self-described assertion. Because assertiveness training advocates tended to rely on self-reports rather than behavioral observations, they failed to transcend their stereotype-based beliefs about differences.

The results of a review on sex differences in assertiveness that appeared in the first decade of the movement (Hollandsworth and Wall, 1977) are worth examining in detail for what they reveal about the staying power of beliefs about difference. Hollandsworth and Wall found 108 studies of assertive behavior in the research literature. Of these, 69 presented methodologically sound assessment data. Of these, 25 used single-sex samples, making gender-related comparisons impossible. Of the remaining 44 studies, only seven reported data separately for females and males. Thus, only 6.5 percent of the original 108 studies were relevant to the question of whether a sex difference can be empirically documented.

These seven studies yielded 14 self-report comparisons, 11 of them on college students, using various paper-and-pencil assertion inventories. The researchers used 14 independent *t* tests to compare males' and females' scores, a method which inflates the possibility of finding a 'difference' that is a statistical artifact. Even so, sex differences were statistically significant for only four of the 14 comparisons.

In a second study, Hollandsworth and Wall compared four samples of women and men on a widely used assertion inventory. The aggregate sample consisted of 408 females and 294 males. Sex differences were compared by computing a total of 192 *t* tests, one for each of the 48 items on the scale for each of the four samples – again, a method that very greatly increases the risk of finding a statistically spurious 'difference.' A scale item was considered to reflect a real sex difference if the comparison was significant for two or more of the four samples. Only 12 of the 48 items met this criterion. Males reported themselves to be more assertive in dealing with bosses and supervisors, and females reported themselves to be more assertive in expressing positive and negative feelings.

It would seem obvious that these two studies do not provide strong support for the idea of a large or meaningful sex difference in assertive behavior. They relied uncritically on self-report measures, although there is a great deal of evidence that beliefs and expectations about sex differences influence self-reports, so that they often reveal more 'differences' than direct observation in laboratory or field settings (MacDonald, 1982; Unger, 1979, 1981). They used lenient criteria (to be counted as a difference, an item had to differentiate between the sexes in only two of four samples) and statistical techniques that greatly inflated the risk of error. Even with these biases in the direction of finding significant differences, the overwhelming finding is one of sex similarity. There were no significant differences in 71 percent (10 of 14) measures in the first study, and no significant differences in 36 of 48 items over four samples in the second study. Yet the authors concluded that 'The results of the two studies suggest that women may be somewhat less assertive than men' (Hollandsworth and Wall, 1977: 220). Research such as this prompted one feminist critic of the movement to speculate that 'the conclusion of veridical differences was based at least as much on the cultural assumption that the expected differences were there to be found as it was on the self-reported sex differences that were observed' (MacDonald, 1982: 267).

Though Hollandsworth and Wall (1977: 221) tempered their conclusion ('that women are less assertive than men may be a misinterpretation, since for three-quarters of the samples, these differences were not significant'), their results are frequently cited as empirical evidence for women's assertiveness deficiency. The methods, conclusions, and interpretation of this work are interesting to analyze because they show how a maximalist stance – one that emphasizes difference – can be justified on the basis of evidence that others might equally well read as justifying a minimalist account, one that emphasizes the similarity of women and men (cf. Hare-Mustin and Marecek, 1990; Unger, 1979). The preoccupation with difference leads researchers to see what they are looking for, and thus to maximize difference.

But perhaps there are other, indirect sources of evidence that women are less able to speak assertively than men? The difference cannot be at the level of basic verbal abilities; national norms show negligible sex differences (Hyde and Linn, 1988). Differences in other aspects of communication accuracy and expressive style favor women, not men. Meta-analyses of the research literature show that women are clearly superior in sending nonverbal cues, recognizing faces, and judging the meanings of nonverbal cues sent by others. Women have more expressive faces; smile, laugh and gaze at their communication partner more; approach and touch others more; and, in general, are more attuned to nonverbal nuance and more interpersonally engaged (Hall, 1978, 1984). Reviews and analyses of the research literature show that women surpass men in social competence (Wine and Smye, 1981). Of course, as with virtually all areas in which the sexes have been compared, between-sex differences in verbal and nonverbal abilities are small compared to within-sex differences on the same measures. Nevertheless, it is clear that even within the difference framework there is no empirical basis, direct or indirect, for assuming a generalized communication deficiency in girls and women. Women as a group are not less competent communicators than men as a group.

Yet the social construction of difference continues. In a recent clinical handbook for professionals (Fodor, 1992), the socialization model is recapitulated under the heading *Male–Female Differences and Assertiveness*. The evidence cited for sex differences consists of two self-help books for women and three empirical studies that used only women participants.

Man as Norm, Woman as Problem
The assertiveness construct encoded a male norm that constructed women's speech as deficient and problematical. I have already shown how assertiveness training manuals drew on female stereotypes which have changed surprisingly little over the past thirty years (for a review, see Unger and Crawford, 1992). The stereotypical woman is easily influenced, submissive, sneaky, tactful, very aware of others' feelings, passive, lacking in self-confidence, dependent, unlikely to act as a leader, unaggressive, and uncomfortable about the possibility of behaving aggressively (cf. Broverman et al., 1970; Franks and Rothblum, 1983; Rosenkrantz et al., 1968).

Assertion versus passivity has been characterized as a 'central and stable component of sex stereotypes' (Locksley et al., 1980). The centrality of the assertiveness dimension can be illustrated by the items from the Bem Sex Role Inventory (BSRI), an instrument that was normed in the early 1970s, and thus gives a window onto perceptions of gender at the time that the assertiveness training movement was gaining momentum. When Sandra Bem (1974) asked a large number of students from two colleges to rate a list of several hundred traits on their typicality in women and men, 17 of the 20 'feminine' traits that emerged were relevant to assertion. Three items (shy, soft-spoken, does not use harsh language) refer directly to communication style. Six (yielding, sympathetic, sensitive to the needs of others, understanding, compassionate, and eager to soothe hurt feelings) describe responsiveness to others' needs and reluctance to refuse others' requests or assert one's own needs in opposition to another. Two items (flatterable and gullible) describe influenceability; five less directly relevant items describe an idealized positive disposition (cheerful, affectionate, warm, tender, and gentle).

In contrast, the speech and behavior that assertiveness trainers recommend bear a strong – and suspicious – resemblance to positive stereotypes of masculinity. BSRI masculine items – that is, traits considered more desirable for men than women by both sexes – include assertive, defends own beliefs, willing to take a stand, forceful, has leadership abilities, self-reliant, independent, strong personality, and dominant. Clearly, linguistic assertion/nonassertion is a central dichotomy in contemporary sex stereotypes. Even when a stereotype does not describe communication style explicitly, the presence or absence of the characteristic is usually inferred from language. 'Willing to take a stand' implies speaking, and speaking in a different style from 'sympathetic.'

Because the prototype of an assertive person is virtually synonymous with the stereotype of masculinity, change efforts directed at women were inevitably toward helping women (at least those who could afford therapy and educational workshops) attain stereotypically masculine behavior. Assertiveness training was prescribed for women with the implicit promise of helping them compete on equal terms with men by adjusting their speech patterns to be more like men's. This is a clear example of the woman-as-problem orientation. Rooted in stereotypes that reflect a discourse of difference, the assertiveness-training-for-women bandwagon went forward led by psychologists despite very little evidence that the stereotypes reflect clinically or interpersonally important differences.

With its attention to documenting and treating women's problems, the assertiveness training movement helped obscure the understanding that women may appear less able to assert themselves because of differences in power, status, and social roles. Women are disproportionately represented in low-power, low-status situations and roles. Speakers thus situated are unlikely to be direct and forceful. It is inherent in the definition and role requirements of a low-status role that in it one is

> nestled . . . precisely inside the most contradictory moments of social arrangements. Indeed, it is often women's work to be stuffed inside such spots and to testify that *no contradiction* exists . . . *Nothing* shatters our coherent social existences. Wives are not supposed to give away the secret of male dependence although they have plenty of evidence; secretaries are not supposed to tell about male incompetence or the incoherence they make presentable; lesbian women are not supposed to 'flaunt' their sexualities . . . mistresses are not supposed to tell about the contradictions inside heterosexuality, monogamy, and the promises of marriage; prostitutes are not supposed to tell about the contradictions of intimacy and sexuality; daughters are not to speak of incest; and maids or domestics are not supposed to talk about the contradictions of the world of paid work and family life . . . Women of all colors and classes are nestled inside these contradictory spots in which the pressures and structures of the economy rub against the pressures and structures of racism, sexism, and heterosexism. Women are sworn to both invisibility and secrecy. (Fine and Gordon, 1989: 162, emphasis in original)

Women's task has been to 'sit inside moments of social contradiction and . . . keep our mouths shut' (Fine and Gordon, 1989: 169). The realities of belonging to a group with little social power – whether women, people of color, gay and lesbian people, or any other marginalized group – and the double bind of assertiveness for members of these groups, are rarely acknowledged in the assertion training literature.

Social Acts without Social Evaluation

The fiction that situations and social roles contribute little to assertiveness is maintained in many ways in the research literature. Assertiveness is frequently measured by paper-and-pencil inventories, and the outcome of assertiveness training programs is assessed by comparing pre- and post-training scores. Thus, assertiveness is measured as a quality within the individual which can be self-assessed and self-modified. Although behaviorist researchers conceptualized assertion as a set of skills, they often essentialized the notion of skill. The idea that interactional problems within relationships that involve status and power can be resolved by changing individual 'communication skills' is an example of the fundamental attribution error in which persons are seen as much more central than situations. If individuals do not succeed in having their wishes heard and respected, it is because they lack assertiveness rather than because the situation does not enable them to exert interpersonal influence.

The trait-versus-behavioral-skill confusion is readily apparent in the assertiveness literature. In this passage, the author veers from behavioral analysis to essential trait descriptors in a single paragraph:

> Although I will use the term 'assertive person,' I do not believe there are many, if at all any, assertive people; nor are there passive and aggressive people. There is passive, aggressive and assertive *behavior*, with most people possessing some of each. Of course, many of us have developed an abundance of one particular class of behaviors and hence may be referred to as passive, aggressive, or assertive people. (Percell, 1977: 61, emphasis in original)

In contrast to the hundreds of studies assessing and training assertive skills and traits, there are very few that explore the effectiveness of assertive training in everyday situations or that ask questions about the effect of assertive speech on recipients. Nor do many studies examine the social reactions of others toward a speaker who uses formulaic assertive techniques.

The lack of outcome research is both conspicuous and puzzling. The behaviorist perspective would predict that changing one's speech style would result in 'reinforcing' or 'punishing' social responses that would affect whether the speaker would use the same speech strategy in the future. Researchers were not unaware of this implication. In the few social evaluation studies published, social learning theory was invariably the rationale provided. Responses to assertion were presumed to be important because they serve as reinforcers or punishers for the behavior, and because they serve as discriminative stimuli for producing the behavior in new situations (Kelly et al., 1980; Rakos, 1979). Researchers also justified social evaluation studies on grounds of clinical relevance, again relying on a social learning framework: if a client knows that assertion may lead to specific reinforcers and punishers, it may be easier for him or her to make the transition ('generalize') from therapy to real-world settings (Keane et al., 1983).

There were plenty of outcome studies in which a group of clients (usually all women) were pre-tested on paper-and-pencil measures of self-esteem, depression, or assertiveness, then attended training sessions for several weeks, then were post-tested on the same measures. These usually showed self-rated improvement. But the movement was promising more than just feeling better about oneself. The social learning perspective underlying assertiveness training clearly predicted that when a woman changed her speech style she could expect reinforcing social responses that would affect her ways of talking in the future. Moreover, self-help manuals promised positive social consequences, from getting one's own way to increased respect. Yet there were virtually no studies on the social consequences of assertive speech. How do people react when they are the recipients of textbook assertive behavior? When one is on the receiving end of the 'broken record' or 'I–me' language, does one respect and admire the speaker or experience frustration, anger, or feelings of having been manipulated? What do recipients think about the person who uses an assertive formula?

I decided to do some research on the social consequences of assertive speech (Crawford, 1988). I designed an experimental analogue study to assess perceptions of women and men who used assertive techniques. Adapting situations from assertion training manuals, I made up scenarios in which either a woman or a man behaved assertively. For example, one scenario takes place in an office where a supervisor habitually refers to an employee as 'kid' or 'kiddo' in front of customers. The asserter expresses mild dissatisfaction and requests that she be called by her name. The speech was identical for male and female asserters in each scenario. Participants, who were students and older adults, rated the assertive person in the scenario on 24 interpersonal assessment items (tactful, considerate, etc.). An exploratory factor analysis showed that participants were judging the assertive models along dimensions of social competence and likability, dimensions that come up consistently in other research on assertion (Kelly et al., 1980).

The most important result was that assertiveness was evaluated differently depending on the sex of the assertive model and the sex and age of the research participant. Assertive women models received the lowest likability ratings of all from older male participants and the highest from older female participants. However, the sex of the assertive model made no difference when competence was being judged.

These results strongly suggest that the meaning of assertion is at least partly in the eye of the recipient. Assertive women were perceived as competent, but less likable, a distinction not made for assertive men (cf. Kelly et al., 1980). They underscore the importance of using more diverse samples of participants than the ubiquitous college sophomores used in American social science research (Sears, 1986). If college students alone had been studied, no gender-related differences would have been revealed. The results also suggest that assertion in real-life settings such as the workplace, where women are highly likely to be interacting with older men in power, may have important, and negative, interactional consequences. It is possible, then, that nonassertion may sometimes be a positive and adaptive strategy for women.

Although there are many studies of interaction that are congruent with my results and those of Kelly et al. (1980), they are rarely, if ever, cited in the assertiveness training literature. These studies have to do with conversational dominance and assertion as gender-role violations for women. Because they measure responses to more varied speech styles than merely formulaic assertive speech, these studies are worth a brief review for what they reveal about the social sanctions imposed on 'dominant' female speakers.

How do people react to women and men who attempt to dominate a partner? To study perceptions of dominance, Cowan and Koziej (1979) constructed four audio tapes of heterosexual interactions in which dominant and submissive behavior were either sex-role congruent (e.g., a dominant husband tells his submissive wife what dress to wear to a party) or incongruent (e.g., a dominant wife tells her submissive husband what suit to wear). Dominant behavior performed by a wife was rated more masculine and less feminine than identical behavior performed by a husband. However, out-of-role (submissive) behavior by a husband was not seen as more feminine or less masculine than submissive behavior by a wife. The dominant woman's behavior was also more strongly attributed to internal causes (mood and personality), and less to situational factors, than the dominant man's behavior. Thus, at least in the context of heterosexual marital interaction, masculine behavior in a woman is more polarized and more essentialized than similar behavior in a man. Applied to the social evaluation of assertion, this result suggests that when a man responds assertively to an infringement of his rights, he might be seen as responding legitimately in that specific situation, while a woman responding in the same way might be judged to be in a bad mood or to have an unpleasant personality.

How do people respond to a woman who assertively attempts to persuade them to her point of view? In a study of the effectiveness and interpersonal consequences of different approaches to persuasion, participants saw video tapes of male or female speakers delivering speeches that were identical except that they ended with an appeal based on either helplessness or expertise (Falbo et al., 1982). The helplessness and expertise approaches had been determined to be gender-stereotyped in previous research. As predicted, speakers who used other-sex power bases were evaluated as less likable, qualified, and competent. This research suggests that one reason assertive women may be less favorably evaluated is that they are using masculine power bases when making direct requests, and that the language they use is considered out-of-role.

There is further evidence of interpersonal costs for out-of-role behavior. In three studies using, respectively, confederates in small-group discussions, audio tapes of simulated professor–student interactions, and written vignettes of therapist–patient interactions, research participants consistently evaluated passive/dependent men and aggressive/dominant women as less popular than their sex-role-congruent counterparts (Costrich et al., 1975). In addition, passive men and aggressive women were seen as more seriously disturbed and more in need of therapy than their stereotyped counterparts. This study implies a paradox for women learning to be assertive, especially since behavior labelled assertive by trainers is often labelled aggressive by recipients. The role of assertive woman, which has been touted as healthy by mental health professionals, may be seen as evidence of disturbance by others.

How do people strive to control and limit women's behavior in working groups? Studies of group process and leadership show sanctions for out-of-role behavior. In a study with male- and female-led small groups, people who behaved role-incongruently (angry female and distressed male group members) were repeatedly attacked (Kahn, 1984). Another, which used diaries, audio tape recordings, and analyses by both participants and observers to assess group process, showed that men's responses to the emergence of women's leadership included withdrawal from active participation, striving to regain leadership followed by resentment and withdrawal, joking and satire, and sexualization of the interaction climate (Bormann et al., 1978).

In a related study, male participants worked on a task with a male or female supervisor whose job title was sex-role congruent or incongruent (Cohen et al., 1978). Although written evaluations of the supervisors and actual task performance were not related to supervisor sex, incongruent female supervisors received unfavorable reactions in the form of participants' spontaneous verbal comments during the task. Thus, in addition to being less liked, women who use out-of-role, assertive behavior may incur other costs: verbal attack, pointed silence, joking, satire, sexual and off-task remarks, and inattention. I will have more to say about joking as a strategy for conversational control in Chapter 5.

Even when a woman is in a formal, high-status authority position, her assertive behavior is interpreted differently from that of her male colleagues. In an analogue study, college students heard audio tapes of university police officers attempting to persuade a student to relinquish an alcoholic beverage that the student was consuming in public. The officers spoke in either demanding or reasoning style; that is, using imperatives and direct orders versus expressions of empathy and requests for compliance. Regardless of their speech style, female officers were seen as more assertive, tenacious, and active than male officers. Students' evaluations of the female officers were affected by the officers' speech style – demanding officers were seen as less feminine – but evaluations of male officers' masculinity was not affected by their speech style. Challenging a female officer was seen as more legitimate than challenging a male, and complying with her requests was seen as more of a failure (Sterling and Owen, 1982).

Recent research shows that gender-based evaluations of speech style have changed little. The use of 'masculine' speech is less effective for women than for men. In a study of the effects of tentative versus assertive speech, both women and men judged a woman who spoke tentatively as less competent and knowledgeable than a woman who spoke assertively; there were no effects for judgments about male speakers. This result would suggest that assertive speech is functional for women. However, men were influenced more by a woman who spoke tentatively than one who spoke assertively. Women, on the other hand, found tentative women speakers less effective (Carli, 1990).

These results indicate one of the double binds of assertive speech for women. If women use tentative language, it compromises their perceived competence and makes it less likely that they can persuade other women. If they use more assertive language, they will find it more difficult to persuade men. This pattern is congruent with the results of my own analogue study, in which assertive women were given the most positive evaluation by women and the least positive by (older) men. In influence attempts that take place in mixed-sex settings, there is no behavior by which a woman can 'win.' Not surprisingly, Carli found that women spoke more tentatively when interacting with men than with women. As competent speakers, they were responding to the differential contingencies in their social environments. How men spoke had no impact on their ability to influence women or other men, and their speech style was therefore less flexible. These studies nicely illustrate processes of 'doing gender' in interaction.

When women behave less assertively than men, their behavior may well be an adaptive choice rather than a deficiency. When women were asked about their expectations for how others might judge their assertive behavior, they expected moderately favorable judgments from other women, and less favorable ones from men (Linehan and Seifert, 1983). Thus these women were aware that women's assertion is not always positively regarded by others, and in fact their expectations accurately reflect the results of the studies I have described. As we have seen, there is no convincing evidence that women do not know how to speak assertively. When asked to role-play assertion in one study, they behaved less assertively than men; however, they were readily able to increase their assertion when asked to do so, indicating no lack of assertive skills (Rodriguez et al., 1980). 'Unassertive' speech, rather than being a (female) deficiency in social skills, may reflect a sensitivity to the social impact of one's behavior. Tentative and indirect speech may be a pragmatic choice for women. It is more persuasive, at least when the recipient is male, less likely to lead to negative attributions about personality traits and likability, and less likely to provoke verbal attack.

*Assertion as a Deviant Speech Style: a Speech Act
Perspective*

Perhaps because it was an invented form of speech, assertiveness has
been studied and analyzed largely without reference to research on
conversation. Theories that emphasize the communicative function of
talk have not, for the most part, been brought to bear on the behaviorist construct of assertion or used to assess its social consequences. In
this section I will introduce a speech act framework that shows how
assertive speech deviates from natural language, accounts for inconsistencies and anomalies in the assertion literature and suggests new
approaches to research (Gervasio and Crawford, 1989).

Speech act theory (Austin, 1962) originated in opposition to the
view that language is an abstract system whose function is to describe
the empirical world (Potter and Wetherell, 1987). Arguing that all utterances both state things and do things, Austin analyzed speech in terms
of meaning, force, and consequences. The statement 'I told you I'll
wash the dishes' has a literal meaning that we comprehend by virtue of
our knowledge of specific objects (dishes) and scripts (household routines). Its force is most likely that of a declarative statement. Its
consequences are less clear. It could have the effect of placating the
hearer, or of annoying her. (And should we consider clean dishes to be
a consequence of the statement? One criticism of speech act theory is
that it provides no systematic way to decide what counts as the consequences of an utterance (Potter and Wetherell, 1987).)

Speech Acts and the Construct of Assertive Speech   As described earlier, assertiveness training manuals specify quite specific verbal
strategies. Speakers are encouraged to use 'I–me' language, to practice
techniques such as 'fogging' or 'broken record,' and to make statements or refuse requests without giving reasons. Other strategies are
labeled nonassertive and are discouraged. These include indirectness,
hinting, and making requests or expressing opinions tentatively.

One way to evaluate these techniques is to analyze them in terms of
Austin's categories of meaning, force, and consequence (Austin, 1962;
Searle, 1969, 1979). The first is perhaps least useful, since the syntax
and semantics of assertive speech, and its literal meaning, are usually
unambiguous. Textbook examples of assertive speech do seem to differ
from examples of 'passive' speech at the grammatical level, though not
always in the ways predicted by definitions of assertiveness (Gervasio,
1988; Gervasio et al., 1983). More interesting are questions of the force
and conversational consequences of assertive speech. How might such
utterances be understood by others and what might they be taken to
imply about the speaker's intentions?

Answering such questions would be easier if utterances always followed a particular form for a particular illocutionary force. If all requests were in the form of questions, and all orders in the form of imperatives, we would have less trouble specifying a speaker's intent. The sentence

(a) It's been a long day

is literally an assertion, but may be used as a request to a guest to go home, while the sentence

(b) I see someone whose papers are not tidy

also an assertion in form, may be heard as an order to tidy up a desk if spoken by a teacher to a class of young pupils. In other words, speech acts can be quite indirect. Yet there must be limits to indirectness. It is unlikely that either of the above sentences would be used to ask someone to join the speaker for a week in Paris. One of the tasks speakers have is to craft utterances that are neither too direct (and thus rude; for example, 'Go home now' to a guest) nor too indirect (and thus not understood).

What conversational rules do speakers follow? H. P. Grice (1975) attempted to set out some general conversational maxims that people use in composing utterances and listeners use in interpreting them. He limited himself to cases where both parties want to communicate efficiently and accurately with each other in exchanging information. Such conversation follows a *cooperative principle*; speakers follow certain conventions that help them to be informative, truthful, relevant, and clear, and listeners interpret their remarks in light of the assumption that this is what the speaker is trying to do.

Grice set out four categories of rules that people follow in adhering to the cooperative principle:

1 *Quantity* Make your contribution only as informative as necessary, neither more nor less.
2 *Quality* Make your contribution one that is true to the best of your knowledge.
3 *Relation* Be relevant to the ongoing topic and dialogue.
4 *Manner* Be brief and orderly; avoid vagueness, ambiguity, wordiness.

These maxims are critical to cooperative communication. When they are adhered to, speakers can imply meanings efficiently and listeners can safely draw correct inferences from what speakers say. In the following exchange, B rightly takes the implication that A would not be telling her about the movie if A had no interest in going, and B can proceed directly to negotiating the details of their plan to attend.

A: The new Spike Lee movie is on at the Ritz.
B: Think we could make the nine o'clock show?

Grice (1975) discussed such *implicature* in detail; the concept is now viewed as one of the most important ideas in pragmatics. It shows how forces outside the structure of language (i.e., principles of cooperative social interaction) have strong effects on language structures. It also provides detailed guidelines for explaining how people mean much more than they actually say. When people speak, others have very strong expectations that they will adhere to the general cooperative principle by following its maxims. Implicatures are triggered in hearers so automatically that they sometimes are confused with core semantic content. Thus, the 'stable semantic core' of talk 'often has an unstable, context-specific pragmatic overlay' (Levinson, 1983: 99).

If speakers violate conversational maxims unwittingly, communication can break down.

A: I'm travelling tomorrow.
B: Really? Where are you going? Off on vacation?
A: No, I'm taking the train to work.

In this exchange, A has violated the maxims of manner and quantity by using the general verb 'travelling' rather than the more specific 'commuting,' and by giving less information than is normally provided by not specifying her destination. B therefore misinterprets her meaning and a rather unsatisfactory exchange ensues.

A second kind of implicature comes when a speaker flouts or exploits the maxims. Because cooperation is so strongly expected, utterances are read as though they are meant to be cooperative at some level if this is at all possible to infer. By overtly breaking a maxim, the speaker can force the hearer to make a complicated set of inferences (Levinson, 1983).

In other words, people involved in conversations usually assume that everyone is trying to follow the cooperative principle. When a speaker says something that seems to violate the maxims, hearers reinterpret the meaning of the utterance so that it is consistent with the maxims. They construct an interpretation that makes sense only if the speaker really is being cooperative and following the maxims. Speakers design their utterances to allow for this process; they rely on recipients' ability to make complex inferences (Nofsinger, 1991). Thus, speakers can violate cooperative maxims in the service of particular interactional goals. Grice (1975: 52) gives a good example: 'A is writing a testimonial about a pupil who is a candidate for a philosophy job, and his letter reads as follows: Dear Sir, Mr. X's command of English is excellent, and his attendance at tutorials has been regular. Yours, etc.' Since the letter-writer is the candidate's teacher, he must know more about the candidate than he is saying in the letter; moreover, he knows that more is expected and wanted by the person to whom he is writing. Therefore, by intentionally violating the maxim of quantity, he is inviting the recipient of the letter to infer that he knows things about the candidate that he is reluctant to write on paper. Such 'damning with faint praise' is a standard violational move that is readily understood by conversational participants:

A: So, you had your first date with that new guy? What's he like?
B: He's very clean.

Thus, speakers can imply meanings by flagrantly violating maxims while remaining committed to the cooperative principle. And listeners can readily make the inferences they are meant to. Sarcasm, for example, can involve deliberately stating an untruth, a violation of the maxim of quality:

A: Have you met the new Provost?
B: A *charming* man.

The various indirect ways of expressing a speech act lead to different interpretations about meaning and therefore different social consequences (Clark and Clark, 1977). For example, being indirect is one important way that people behave *politely* in conversation (Brown and Levinson, 1978). The following request forms (from Clark and Clark, 1977) cover a range from rude to overly polite in normal circumstances:

(a) Open the door.
(b) I would like you to open the door.
(c) Can you open the door?
(d) Would you mind opening the door?
(e) May I ask you whether or not you would mind opening the door?

We can envision even less direct requests for the same action:

(a) Do you usually keep the door closed on a hot day?
(b) It sure is hot in here.
(c) When I stayed in Italy, I liked the way people flung the doors open to let the fresh air in.

In choosing among alternatives that vary in directness, a speaker must take many factors into account. What is her authority with respect to the listener? Does she want to be rude or polite, and to what degree? Is the situation an emergency that calls for urgent direct communication? And she is constrained by the immediate context – the sentences that immediately preceded her turn. In summary, the speaker, having decided what speech act she intends, must decide its form by bringing to bear nuanced linguistic and social judgments. Speech acts in context can be quite indirect, *and they are indirect for good reasons*. For example, we have seen that direct requests are easily seen as rude. Indirect requests allow the hearer to refuse equally indirectly while both parties avoid loss of face. Suppose A's car is in the garage for repairs and A would like to borrow B's. A might say:

(a) Lend me your car.
(b) Could I please borrow your car?
(c) It's going to be tough to get to work until I get my car back.

The most direct form (a) demands a direct acquiescence or refusal. The least direct (c) could lead to

(d) I know, it's really a hassle. I'd loan you mine but I have to take my son to his dancing lessons.

In this exchange, empathy is offered, personal disclosure is used to decrease social distance, and the request is neither baldly stated nor baldly refused, so that personality attributions such as 'aggressive' or 'rude' are unlikely to be made. Speakers know what they are doing when they talk in these indirect ways.

Assertiveness training techniques attempt to solve communicative decision-making problems by prescribing formulaic patterns through which the speaker is supposed to express her needs and wishes. The limitations of assertion formulae can be seen when they are analyzed in terms of speech act theory. Some assertion techniques may violate conversational maxims in ways that are socially inept and that could cause listeners to make inferences that speakers did not intend.

Amy Gervasio (1987) analyzed 13 assertive techniques in terms of Grice's (1975) conversational maxims and sociolinguistic theories about rules for polite requests and refusals (Labov and Fanshel, 1977). In *clipping*, for example, the asserter gives a minimal response to an indirect request:

Mother: The dishes aren't washed.
Daughter: That's right.

This technique violates conversational norms by denying the validity

of an indirect request. Rather than furthering conversational understanding, it would likely be perceived as a passive aggressive response
or as a joke, because it takes an ambiguous request as a literal statement. 'One difficulty with changing an individual's conversational rules
is that communication may become ineffective when two speakers no
longer share the same conversational postulates' (Gervasio, 1987: 115).
One client in an assertion training course put it more succinctly. 'You're
teaching me a whole new language,' he told the psychologist in charge
of his group. 'But the people I talk to don't speak it' (White, personal
communication).

Research on the social evaluation of assertion tells us that formulaic
assertive speech is not wholly acceptable as a conversational norm. It is
not considered likable or sensitive, perhaps because it violates the cooperative principle. Moreover, what therapists and researchers call
'standard assertion' (i.e., no justifications or empathy allowed) is the
least acceptable type. Not surprisingly, 'polite assertion' and 'empathic
assertion,' which are less direct and closer to ordinary conversational
norms, are better received.

New Approaches to Assertiveness

What would research on assertive speech and the clinical practice of
assertiveness training look like if they were grounded in a more
dynamic and context-sensitive view of language use? In what follows, I
will suggest ways to insure more relevant and useful projects of research
and therapy.

Toward more Ecologically Valid Research

The process of doing my own (1988) analogue study led me to become
more aware of the limitations of analogue research in this area. I went
on to examine the social evaluation research to assess whether this
research was relevant to clinicians and consumers of assertiveness
training (Gervasio and Crawford, 1989).

In order for research to be clinically relevant, it must have high ecological validity. Ulrich Neisser (1976: 2) has defined ecologically valid
theory and research as that which 'has something to say about what
people do in real, culturally significant situations. What it says must not
be trivial, and it must make some kind of sense to the participants in
these situations themselves.' Neisser also wryly observes that the
demand for ecological validity

> is not always as clear or helpful as it seems. Like so many admonitions to
> virtue, it emphasizes the superior righteousness of the moralizer without giv-
> ing much guidance to the moralizee . . . Demands for ecological validity are
> only intelligible if they are specific. They must point to particular aspects of

ordinary situations that are ignored by current experimental methods, and there must be good reason to suppose that those aspects are important. (Neisser, 1976: 33–4)

We attempted to meet Neisser's critical criteria by providing a detailed conceptual and methodological critique of research on the social outcomes of assertion. The literature we found consisted of experimental analogue studies similar to my own work described earlier (Crawford, 1988). In them, participants (usually college students) view or read brief video tapes, audio tapes, or written vignettes in which someone behaves assertively in interpersonal situations. Often, these are contrasted with vignettes representing passive or aggressive behavior; or perhaps different styles of assertion are compared. The respondent then rates the assertive speaker on adjective checklists describing personality traits or attributes such as 'assertive,' 'likable,' or 'intelligent.' Respondents may also be asked to rate their willingness to interact with the model in a variety of situations such as work settings or parties (cf. Kelly et al., 1980).

We found that, given its basic assumptions, most research on this topic was methodologically sound in the traditional sense, using validity checks on stimulus materials, standardized stimuli and dependent measures, and sophisticated statistical techniques. However, this methodological uniformity – and the consistency of results it achieved – may have been purchased at the expense of ecological validity. Three aspects of research design limited ecological validity:

Choice of Stimuli   Stimuli are heavily weighted in favor of relatively inconsequential and impersonal situations. For example, participants may be asked to evaluate a model who returns a poorly cooked steak to a waiter or speaks assertively to someone who has cut into a queue. Failure to assert oneself has few serious consequences in these situations. They are not at all representative of the concerns of clients in assertiveness training, who usually want help in dealing with problems in ongoing relationships where changes in one person's behavior may alter a complex interaction dynamic. Moreover, in terms of the research situation itself, the triviality of the issues presented to the participants may encourage them to view the entire experience of being a 'subject' as trivial and inconsequential. From a social constructionist framework, experimental settings are not socially neutral situations. Rather, they are occasions of social interaction invested with meaning by participants.

There is an almost complete lack of attention to 'race,' class, and status in stimuli. There were no published studies with Asian or Hispanic women or men as models, although one might expect that stereotypes about expected submissive and compliant behavior in Hispanic and

Asian women might lead to differential evaluation of their assertive speech. Behaviors defined by white psychologists as assertive might not be relevant to non-white groups. For example, direct eye contact, refusing to comply with a request, and a firm voice tone might be considered disrespectful within Asian-American or African–American cultures (Cheek, 1976). Lillian Comas-Diaz (1985) has pointed out that traditional assertiveness training ignores the carefully constructed rituals of *personalismo* (personal, friendly, repeated contact with helpers, salespeople, doctors, etc.) in Hispanic cultures. Interactions of ethnicity and gender should receive more attention. There is evidence that black and white women who are friends agree that the black woman is usually the more assertive of the two (McCullough, forthcoming) and that expected levels of assertion for women differ in black and white social groups (Stanback, 1985). Cheek (1976) suggested that African–Americans who act assertively might be perceived as aggressive by whites, while those who act passively would be more favorably evaluated.

Representation of status and power differentials is entirely absent from the stimuli used in evaluating assertive behavior. Stimulus materials typically describe the recipient of assertion as a 'friend,' 'co-worker,' or 'stranger.' In the limited interactional worlds of assertion experiments, models virtually never assert to an authority figure, someone who possesses greater economic or social power, or a partner in a long-term intimate relationship. The lack of recognition of status and power effects is particularly important because women disproportionately occupy lower-power social positions. As Fine (1985: 168) pointed out, 'the fact that *being female* often means *being in a low power position* is obfuscated in studies that examine gender as an explanatory rather than a descriptive variable . . . .'

Dependent Measures   Given that assertion is a social behavior, it would seem that the best measures of its social impact would involve interaction with an assertive model. However, research participants rarely interact with or even see a live person behaving assertively. Rather, they rate a model they have viewed on video tape, heard on audio tape, or read about in vignettes, by completing adjective checklists or similar paper-and-pencil measures. Almost without exception, they have viewed, heard, or read about the model only once, and make their decisions after being presented with a single two-utterance example of the model's assertive behavior. They may be asked to rate how much they would like to interact with the model, but there have been no direct measures of their choice of whether to do so. In summary, there are no studies of how people behave when they are around someone who uses assertive techniques.

There are no studies of how their behavior might change over time in response to the repeated use of these techniques. This omission is surprising since one consistent finding in the analogue research is that even one exposure to experimenter-defined assertive behavior leads to judgments that the model is less sensitive and likable than a nonassertive model. Would repeated use of the techniques make the model even less likable, or undermine the generally positive evaluations of competence?

Participants   The great majority of studies have used college students as participants, a limitation that is certainly not confined to this research area (Sears, 1986). While there may be research topics for which the behavior of college students can be taken as representative of people in general, the social evaluation of assertiveness is not one of them. Relying on college students constrains investigators to using situations that are not potentially controversial or upsetting and that students will find familiar and interpretable (asking a neighbor to turn down a stereo, preventing someone from cutting into a queue) rather than situations that may be closer to clinically significant problems in assertion (dealing with sexual harassment by an employer or verbal abuse by an alcoholic spouse).

The importance of varied participants is underscored by the results of the few studies that have asked people other than college students for their evaluations. In one, employers rated the likelihood that assertive job-seeking behaviors would increase an applicant's chance of being offered a job (Cianni-Surridge and Horan, 1983). Contrary to suggestions from psychologists that these strategies would increase employability, employers reacted positively to only about one-third of the assertive behaviors. In my own study, the least positive evaluations were given by older men to female models (Crawford, 1988).

Is experimental analogue research useless in furthering understanding of social interaction? This question connects to the larger question of whether some methods of inquiry are better than others for research in gender. Feminist theorists have reminded researchers that methods are not neutral tools; the choice of method always shapes and constrains what can be found (Marecek, 1989), and have criticized psychology for overusing experimental methods (Sherif, 1979). They point out that in an experiment the researcher creates an artificial environment and manipulates the experience of the 'subjects.' Experiments strip behavior from its social context and create an inherently hierarchical situation (Parlee, 1979; Peplau and Conrad, 1989). Therefore, behavior in the laboratory may not be representative of behavior in more naturalistic settings. Although laboratory studies isolate variables from the contaminating influence of subtle social processes, gender is played out in exactly those processes (Crawford and Marecek, 1989).

In the case of the social evaluation of assertion, the research was intended to measure the social consequences of different kinds of speech, but the experiments failed to use realistic conversations or to measure actual responses to diverse speakers. Moreover, the experimental interaction scenarios have little social significance and therefore little relevance to therapists and their clients. In short, the methods used to assess the social impact of the newly invented behavior 'assertiveness' were heavily influenced by a tradition of reductionism and insufficiently sophisticated to study social interaction. Social processes were reduced to individual behaviors and private responses, allowing essentialism to linger unanalyzed in the construct. The social act of conversation became reduced to a matter of individual traits and trans-situational skills.

On the other hand, many important advances in understanding women and gender have come about because of experimental results. For example, experimental research on sex stereotypes, perceptions of leadership, attributions about women's and men's performance in work settings, and the denial of personal disadvantage has demonstrated in detail how sex discrimination occurs and why it is so difficult to eliminate (for a review, see Unger and Crawford, 1992). Experimental research on assertiveness (and other speech strategies) could be made more ecologically valid.

The following steps could generate more ecologically valid research on the social impact of assertiveness (Gervasio and Crawford, 1989). First, studies should involve actual interactions with an assertive model. Second, the stimuli presented should deal with non-trivial events. Third, responses to interactions should be evaluated over time and after repeated (but different) interactions. The social meaning of a single encounter with a stranger may be quite different from the meanings assigned in ongoing relationships; a person who repeatedly uses assertive techniques may become labeled as aggressive or 'hard to get along with.' Fourth, researchers must attend more closely to personal and interpersonal characteristics of interactions such as age, 'race,' and especially status differences between speakers. At present, assertiveness research is situated in a mythical world of social equality. Finally, methods for measuring the social impact of assertiveness must go beyond attitude scales to more realistic socially derived measures. Some possibilities are suggested by the speech act framework. How do people behave in response to 'I–me' statements or 'broken record' techniques? How do they respond when a speaker refuses to give a reason or justification for a decision? Do they distance themselves linguistically and behaviorally?

Speech Acts and Social Roles

The legacy of the general theory of speech acts is that it reminded philosophers and psycholinguists that sentences *do* things as well as describe the world, and that social conventions and rules must be met for speech acts to be carried out (Potter and Wetherell, 1987).

Grice (1975) and others (Hassan, 1973; Searle, 1969, 1979) further explored the social conventions of conversation. For example, they examined how certain roles are enacted through language. A particular kind of language can be an important attribute of a role, and a particular combination of speech acts can create a role. A simple case concerns the roles of *interviewer–interviewee*, which are largely created by verbal interaction. They can be characterized by the number and type of questions one participant asks and the number and type of statements provided by the other participant in return. If the verbal behavior departs from the norm, the role is not fulfilled. (A student of mine recently complained about her job interview at a social service agency, 'He [the interviewer] didn't ask me any questions, he just talked on and on about the agency.' Her indignation was that the interviewer had not fulfilled his role and the interaction could not properly be called an interview.)

Speech act theory has been very influential in the general theory of language use. Levinson (1983) cites work applying it to language acquisition, the study of genre and textual subtlety in literature, the study of spells and ritual in anthropology, the philosophical study of ethical statements, and, within linguistics, syntax, semantics, and second language learning. Yet the analyses provided by natural language philosophers remain decontextualized. What is missing from them is an understanding that roles, and the language that characterizes them, are often related to gender, status, and power; and that observers often infer personality characteristics from verbal behavior. Research on out-of-role behavior reviewed earlier in this chapter tells us that if a particular kind of speech is expected as part of a low-status social role, failure to produce this kind of speech will lead to social sanctions. A woman's failure to use particular speech forms such as tentative hedges, justifications, or expressions of empathy may result in the listener attributing aggressive intent to her. The label 'aggressive' may be applied not only to the speech but to the person: 'She's the aggressive type.'

Though speech act theory *in principle* can be applied to problems of women's speech (or, more generally, to problems of social status, power, and speech) it has not been developed along these lines, perhaps because of its origins:

Austin offers a highly social view of language. He draws our attention to the role played by the web of social conventions in the achievement of actions through talk and thus sensitizes the researcher to features of the social *context* surrounding language use. Despite these positive aspects, however, his theory was primarily developed to combat alternative philosophical views and little consideration was paid to the practicalities of actually applying it to everyday talk in natural situations. (Potter and Wetherell, 1987: 18)

Future work grounded in natural language philosophy must deal more directly with language in social context. Linguistic attempts to answer questions of why people so often use indirect, allusive, wordy or vague speech styles may lead to the radical abandonment of the idea that there is a literal semantic force at all. In other words, meaning may reside in social context rather than in language form. Thus, speech act theory may be superseded by a complex pragmatic theory of the functions that utterances achieve – a move to conversational analysis, discourse analysis, and other related approaches such as ethnography of speaking (Levinson, 1983; Potter and Wetherell, 1987). In Chapter 5, I will present a discourse approach to one important indirect speech mode, conversational humor.

Clinical Implications: Assertiveness Training and Feminist Therapy

Assertiveness training was developed originally as a therapeutic technique. Many of its earliest proponents claimed that its origins were in the women's movement and that it was a feminist therapy. For example, Flowers et al. (1978) stated that the popularity of assertiveness training was due to the recognition by people in the women's and gay rights movements that changing individual beliefs and behaviors can help deal with social oppression.Other authors viewed assertiveness training as part of a progressive chain of liberation techniques:

> Spurred on by various social liberation doctrines, in particular the women's movement, assertiveness training has supplied useful technology for behavior change and a natural sequel to consciousness-raising rhetoric and group meetings. The authors' own experience supports this phenomenon as women have outnumbered men in our groups almost two to one. (Shoemaker and Satterfield, 1977: 49–50)

Still others emphasized assertiveness training as a preventative against more radical methods of social change:

> When assertive rights are not exercised, they can be, and often are, taken away. Women, children, employees, and even citizens often have to reclaim their assertive rights after a period of disuse. Philosophically, assertive behavior and assertion training have social as well as individual consequences. When the assertive alternative is lost to the individual, assertiveness training is a treatment of choice. When the assertive alternative for social change is lost to a group or a society, the more radical interventions that finally result are often painful and can be destructive. (Booraem and Flowers, 1978: 17)

Is assertiveness training a viable and legitimate mode of feminist therapy? Or is it merely a way of diverting women's attention from social structural issues and the need for collective action, an inevitably ineffective individual 'solution' to structural power imbalances? As Fodor (1985: 258) asked, 'Is assertiveness training yet another "treatment" that is directed at the victim of social injustice, placing the burden for social change on the backs of individual women?'

For the most part, feminist therapists have not taken the more radical stance of rejecting assertion training. Some have accepted its clinical value relatively uncritically. Many of the self-help manuals, continuing education courses, and corporate workshops were (and are) conducted by women, most self-described feminists. Others have recognized the conceptual weaknesses of the assertiveness construct and the lack of empirical evidence on key questions within it. In writings aimed at behavior therapists and assertion trainers as well as at their feminist clinical colleagues, they have questioned some of the implicit assumptions of the movement: that women as a group have a skills deficit that requires intervention; that effective language behavior can be prescribed and taught easily; and that if women become more assertive they will reap positive social consequences (Fodor, 1985; Fodor and Epstein, 1983; Stere, 1985).

One of the earliest feminist critics of the movement was Nancy Henley, who argued that it paid insufficient attention to social context and structures. Henley (1980) addressed clinicians and assertion trainers directly with the charge that, within the assertiveness training movement, both the blame and the responsibility for a solution was placed on the individual when women experienced trouble in making others understand and respect their talk.

As the research and clinical literature on assertiveness expanded, feminists began to enumerate its limitations. In a volume aimed at behavior therapists, Fodor and Epstein (1983: 137) pointed out that there was an overemphasis in the literature on the success of assertiveness training and a 'pointed neglect of the issue of dropouts and failures.' They took assertion trainers to task for ignoring issues of power and authority in women's lives. For example, one of the most frequently reported 'failures' among clinical clients is that after assertiveness training their relationships seem to be worse rather than better. Assertiveness training may lead to a power struggle with a resistant partner in which 'backing down' for the woman leads to self-blame. Moreover, the evidence on factors that affect the likelihood of physical battering is mixed: '[G]iven the contradictory findings on triggers for husbands' abusive behaviors, there is a high risk that if we train such women to be more assertive, we may be subjecting them to further abuse . . .'(1983: 151).

Feminist clinicians have called for two kinds of change to ensure that assertiveness training is good feminist practice (Stere, 1985). One is to develop better methods of working with women who seek personal change through individual and group therapy: that is, assertiveness training techniques that do not reflect negative assumptions about women and their social worlds. The second is to focus less on women and more on social structures and men.

The first strategy, that of improving therapy, is exemplified by the work of Stere (1985) who argued that most of the clinical pitfalls of assertiveness training groups for women arise from overemphasis on the expert status of the leader. She illustrates several ways in which leaders reinforce their expert status, thereby neglecting the strengths and resources of clients, and offers alternative methods. Her examples include:

1   *Defining assertiveness and evaluating responses*   When the therapist uses prescribed definitions of 'appropriate' assertive behavior and evaluates client's attempts, women may become preoccupied with making a 'correct' response. Instead, the therapist should acknowledge that, given the complexities of human interaction, there is no general 'right' way to speak. Group members should be treated as a valuable resource for suggestions on how to respond in a variety of situations.

2   *Implying that assertiveness leads only to positive social consequences*   By failing to discuss the limitations of individual change, the therapist encourages women to blame themselves if their attempts to 'speak up' are unheard. Instead, the therapist should discuss and acknowledge gender inequities including the fact that 'people generally are not oriented toward taking the needs and interest of women seriously' (1985: 53).

3   *Handing out lists of 'irrational beliefs'*   The emphasis on cognitive restructuring in assertiveness training has led many therapists and group leaders to challenge apparently self-limiting beliefs in clients by labeling them irrational. However, women have a long history of being told by the psychiatric establishment that their beliefs and experiences are irrational; thus this technique risks perpetuating one of the most common ways that women's thoughts are invalidated. In addition, 'irrational' beliefs (such as 'If I assert myself, people won't like me') are shown by research to be quite rational. She suggests that groups of women should be encouraged to examine beliefs and values without the use of the label irrational.

4   *Rehearsing leader-contrived role-plays*   Practicing contrived situations has little value because the everyday assertion dilemmas of women are usually quite different from those depicted in training

exercises. Instead, group members should contribute actual situations from their own experience for role-play and analysis by the group.

Some feminist critics have advocated a shift to a societal focus that addresses social structural inequities (Henley, 1980). Fodor (1985: 261–2) notes that

> Going beyond individual work, toward creating an environment receptive to strong, assertive women, we need to take our methodology into a broader, more difficult area and address power issues and male domination . . . we need to go beyond work with individual women and their personal assertiveness issues and begin to use assertiveness techniques to challenge male patriarchal structure.

She suggests four strategies toward that end:

1 *Go beyond treating individual women*   Instead, groups of women should be educated to understand the assertive strengths they already possess and to work together to develop woman-defined assertive behavior.
2 *View men's negative response to women's assertiveness as a problem requiring change*   This would entail the development of support groups for women who are challenging the patriarchal system as well as working directly with men as clients.
3 *Feminist clinicians should enter the business and corporate sectors as trainers*   Research and training workshops within the business community could be used to educate managers to accept women's assertion and to reflect on the communication style they consider optimal for advancement.
4 *Focus on the media*   The mass media play a leading role in perpetuating negative stereotypes of the assertive woman. They frequently distort the work of psychologists. For example, *New York* magazine's cover article on assertiveness training featured a cartoon of a woman slapping a man after attending an assertiveness workshop. *Philadelphia* magazine's cover story on sex differences featured a woman standing triumphantly over a man who has been knocked to the ground, her foot on his body. Feminist clinicians must develop effective strategies for educating media representatives and countering the negative stereotypes they present.

At least some recent work seems to reflect a more sophisticated and nuanced approach than earlier 'bandwagon' research on self-referred, nonclinical populations of middle-class white women. For example, Iris Fodor (1992), in a volume on social skills training for adolescents, deals extensively with ethical and sociocultural aspects of assertiveness training and reports work with diverse ethnic groups including

Asian–Americans, African–Americans, and Latinos. She includes class
diversity by reporting work with disadvantaged high-risk groups and
middle-class suburban substance abusers. Significant, nontrivial issues
and situations are addressed, such as using assertiveness training as a
tool for advocacy by helping teenage mothers assert their educational
needs to school authorities. Throughout the volume there is an awareness that concepts such as 'social competence' are inherently
value-laden and that 'social skills training' in adolescents has sometimes been used in attempts to change behaviors considered
problematic by the agents of society rather than by the young people
themselves.

**The Social Construction of the New Assertive Woman:
Summary and Conclusions**

One of the most often-voiced criticisms by feminist psychologists of
mainstream psychology is that its ideal of objectivity – in the traditional, observer-from-Mars, definition – is a myth. However, it is not
sufficient simply to make that claim. Feminist psychologists must do
critical historical research to show exactly how cultural influences
impinge on psychological research. In analyzing the unexamined
assumptions about masculinity and femininity that underlie the psychological construct of assertive speech and the research associated
with it, I have shown specific ways in which psychology has participated in the social construction of difference and become an agent of
self-fulfilling prophecy with respect to gender. The beliefs that women
as a group are uniquely in need of communication skills training, that
an effective language style can be invented and taught, and that such
intervention would lead to a better life for women were uncritically
assumed by many researchers and therapists as well as by popularizers
of psychology.

In the assertiveness training movement we can see complex interre-
lationships between the discipline of psychology and the larger culture
in which it is embedded. Psychologists invented the construct of
assertiveness and participated in its mass dissemination. Thus they
made available a new 'scientific' explanation of women's low social status and a new pejorative label for women. Women were encouraged by
mass-market books, educational workshops, and therapy groups to
internalize the image of themselves as passive, inept communicators
and to find a cure for this invented deficiency through psychology. The
assertiveness training movement functioned to deflect attention from
the fact that women are over-represented in low-power, low-status
social roles and situations. It obscured the double bind of female
authority. It constitutes an example of 'woman-as-problem' thinking in

which women are blamed for the consequences of their low social status. Even more important, it illustrates how such thinking can contribute to the continued powerlessness of women by channeling energy into individual change efforts rather than collective action. And it shows how gender relations are constructed and maintained at all three levels – individual, interactional, and social structural.

Its success should encourage feminist theorists to examine further the interaction of disciplinary perspectives and the mass media. Which psychological constructs become bandwagons, ending up on television talk shows and the *New York Times* best-seller list, and which research is never mentioned in the popular media? What are the assumptions about human nature that underlie popular psychology? The assertiveness training movement would be an interesting case study even if it were an isolated example, but unfortunately it is not. Feminist psychologists have noted many other bandwagons, such as fear of success, the Cinderella complex, androgyny, co-dependency, the different moral voice, women's ways of knowing, and mother–infant bonding (Brown, 1990; Crawford, 1989a; Crawford and Marecek, 1989; Eyer, 1993; Mednick, 1989). In Chapter 4, I turn to the newest bandwagon in gender and language: the notion that women and men are so opposed in conversational goals and styles that talk between them is cross-cultural communication.

4

Two Sexes, Two Cultures

Cross-cultural Talk

Both the 'genderlect' approach and the assertiveness training movement were based on the premise that women's language and speech
style are less adequate than men's. As the crucial differences proved elusive, and assertiveness training failed to solve women's problems of
being heard and respected, an alternative approach gained popularity.
This approach maintains that communication between women and
men is, in effect, communication across cultures. Consider the difficulties of talk between, say, a person of Italian background and one from
Japan. Even if the two share a common language, they may have trouble communicating because they are likely to have different ways of
expressing politeness, conversational involvement, and so forth. The
'two-cultures' approach proposes that talk between women and men is
fraught with potential misunderstanding for much the same reasons
that communication across ethnic groups is.

The two-cultures approach, like the assertiveness training approach
before it, has become a bandwagon. Talk shows and best-sellers pro-
claim the frustrations of cross-sex talk (*You just don't Understand*) and
describe a gender gap so great that the two sexes might as well be from
different planets (*Men are from Mars, Women are from Venus*). In this
chapter I will examine the origins of this latest bandwagon and provide
a feminist analysis of its precepts and its potential. I will analyze reasons for its popularity and discuss some troubling implications of its
widespread acceptance as an account of acquaintance rape.

Talking across the Ethnic Divide
The origins of the two-cultures model lie in the work of the linguist
John Gumperz (1982a). Gumperz was critical of the speech act
approach to conversation on much the same grounds I have discussed
in Chapter 3. He saw it as insufficiently dynamic to capture the shifting,
goal-directed nature of conversation. In his own approach, he emphasized interactive conversational goals and the importance of
communication flexibility in an increasingly diverse and bureaucratic
society. With students and colleagues, Gumperz (1982b, 1992) explored
the idea that distinct groups of people develop within-group communication styles. Norms for interacting, the way talk is structured, and so

on – all the subtle components of conversational style – are developed within one's social reference group. Consequently, people who are socially distant from each other may experience frustration and misunderstanding in trying to communicate. Conversation proceeds on the basis of shared assumptions about what is taking place, and miscommunication results when conversational partners do not share the same assumptions. Seemingly minor stylistic differences, such as whether a speaker uses a rising inflection with a question, can determine whether he or she is perceived as rude and hostile or polite and friendly.

In Gumperz's work, the focus was on ethnic groups. In the interethnic communication situations he studied, inaccurate perceptions of a speaker's intentions were not usually recognized as problems in communication. Rather, they were attributed to personality problems (in much the same way that formulaic 'assertive' speech may lead to the attribution, 'She's an aggressive person'). Or they were interpreted in terms of racial stereotypes (in much the same way that women's speech may be judged with reference to stereotypes about femininity). Indian speakers of English who were trying to deal with British bureaucrats in order to receive a social stipend, for example, were characterized by the bureaucrats as ineffective, deficient communicators. Gumperz's approach does not assume that inter-ethnic communication problems are the result of bad faith or bad intentions. Miscommunication can result even when people with good intentions are trying their best to understand each other.

Talking across the Gender Divide

While the Gumperz approach seems to capture much about communication difficulties between people of different ethnic groups, it is less than self-evident as a model of gendered speech. While it may make sense to say that Indian and Anglo speakers of British English constitute two distinct cultures – they live in different neighborhoods, have different religious and social customs, are distributed differently in the class structure, and so forth – to say that North American women and men constitute two cultures seems at first hearing puzzling. When we think of distinct female and male subcultures we tend to think of societies in which women and men spend virtually their entire lives spatially and interactionally segregated; for example, those which practice purdah. In Western societies, however, girls and boys are brought up together. They share the use of common space in their homes; eat, work, and play with their siblings of both sexes; generally attend coeducational schools in which they are aggregated in many classes and activities; and usually participate in religious meetings and activities together. Both sexes are supervised, cared for, and taught largely by women in infancy and early childhood, with male teachers and other authority figures becoming more visible as children grow older. Moreover, they see these social patterns mirrored and even exaggerated in the mass media. How can the talk of Western women and men be seen as talk across cultures?

The two-cultures model was first applied to the speech of North American women and men by Daniel Maltz and Ruth Borker, who proposed that difficulties in cross-sex and cross-ethnic communication are 'two examples of the same larger phenomenon: cultural difference and miscommunication' (1982: 196). Maltz and Borker acknowledge the argument that American women and men interact with each other far too much to be characterized as living in different subcultures. However, they maintain that the social rules for friendly conversation are learned between the ages of approximately 5 and 15, precisely the time when children's play groups are maximally segregated by sex. Not only do children voluntarily choose to play in same-sex groups, they consciously exaggerate differences as they differentiate themselves from the other sex. Because of the very different social contexts in which they learn the meanings and goals of conversational interaction, boys and girls learn to use language in different ways.

Citing research on children's play, Maltz and Borker (1982) argue that girls learn to do three things with words:

1 to create and maintain relationships of closeness and equality;
2 to criticize others in acceptable (indirect) ways;
3 to interpret accurately and sensitively the speech of other girls.

In contrast, boys learn to do three very different things with words:

1 to assert one's position of dominance;
2 to attract and maintain an audience;
3 to assert oneself when another person has the floor.

The Two-cultures Approach as Bandwagon

Maltz and Borker's attempt to bring together developmental psychology and sociolinguistics has not remained a mere academic footnote to the Gumperz theory of inter-ethnic communication. Instead, a mass-market version of the two-cultures model has become a metaphor for all the interactional problems of North American women and men (Freed, 1992).

Some of the bandwagon books show all the classic features of the relationship self-help genre. The formula for success in this lucrative genre is to gently lead the reader on a 'journey of a thousand anec-dotes' (Cameron, in press) in which relationship difficulties are identified, labeled, reduced to formulaic patterns, and finally overcome.

Like assertiveness training books, relationship improvement books are aimed largely at heterosexual women. As I noted in Chapter 3, many encode a deficiency model that identifies women as the source of relationship problems and blames them for not achieving happiness in hetero-pairings (Worell, 1988). Like pop-psychology assertiveness training books, they promise that if women change their ways of relating to others they will achieve both love and respect.

The new twist in the two-cultures model of communication is to conceive relationship difficulties not as women's deficiencies but as an inevitable result of deeply ingrained male–female differences. The self-help books that encode a two-cultures model make the paradoxical claim that difference between the sexes is deeply socialized and/or fundamental to masculine and feminine natures, and at the same time subject to change and manipulation if the reader only follows prescribed ways of talking. Instead of catchy slogans and metaphors that stigmatize women (*Women who Love too Much*, Doris Doormat v. Agatha Aggressive) the equally catchy new metaphors glorify difference.

A best-selling exemplar of the genre is *Men are from Mars, Women are from Venus* (Gray, 1992). As its title proclaims, this book dichotomizes and stereotypes women and men to extremes:

> Centuries before the Martians and Venusians got together they had been quite happy living in their separate worlds. Then one day everything changed. The Martians and Venusians on their respective planets suddenly became depressed . . . When the Martians became depressed, everyone on the planet left the cities and went to their caves for a long time. They were stuck and couldn't come out, until one day when a Martian happened to glimpse the beautiful Venusians through his telescope. As he quickly shared his telescope, the sight of these beautiful beings inspired the Martians, and their depression miraculously lifted. *Suddenly they felt needed.* They came out of their caves and began building a fleet of spaceships to fly to Venus.
>
> When the Venusians became depressed, to feel better they formed circles and began talking with one another about their problems. But this didn't seem to relieve the depression. They stayed depressed for a long time until through their intuition they experienced a vision. Strong and wondrous beings (the Martians) would be coming across the universe to love, serve, and support them. *Suddenly they felt cherished.* As they shared their vision their depression lifted, and they happily began preparing for the arrival of the Martians . . . Men are motivated and empowered *when they feel needed* . . . women are motivated and empowered *when they feel cherished.* (Gray, 1992: 42–3, emphasis in original)

Every aspect of personality, motivation, and language is polarized. Women's speech is indirect, men's is direct. Women respond to stress by becoming overwhelmed and emotionally involved, men by becoming focused and withdrawn. Women and men even lunch in restaurants for different reasons: for men, it is an efficient way to approach the task of eating; for women, it is an opportunity to build a relationship.

Women and men are so irredeemably and fundamentally different that they need translators to help them communicate (a Martian/Venusian phrase dictionary is provided). They also need rules and routines to bridge the gender gap. (Oddly, some of these rules and routines are opposite to those endorsed in assertiveness training books. Instead of 'I would like you to take out the trash,' a wife is exhorted to ask, 'Would you take out the trash?' Like assertiveness prescriptions, however, they are promulgated with detailed specificity and total conviction. If she unthinkingly asks '*Could* you take out the trash?' the wife has doomed her relationship to a period of resistance and resentment.) The reader's head begins to spin with lists: 23 things not to say, 101 ways to score relationship points with a woman (offer to carry the groceries), five points to include in love letters, five tips for motivating a man, 15 things to do when your man won't talk to you (go shopping, take a bubble bath), the six (different) primary love needs of women and men (she needs devotion, he needs admiration).

Although the book makes prescriptions for both sexes, it leaves little doubt about its intended readership: women in middle-class heterosexual marriages. In this book, Martians come home after a long day at the office to waiting Venusians. Martians are obsessed with paid work and money, Venusians with home and feelings. Venusians seem to do almost all the domestic work, from taking children to the dentist to cooking, cleaning, and calling elderly relatives. Martians may be asked to help, but only if Venusians use carefully circumscribed request forms and recognize that Martians have every right to refuse. Helpful tips are provided for 'Programming a Man to Say Yes' and 'The Art of Empowering a Man.' If all else fails, one can read the section on 'How to Give up Trying to Change a Man.'

The norms of the self-help genre allow for exaggerated claims of effectiveness, and *Men are from Mars, Women are from Venus* is no exception. Twenty-five thousand people have attended the author's relationship seminars, and at least 90 percent of them have recognized themselves in the Martian/Venusian metaphor, John Gray claims; 'literally thousands . . . saw their relationships dramatically transform overnight' (1992: 3). Despite the endless lists of how to change each other, the ultimate promise is that women can earn love through acceptance of the status quo. Individual change is not really necessary, much less the restructuring of masculinity and femininity. 'Through understanding the hidden differences of the opposite [sic] sex we can . . . give and receive . . . love. Love is magical, and it can last, if we remember our differences' (Gray, 1992: 14).

Academic psychologists and linguists have tended to ignore self-help materials. The path along the journey to enlightenment and communication heaven in these books is not likely to be cluttered with any actual references to research. Although the author's PhD is always writ large on the cover, few prominent psychologists write self-help books. And although these works may be analyzed critically in feminist journals, they are rarely even reviewed in mainstream professional journals. For linguists, they violate a strong disciplinary stricture against prescribing how people should talk (Cameron, in press). For these reasons, there has been very little critical evaluation of self-help books on relationships.

The situation would be different if a prominent and well-respected academic were to claim expertise in male–female communication and write about it for the general public. And that is just what has happened with Deborah Tannen's *You just don't Understand: Women and Men in Conversation* (1990), which has become a phenomenal success in the US. Acclaimed in the popular press as the 'Rosetta Stone that at last deciphers the miscommunication between the sexes' and as 'a Berlitz guidebook to the language and customs of the opposite gender [sic],' *You just don't Understand* has been on the *New York Times* best-seller list for over three years and claims over one million copies in print. Neither Lakoff's work nor any of the dozens of popular books that emerged from the assertiveness training movement could claim this level of popularity. It seems that the state of gender relations among the middle-class book-buying public demanded an explanation of communication difficulties and frustrations, an explanation that books like *Men are from Mars, Women are from Venus* and *You just don't Understand* promised to provide.

Although Tannen is a much-published and respected linguist, this particular work has been quite controversial among her peers. Scholarly review and commentary have been mixed:

> This book is an anachronism . . . part of . . . a backlash against women and feminism. Its popularity and overwhelming acclaim are both astonishing and troubling . . . Now the general public, already ignorant about fundamental principles of language and rather tolerant of male dominance, embraces a theoretical model of communication which simultaneously perpetuates negative stereotypes of women, excuses men their interactive failings and distorts by omission the accumulated knowledge of our discipline. (Freed, 1992: 1–2)

> [G]enuinely exciting and immediately relevant . . . a delight to the eye and ear . . . should be required reading for all incoming freshpeople in their first social science course; few books will better prepare them for the worlds of education and work ahead of them. (Boden, 1991: 851)

> I find this book not only flawed in its arguments but intellectually and politically dishonest . . . The current salience (and marketability) of gender-related topics is exploited to propound a message that is depoliticized at best; at worst it is downright anti-feminist. (Cameron, 1992: 467)

> That such a deeply reactionary book should appeal to so many readers informs us, disconcerting as it may be, that what is non-threatening to the

status quo sells better than critical analysis. This is a dishonest book . . . It veils and conceals the political analysis to which women have given their energy during the last 30 years, and the changes they have brought about with the help of fair men. (Troemel-Ploetz, 1991: 490)

What claims have produced such unprecedented popularity with the general public and such contradictory and passionate evaluations from academic critics? I will briefly describe the tenor of *You just don't Understand* and summarize its main arguments before proceeding to a more general feminist critique of the two-cultures model.

A banner heading in Chapter 1 proclaims that 'Male-Female Conversation is Cross-cultural Communication.' Citing Maltz and Borker (1982), Tannen claims that childhood play has shaped world views so that, when adult women and men are in relationships 'women speak and hear a language of connection and intimacy, while men speak and hear a language of status and independence' (1990: 42). The contrasting conversational goals of intimacy and independence lead to contrasting conversational styles. Women tell each other of their troubles, freely ask for information and help, and show appreciation of others' helping efforts. Men prefer to solve problems rather than talk about them, are reluctant to ask for help or advice, and are more comfortable in the roles of expert, lecturer, and teacher than learner or listener. Men are more talkative in public, women in private. These different styles are labelled 'report talk' (men's) and 'rapport talk' (women's).

Given the stylistic dichotomy between the sexes, miscommunication is almost inevitable; however, no one is to blame. Rather, another banner proclaims, 'The Key is Understanding:' 'Although each style is valid on its own terms, misunderstandings arise because the styles are different. Taking a cross-cultural approach to male–female conversations makes it possible to explain why dissatisfactions are justified without accusing anyone of being wrong or crazy' (1990: 47).

You just don't Understand makes its case for the two-cultures model skillfully and well using techniques that have become standard in popular writing about behavior: characterizations of 'most' women and men, entertaining anecdotes, and the presentation of research findings as fact. However, it is better written than most. In comparison, the popular psychology books on relationships, the assertiveness training books described in Chapter 3, and especially *Men are from Mars, Women are from Venus*, seem contrived in their examples, divorced from systematic research, and heavy-handed in their prescriptive formulae for change. Tannen's book is much more sophisticated than the Doris Doormat and April Assertive of an earlier era, and much less didactic. It is engagingly written; its anecdotes have the ring of truth. Instead of advocating conversational formulae or regimented training programs for one sex, it recommends simply that people try to understand and accept sex differences and to be as flexible in style as possible. Like Gray's book, it ends with a call for nonjudgmental acceptance of differences; the final chapter is titled 'Living with Asymmetry.' If we can't change gender-linked ways of communicating, we can learn to accept them graciously – a comforting, if vague, recommendation.

The Two-cultures Approach: an Evaluation

Beyond Deficiencies and Blame

Proponents of the two-cultures model maintain that it is an advance over approaches that blame particular groups for miscommunication. When inter-ethnic misunderstanding occurs, the reason is incompatible styles, not unscrupulous motivations. In applying the model to cross-sex talk, Maltz and Borker (1982) expressed the hope that it would help researchers realize that conversational rules are culturally determined and learn to interpret them with sensitivity.

Unlike earlier approaches, the two-cultures model does not characterize women's talk as deficient in comparison to a male norm. In contrast to the notion of an ineffectual 'female register' or the prescriptive masculine ideals of the assertiveness training movement, the two-cultures model problematizes the behavior of men as well as women. To John Gray, neither Mars nor Venus is a superior home. To Deborah Tannen, 'report talk' and 'rapport talk' are equally limiting for their users in cross-sex communication. The speech style attributed to men is no longer 'standard' speech or 'the language,' but merely one way of negotiating the social landscape.

A model of talk that transcends woman-blaming is less likely to lead to woman-as-problem research programs or to widespread attempts to change women through therapy and skills training. Moreover, ways of talking thought to characterize women can be positively revalued within this framework. In a chapter on gossip, Tannen notes that the negative connotation of the word reflects men's interpretation of women's ways of talking. But gossip can be thought of as 'talking about' rather than 'talking against.' It can serve crucial functions of establishing intimacy and rapport.

Language Flexibility

The two-cultures model avoids the problem of equating form with function. In earlier chapters I showed how researchers seeking empirical evidence for Lakoff's claims often assumed that all tag questions (or hedges or fillers) had the same meaning, leading to simplistic exercises in feature-counting. Similarly, assertion trainers assumed that particular techniques ('I–me language' or 'broken record') could be counted on to convey equivalent meanings across settings and participants. Although *Men are from Mars, Women are from Venus* prescribes rigid rules for talk, the much more sophisticated *You just don't Understand* presents a view of language that stresses its flexibility, an approach more compatible with social constructionist views. As my earlier discussion of conversational implicature and speech act theory showed, speakers can use many different forms to convey (for example) a polite request. And hearers strive to interpret utterances in ways that do not violate conversational maxims. The same intention can be expressed many ways, and different, even conflicting, intentions can be expressed in identical ways.

One of the criticisms of speech act theory as applied to gendered talk is that it has remained decontextualized, its conceptualization of roles and their demands abstract. In contrast, the two-cultures model, grounded in practical studies of mundane talk across ethnic groups, might be more useful in analyzing everyday talk and more sensitive to how social differences of all sorts position speakers in particular roles. Potentially, then, it can address the types of diversity of most interest to feminist analysts.

Ambiguities of the Self

Within a social constructionist framework, differences between women and men (or in other subjectivities) are viewed as transactional. That is, women behave in particular ways not because they are women, but because they are members of a distinct, culturally salient group who are placed in particular situations and interactions that enable certain behaviors and suppress others. The two-cultures approach could show how the interactional contexts of same-sex play groups position boys and girls differently and render different aspects of their identities salient. Thus, (some) girls and boys come to experience intimacy and autonomy differently because the gender system, operating at the social structural and interactional levels, recreates the ideology of gender within individuals.

However, the approach does not address *why* and *how* girls and boys come to be in sex-segregated groups except to suggest that it is voluntary. The differences that create same-sex play groups in the first place must be prior to the differences created by talk. To claim that girls' and boys' different worlds create two conversational cultures requires the 'startling assumption that the gender-differentiated behaviors came first, alinguistically, and the speech came later, and was shaped to fit the behaviors' (Henley and Kramarae, 1991: 30). And why are certain interactional strategies, and not others, associated with each sex? The relationships between particular features or strategies (e.g.

interruption) and power provide a better explanation for who uses those features than the essentialist assumption that they are somehow characteristic of men because of early socialization.

In earlier chapters I discussed how women's 'ineffectual style' and 'lack of assertiveness' were attributed to early socialization. A generic 'society' was blamed for conditioning girls and women to speak and behave in passive, self-defeating ways. Locating responsibility in a reified 'society' and placing it in the distant past ensures that people in power need not change their current behavior. It deflects attention from the ongoing ways in which gender conformity is enforced and gender inequality perpetuated.

The two-cultures model excises the notion of responsibility altogether. Women's and men's styles are equally valid. Moreover, their origins are benign and inevitable. Children are not reinforced, shaped, or coerced into playing with same-sex peers. Instead, the peer-group sex segregation that underlies adult communication difficulties is *voluntary*. If the socialization explanations of earlier eras taught readers to expect change to be slow and laborious, as each generation revised childhood gender roles, the *self*-socialization explanation behind the two-cultures model teaches us to expect no change at all. If children segregate themselves *naturally*, how could matters ever change?

The idea that children are willing agents of their own gender socialization stems from cognitive developmental theory (Kohlberg, 1966). The theory has gained wide acceptance partly because it does provide an account of how children often seem to develop gender-stereotyped preferences in the absence of direct pressure from adults. Many parents can offer examples: the little girl who insists on wearing dresses to playschool, though her parents would prefer her to wear more practical trousers; the little boy who rejects the doll his parents have provided in an attempt at nonsexist childraising. The cognitive developmental approach theorizes that, once children understand that there are two sexes and assignment to one of them is permanent, they become motivated to become the best possible (most prototypical) exemplar of their sex.

However, the theory has never been able to explain satisfactorily why girls should be motivated to assume a gendered identity that is also associated with powerlessness and devaluation (Unger and Crawford, 1992). It does not take into account the coercion, persuasion, and closing of options that underlie girls' acceptance of their subordinate status. It is only recently that feminists have developed critical analyses of how developmental theories that posit voluntary sex segregation and girls' self-motivated adoption of feminine characteristics naturalize girls' relegation to the feminine (Bem, 1993).

Doing Gender, Doing Power

The two-cultures approach fails to theorize how power relations at the structural level are recreated and maintained at the interactional level. The *consequences* of 'miscommunication' are not the same for powerful and powerless groups. As Deborah Cameron (1985: 150) points out, 'The right to represent and stereotype is not mutual.' Stereotypes of less powerful groups (immigrants, people of color) as inadequate speakers serve to ensure that no one need take seriously what these people say. People of color may have their own set of negative stereotypes of white people, but 'these are the ideas of people without power. They do not serve as a base for administrative procedures and decisions, nor do they get expressed routinely in mass media.' Recent research on the relationship between power and stereotyping suggests that people in power stereotype others partly as a cognitive 'shortcut' that minimizes the need to attend to them as individuals. People without power, of course, must attend carefully to their 'superiors' in order to avoid negative judgment or actual harm and cannot afford to use schematic shortcuts (Fiske, 1993).

'Negotiating status' is an evaluatively neutral term for interpersonal behaviors that consolidate power and maintain dominance. Ignoring the enactment of power and how it connects to structural power in gender relations does a disservice to sociolinguistics, distorting its knowledge base and undermining other more legitimate research approaches (Freed, 1992). Moreover, it badly misrepresents communication phenomena. Nancy Henley and Cheris Kramarae (1991) provide a detailed analysis of six 'cultural differences' in female–male speech styles taken from Maltz and Borker (1982), showing that they may be more plausibly interpreted as manifestations and exercises of power. For example, men's tendency to interpret questions as requests for information, and problem-sharing as an opportunity to give expert advice, can be viewed as prerogatives of power. In choosing these speech strategies, men take to themselves the voice of authority.

This failure to recognize structural power and connect it with interactional power has provoked the strongest criticisms of the two-cultures approach. In a review of *You just don't Understand*, Senta Troemel-Ploetz (1991) pointed out that if the majority of relationships between women and men in our society were not fundamentally asymmetrical to the advantage of men,

> we would not need a women's liberation movement, women's commissions, houses for battered women, legislation for equal opportunity, antidiscrimination laws, family therapy, couple therapy, divorce . . . If you leave out power, you do not understand any talk, be it the discussion after your speech, the conversation at your own dinner-table, in a doctor's office, in the back yards of West Philadelphia, in an Italian village, on a street in Turkey,

in a court room or in a day-care center, in a women's group or at a UN conference. It is like saying Black English and Oxford English are just two
different varieties of English, each valid on its own; it just so happens that
the speakers of one variety find themselves in high-paying positions with a
lot of prestige and power of decision-making, and the others are found
more in low-paying jobs, or on the streets and in prisons. They don't always
understand each other, but they both have the best intentions; if they could
only learn a bit from each other and understand their differences as a matter of style, all would be well. (Troemel-Ploetz, 1991: 497–8)

No one involved in debating the two-cultures approach denies that
men have more social and political power than women. Maltz and
Borker (1982: 199) acknowledge that power differentials 'may make
some contribution' to communication patterns. However, they do not
theorize the workings of power in interaction or advocate structural
changes to reduce inequity.

The Bandwagon Revisited

There is no inherent limitation to the two-cultures approach that would
prevent its development as a theory of difference *and* dominance, a
theory that could encompass the construction of gendered subjectivities, the reproduction of inequality in interaction, and the role of
interaction in sustaining gendered social structures. It is therefore the
more disappointing that in the popularized versions that have influenced perhaps millions of people, it is flattened into an account of sex
dichotomies. And this is why the model has been so harshly evaluated
by feminist scholars. Perhaps unfortunately, the more egregious versions have been largely ignored and the more scholarly one attacked.
Deborah Tannen's critics have charged that, despite the absence of
overt woman-blaming and the positive evaluation of 'feminine' modes
of talk, the interpretations she offers often disguise or gloss over
inequity, and privilege men's interpretations (Freed, 1992; Troemel-
Ploetz, 1991). They have accused her of being an apologist for men,
excusing their insensitivity, rudeness, and dominance as mere stylistic
quirks, and encouraging women to make the adjustments when needs
conflict (Freed, 1992). Indeed, the interpretations Tannen offers for
the many anecdotes that enliven her book often read as though the past
two decades of women's studies scholarship had never occurred, and
there were no feminist analyses available with which to contextualize
gendered behavior (Troemel-Ploetz, 1991).

You just don't Understand is apolitical – a choice which is in itself a
political act, and a significant one at that, given that the book has sold
well over a million copies. Like the popular psychology of the assertiveness training movement, it does not threaten the status quo

(Troemel-Ploetz, 1991). Like its pop-psychology companions on the bookstore shelves, it offers something to both the powerful and those over whom they have power: to men, a compelling rationale of blame-free difference and to women a comforting promise of mutual accommodation.

Let us consider three examples, from three types of conversational setting, to illustrate how the accounts of interaction in *You just don't Understand* might be reinterpreted in light of research on women and gender. The first is an anecdote about Josh and Linda. When an old friend calls Josh at work with plans for a visit nearby on business, Josh invites him to spend the weekend and makes plans to go out with him Friday night. These plans are made without consulting with Linda, who protests that Josh should have checked with her, especially since she will be returning from a business trip herself that day. Tannen's explanation of the misunderstanding is in terms of an autonomy/intimacy dichotomy. Linda likes to have her life entwined with Josh's, to consult and be consulted about plans. Josh feels that checking with her implies a loss of independence. 'Linda was hurt because she sensed a failure of closeness in their relationship . . . he was hurt because he felt she was trying to control him and limit his freedom' (1990: 27).

No resolution of the conflict is provided in the anecdote; the implication is that Josh's plans prevail. Interpreting this story in terms of women's needs for intimacy and men's for autonomy glosses the fact that Josh has committed mutual resources (living space, food, the time and work required to entertain a houseguest) on behalf of himself and his partner without acknowledgement that the partner should have a voice in that decision. His behavior seems to reflect the belief that the time and energy of others (women) are to be accommodated to men. As a test of the fairness of his behavior, imagine that Josh were living with a male housemate. To invite a mutual weekend guest without consulting the housemate would be considered overtly rude. The housemate (but not the woman in a heterosexual couple) would be warranted in refusing to cooperate, because he is seen as entitled to make his own plans and control his own resources. A sense of entitlement to act entirely on one's own and make decisions unilaterally is 'part of the social empowerment that men enjoy. It has precious little to do with communicative style or language' (Freed, 1992: 4).

Josh's behavior could also be analyzed as a form of covert *dependence*. Assuming his entitlement to his partner's time and work, he gains benefits that he need never overtly acknowledge. Far from being autonomous, he has enlisted the resources of another person to his own ends. Josh, and other members of socially privileged groups, can constitute themselves as independent and autonomous in conversation (and in their self-concept) because the social structure is arranged in ways that provide help and support that is naturalized and rendered invisible. The Josh-and-Linda anecdote recalls Brinton Lykes' (1985) research which I discussed in Chapter 3: individuals from privileged groups, whose material conditions and social relations are consistent with individualistic accounts of the self, are more likely to see themselves as autonomous. And, as Michelle Fine and Susan Gordon (1989) noted, women – secretaries, wives, mothers – are expected to collude in the fiction of male autonomy and keep the secrets of male dependence.

In a section titled 'First Me, Then Me,' Tannen describes her own experience of discourse in a professional setting. Seated at a faculty dinner next to a woman, she enjoyed a mutually informative and pleasant discussion in which each talked about her research and explored connections and overlaps. Turning to a male guest, she initiated a conversation in a similar way. However, the conversation proceeded very differently:

> During the next half hour, I learned a lot about his job, his research, and his background. Shortly before the dinner ended there was a lull, and he asked me what I did. When I said I was a linguist, he became excited and told me about a research project he had conducted that was related to neurolinguistics. He was still telling me about his research when we all got up to leave the table. (1990: 126)

Lecturing, says Tannen, is part of a male style. And women let them get away with it. Because women's style includes listening attentively and not interrupting, they do not jump in, challenge, or attempt to deflect the lecturer. Men assume that if their partner had anything important to say, she would say it. The two styles interact to produce silent women, who nod and smile although they are bored, and talkative men, who lecture at length though they themselves may be bored and frustrated by the lack of dialogue. Thus, apparent conversational dominance is not something men deliberately do to women. Neither is it something women culpably permit. The imbalance is created by 'habitual styles.'

The stylistic interpretation discounts the possibility that the male academic in this example did not want to hear about his female dinner companion's research because he did not care about it. That women and what they do are valued less than men and what they do is one of the fundamental insights of feminism. The history of women in the professions provides ample evidence of exclusion, discrimination, and marginalization. Methods vary: plagiarizing women's work (Spender, 1989), denigrating them as unfeminine while stealing their ideas (Sayre, 1975), denying them employment (Crawford, 1981; Scarborough and Furumoto, 1987) and recognition (Nochlin, 1971). When women compete successfully in male domains, they are undermined by sexual harassment (Gutek, 1985) and by being represented as sex objects (a long-running 1980s ad campaign featured female physicians and attorneys making medical rounds and appearing in court in their underwear) (Lott, 1985). In short, there is not yet much reason to believe that women in the professions are routinely taken as seriously as their male peers. And the academy is no exception. What Tannen explains as mere stylistic differences have the effect of keeping women and their work invisible, and have had documented consequences on women's hiring, promotion, and tenure (Caplan, 1993).

Accounts of the careers of our foremothers in the arts and professions can provide a basis for exploring the structural reasons for their absence of visibility (Crawford and Marecek, 1989). Moreover, there is an abundance of research showing that work attributed to women is still systematically devalued (Lott, 1985; Unger and Crawford, 1992). Relying on a 'conversational style' interpretation forecloses the opportunity to use the insights of this research and the lessons of women's history in understanding talk.

The third anecdote is meant to illustrate that sharing secrets is an essential part of friendship for women. When women have no secrets to tell, their friendships may falter:

> [A] woman I'll call Carol had several women friends she talked to every few days, exchanging stories about dates with men. They would share their excitement before a new date, and after the date took place, they would report in detail what had been said and done. So when Carol fell in love and formed a lasting relationship with a man, she ran out of material for talks with her friends. She also had less time to talk on the phone, since she now spent most of her free time with the man. This put a strain on her friendships; it was as if she had gathered up her marbles, reneging on her part in the partnership of talk that constituted the friendship. (1990: 98–9)

In this story, the fact that Carol apparently unthinkingly privileges her relationship with a man over her relationships with other women is not questioned. We learn that she has no time to talk with women because she is spending her time with her man, but this choice (which involves much more than conversation) is not problematized.

There are more important questions here than whether one has a secret to tell today. One of the ways that gender ideology is maintained is through the culture of romance. Mass media such as the romance novel and popular magazine fiction provide narratives of women who find self through their heterosexual romantic relationships, which are all-consuming (Modleski, 1980; Radway, 1984). Young women learn to judge themselves in terms of their conformity to this culture (Holland and Eisenhart, 1990) and to decide that their romantic relationships are more valuable than their friendships. Women's talk with women can be subversive of prevailing gender relations only when they start to privilege it over their talk with men (Cameron, 1985). Instead of engaging the politics of Carol's choice about talk, Tannen's analysis encourages the reader to stereotype women as people who have no other interests in common than the care and maintenance of their heterosexual romantic relationships. When girls can't tell secrets about guys, their talk dries up.

These three anecdotes and my contextualizations of them highlight some of the most frequently voiced feminist criticisms of the two-cultures model and especially with self-help versions of it. By ignoring feminist scholarship that could provide a sociocultural context for gendered behavior, it obscures and erases the structural inequalities that define gender. Interactional processes are treated neutrally, as though they did not involve differential power. With sociocultural context obscured, the 'cross-cultural differences' between women and men readily collapse into essential differences.

Differences and Dichotomies

In both *You just don't Understand* and *Men are from Mars, Women are from Venus*, women and men are presented as having non-overlapping and inherently conflictual conversational goals and styles. Most readers could probably generate counter-examples to the status-obsessed men and intimacy-obsessed women they portray. Yet rhetorically, the notion of gender as difference is very effective. As I discussed in Chapter 1, it connects to common wisdom, it is endorsed in much traditional social science research, and it is authorized as a legitimate explanation by the dominant culture. The difference schema is accessed and reinforced in several ways.

Both books position cross-sex communication as fundamental. They do not set out to deal with communication across other categories that separate people: class, 'race,' ethnicity, age, sexual orientation, and so on. None of these is addressed as an analytical category, a particularly noticeable omission since the two-cultures model originated with inter-ethnic studies (Cameron, 1992). With their erasure, the complexities of social position and situation are backgrounded; women become a global category and sex can take center stage. In Chapter 2, I described the 1970s conceptualization of women as a homogeneous category as perhaps a necessary stage in theorizing gender. There is now a great deal of research showing that questions of women's language must be addressed in terms of *which women* in *which* social groups (Coates and Cameron, 1988; Nichols, 1980), and less justification for maintaining this stance.

When sex is the only conceptual category, differences attributable to situations and power relationships are made invisible. If sex were the determining factor in relationship goals and styles, the relationships of lesbians and gay men would each involve two partners with similar styles. Gay male partners, both concerned with status and autonomy, would have very different relationship dynamics than lesbian partners, both concerned with intimacy and connection. However, the accounts that people give of their relationships do not fit these expectations. When people were asked to describe the influence strategies they used in close relationships, sex was related to the type of strategy used only among heterosexuals. Gay men and lesbians did not use sex-differentiated strategies. This suggests that power differentials within the relationship are a more important determinant of communication strategy than whether the partners are male or female. Regardless of whether they were gay or straight, people who saw themselves as the more powerful partner in their relationship used more direct, interactive strategies (the prototypical heterosexual male strategy) and lower-power partners used indirect, 'feminine' strategies (Falbo and Peplau, 1980).

The rhetorical stance of dichotomization is buttressed when the two-cultures model is treated as fact. Gray (1992) sidesteps the question of how women and men could come to be so different; it's a complex issue, he says, and best to take his word for it that difference is categorical. Tannen presents the research origins of the model appropriately, but does not go on to evaluate it critically or even to suggest to the reader that it might be so evaluated. The effects of childhood play groups becomes a totalizing account of women's and men's styles.

The language of both books further constructs gender as difference. Gray repeatedly characterizes men and women as 'opposite sexes,' describes gender-differentiated behavior as 'instinctive,' and indulges in classic gender polarities: Martians are hard, Venusians soft; Martians are angular, Venusians round; Martians are cool, Venusians warm. 'In a magical and perfect way their differences seemed to complement each other' (1992: 44). Tannen's much more responsible and scholarly work is guilty of none of these excesses; it constructs gender as difference more subtly. The overlap between women and men is obscured by chapter titles ('Different Words, Different Worlds') and banner headings ('Male–Female Conversation is Cross-Cultural Communication') that suggest categorically different speech styles. The demands of mass-market writing preclude the use of numbers, tables, statistical analyses, graphs of distributions of results, or discussions of how persons and situations interact. Without these aids to conceptualizing *degrees* of differences and fluctuation, difference cannot readily be described except in terms of most/many women/men. This contributes to the fundamental attribution error. Instead of a flexible, situation-specific behavior, speech style becomes a static personality trait.

As I maintained in Chapter 1, a 'different-but-equal' rhetorical stance cannot be sustained. As academic theories of differences enter the popular culture they join a discourse that hierarchizes. *Difference* becomes *female deficiency* (Crawford, 1989a). Although Tannen notes that some women fear *with justification* that 'different' will be heard in reference to an implicit male norm, and that the conceptual step between 'different' and 'worse' is a short and perhaps inevitable one (1990: 14–15), she never develops these insights. Like the acknowledgment of status and power disparities, acknowledgment that difference may be read as women's deficiency appears, then disappears, without becoming a vehicle for further analysis.

Asymmetries of Power

In earlier chapters I have noted two recurring themes in research on male–female communication. First, there is considerable research showing that males talk more in a variety of settings, interrupt women, control topic development, and withhold expressive feedback. These findings have usually – and reasonably, I think – been interpreted in terms of conversational dominance, the 'micropolitics' of greater male power and status. Secondly, there is the double bind of speech style for women. Stereotypically feminine speech features are devalued, but when women use stereotypically masculine styles, such as direct assertion, their speech and personalities may be negatively evaluated. How does Tannen incorporate this research and theory into the two-cultures account?

In a chapter titled 'Who's Interrupting? Issues of Dominance and Control,' Tannen argues against attributing conversational dominance to men on two grounds. The first is the form/function problem. Like tag questions or any other speech feature, simultaneous talk can have many different functions. It can be a kind of cooperative overlap, for example, rather than an attempt by one speaker to silence the other. She maintains that studies of interruption have used mechanical criteria for counting an utterance as an interruption rather than attending to the substance of the talk at hand: the topic, speakers' intentions, their reactions to each other, and the conversational consequences of the interruption. All these factors influence whether or not anyone's speaking rights have been violated and whether anyone should take offense.

Secondly, she points out that the crucial insight of the two-cultures model, based on inter-ethnic research, is that *no one is to blame* for miscommunication. Some groups (New Yorkers, Jews) have a 'high involvement' style that may seem 'pushy' and rude to speakers who do not share it. But, if it is inappropriate to claim that speakers of certain ethnic groups are pushy, dominating, or inconsiderate because they appear to interrupt people from more 'mainstream' ethnic backgrounds, it is equally inappropriate to claim that men dominate women because they appear to interrupt them in conversation.

Though she professes sympathy for the dominance view and acknowledges that women as a class are dominated by men in our culture, she maintains that accepting the dominance explanation for asymmetries in male–female style logically demands the acceptance of a similar explanation for inter-ethnic communication – if we argue that men try to dominate women in conversation, we are logically bound to argue that some ethnic groups are pushy or aggressive. It is this argument that reveals the limits of the analogy between sex differences and ethnic differences. The prototypical ethnic representatives used to illustrate the two-cultures model (Japanese and American executives, New Yorkers and Nebraskans) are not embedded in a system that dictates a complementary *and unequal* relationship between them. However, women and men are placed in just such a system. 'Gender differences service a whole social, economic, and moral order' (Cameron, in press). Many racial and ethnic differences are also constructed in such hierarchies. This is the point of Senta Troemel-Ploetz's comparison between Black English and Oxford English that I quoted earlier. The ethnic examples chosen to illustrate the two-cultures model are often selective, and conveniently naive about social hierarchies of 'race,' class, and color.

In a chapter titled 'Damned if You Do,' Tannen reviews some of the research showing that the same behavior may be interpreted differently depending on whether it is done by a woman or a man, and that such interpretation is usually to women's disadvantage. The styles more typical of men, she acknowledges, are taken as the norm. Moreover, when women and men interact in mixed-sex groups, men's norms prevail. Women adjust to them, and it is this that gives the *appearance* of male dominance. Women who attempt to emulate the male norms may be disliked and disparaged as unfeminine and aggressive. Although Tannen makes the poignant observation that 'The road to authority is tough for women, and once they get there it's a bed of thorns,' this observation *ends* her chapter on the double bind rather than providing a starting point for further analysis.

In response to a strongly worded critique of *You just don't Understand* (Troemel-Ploetz, 1991) Tannen defends her choice not to write about dominance, control, and the politics of gender:

> These are important areas of research, and many books have been written about them; they are not new, and they are not the field in which I work. I wrote a book about the role of what I call 'conversational style' in everyday conversation, especially in the context of close relationships, because that has been the subject of my research throughout my academic career. (Tannen, 1992: 249)

The two-cultures model does not apply to situations in which women are victimized and should not be used to justify them, she asserts. She writes not about inequities but about what she terms *quotidian conversational frustrations* (1992: 252).

This dialogue between reviewer and author reveals what I view as the crucial flaw of the mass-market version of the two-cultures approach: it assumes that some interactions – the everyday, the quotidian, those between people in close relationships – exist outside the power relations that define and construct gender. It is as though the social structures that award greater power and influence to males exist on another plane (or another planet) and do not intrude into personal relationships. But this is patently false. The structural inequalities of gender *are* reproduced in individual relationships. Thirty years of social science research has shown that men have more power in heterosexual marriage and dating relationships due to their ability to access external resources and their higher social status generally (Unger and Crawford, 1992). One gendered resource is earning power. Gray takes this for granted; in *Men are from Mars, Women are from Venus*, men are almost always away at paid work, women complain that men are never home or always tired, and men maintain that their love is expressed through the money they bring home. Though Tannen briefly and belatedly (on p. 292 of 298 pages of text) acknowledges research showing that earning more money is probably the greatest source of marital power, she does not appear to recognize that the actual result of this phenomenon, which she presents as a gender-neutral fact, is greater *male* power. To put it simply, in the middle-class United States families these books address, women earn less money than men. This holds true for full- and part-time, white, African–American, Asian–American and Hispanic workers. No subgroup of women has a median income that comes close to the median for white men; none even has a median income equivalent to the comparable subgroup of men. The wage differential by sex has remained fairly constant over the past 50 years with women earning about 60–68 percent of men's earnings (Rix, 1991). Even in the rare cases when women gain significantly greater economic power by earning higher incomes than their marital partners, the overall power imbalance is not eliminated, only lessened (Steil and Weltman, 1991). Though these data are from the United States, men's greater control of material resources is a worldwide phenomenon (United Nations, 1991).

Gender, like 'race,' is best conceptualized as a system of social classification that governs access to resources (Crawford and Marecek, 1989). In comparing Black English and Oxford English, Troemel-Ploetz illustrates that interactions between members of powerful/powerless 'racial' or ethnic groups take place, inevitably, in the context of that power hierarchy. No cross-sex conversation is quotidian in the sense that it exists outside the gender system. No cross-sex relationship is unaffected by the fact that women are second-class citizens.

A Rhetoric of Reassurance

The rhetoric of difference makes everyone – and no one – responsible for interpersonal problems. Men are not to blame for communication difficulties; neither is a social system in which gender governs access to resources. Instead, difference is reified: 'The culprit, then is not an individual man or even men's styles alone, but the difference between women and men's styles' (Tannen, 1990: 95).

One of the most striking effects achieved in these books is to reassure women that their lot in heterosexual relationships is normal. Again and again, it is stressed that no one is to blame, that miscommunication is inevitable, that unsatisfactory results may stem from the best of intentions. As these explanations dominate the public realm of discourse about gender, they provide 'one more pseudo-explanation' and 'one more ingenious strategy for not tackling the root causes of women's subordinate status' (Cameron, in press).

Its very ubiquity has made inequality of status and power in heterosexual relationships seem unremarkable, and one of the most important contributions of feminist research has been to make it visible (Wilkinson and Kitzinger, 1993). In the discourse of miscommunication the language feminists have developed to theorize status and power is neutralized. Concepts such as sexism, sex discrimination, patriarchy, and gender inequity are barely mentioned, and conversational strategies that have the effect of silencing women are euphemized as stylistic 'asymmetries.' For example, Tannen explains that when men do most of the talking in a group, it is not because they intend to prevent women from speaking or believe that women have nothing important to say. Rather, they see the women as *equals*, and expect them to compete in the same style they themselves use. Thus, an inequity that feminists have conceptualized in terms of power differentials is acknowledged, but explained as an accidental imbalance created by style and having little to do with a gendered social order.

Power dynamics in heterosexual relationships are obscured by the kinds of intentions imputed to speakers. Both books presume an innocence of communicative intent. In the separate and simplistic worlds of Martians and Venusians, women just want to be cherished and men just want to be needed and admired. In the separate worlds of 'report talk' and 'rapport talk', the goal may be sex-specific but the desire is the same: to be understood and responded to in kind. In *You just don't Understand*, each anecdote is followed by an analysis of the intentions of *both* speakers, a practice that Tannen (1992) feels reflects her fairness to both sexes. But this symmetry is false, because the one kind of intention that is never imputed to any speaker is the intent to dominate. Yet people are aware of such intentions in their talk, and, when asked, can readily describe the verbal tactics they use to 'get their own way' in heterosexual interactions (Falbo, 1982; Falbo and Peplau, 1980; Kelley et al., 1978). Tannen acknowledges the role of power in conversational dynamics (cf. p. 283, 'We enact and create our gender, and our inequality, with every move we make'). But the rhetorical force of the anecdotes is about difference. When an anecdote seems obviously explainable in terms of dominance strategies, the possibility of such an account is often acknowledged but discounted. The characteristics that the two-cultures model posit for females' speech are ones appropriate to friendly conversation, while the characteristics posited for men's speech are not neutral, but indicate uncooperative, dominating and disruptive interaction (Henley and Kramarae, 1991). Whose needs are being served when intent to dominate is ruled out *a priori* in accounting for cross-sex conversation?

Many of the most compelling anecdotes describe situations in which a woman is hurt, frustrated or angered by a man's apparently selfish or dominating behavior, only to find that her feelings were unwarranted because the man's intentions were good. This is psychologically naive. There is no reason to believe that *post hoc* stated intentions are a complete and sufficient description of conversational motives. Accounts of one's intentions are a socially constructed product in which face-saving and self-justification surely play a part. And even if intentions are innocent, language is a form of social action. Speech acts do things, and these things cannot be undone by declaring good intentions (Potter and Wetherell, 1987; Trocmel-Ploetz, 1991).

The emphasis on interpreting a partner's intentions is problematic in other ways as well. As Nancy Henley and Cheris Kramarae (1991: 42) point out, '[F]emales are required to develop special sensitivity to interpret males' silence, lack of emotional expressiveness, or brutality, and to help men express themselves, while men often seem to be trained deliberately to misinterpret much of women's meaning.' Young girls are told that hitting, teasing, and insults are to be read as signs of boys' 'liking.' Adolescent girls are taught to take responsibility for boys' inexpressiveness by drawing them out in conversation, steering talk to topics that will make them feel comfortable, and being a good listener. Girls and women learn from the discourse of popular fiction to reinterpret men's verbal and physical abuse. Indeed, a central theme in the romance novel is that cold, insensitive and rejecting behavior by men is to be read as evidence of their love (Unger and Crawford, 1992). Interpreting their partners' behavior in these ways may function to keep women in unrewarding relationships by making them more bearable (Radway, 1984).

Analyzing conversation in terms of intentions has a very important implication: it deflects attention from *effects*, including the ways that everyday action and talk serve to recreate and maintain current gender arrangements. Instead, readers are left to analyze what goes on in people's heads – what they say they intend to accomplish, not what they do accomplish, when they are engaged in 'doing gender.' Entering a larger discourse in which women are blamed for the consequences of societal sexism and for their own powerlessness, popularizations of the two-cultures model may be used to deflect responsibility from men. This is especially salient in explanations of violence against women. Deborah Tannen (1992: 252) articulately expresses her view that the approach should *not* be applied in this way: 'There is no reason . . . to think I would seek to explain away rape, domestic violence, sexual harassment or sexual abuse as conversational misunderstandings . . . I have had occasion to refute and decry such attempts in recent press interviews.' Unfortunately, the miscommunication model has become the culturally dominant account of acquaintance rape, informing 'expert' explanations and popular accounts alike. In the following section I will show how prevalent it has become and how difficult to disrupt.

Miscommunication and Rape

The notion that women and men are fated to miscommunicate has been used to account for many sites of gender struggle including sexual violence and aggression. Academic evidence is enlisted to support the claim that misunderstood signals between the sexes may be the underlying cause of job discrimination, rising divorce rates, sexual harassment and date rape (Henley and Kramarae, 1991).

From the two-cultures perspective, acquaintance and marital rape can be viewed as extreme examples of miscommunication. Neither the man nor the woman involved is able to interpret the other's verbal and nonverbal cues accurately, and the resulting communication breakdown ends in rape. This view is not entirely implausible. As I discussed in Chapter 3, people use indirect speech styles when they are making and refusing requests precisely because these are sensitive areas in which it is necessary to allow for face-saving. Communication about sexual activity is a sphere in which partners are especially vulnerable, and there is a need to make and refuse requests in ways that avoid overt disagreement. Moreover, sexual scripts that position men as the aggressors and women as reluctant, passive recipients of sexual activity encourage divergent communication patterns in sexual encounters. Because sexual communication is indirect, subtle, complex, and shaped by gendered norms for interaction, genuine miscommunication undoubtedly does take place (Henley and Kramarae, 1991; LaPlante et al., 1980).

The miscommunication model can be compared to two other models commonly used to account for rape (Corcoran, 1992). The *victim precipitation* model places responsibility on the woman who is raped. Her behavior is said to invite sexual aggression (Amir, 1967). The implication is that if women monitor and control their behavior, they can avoid rape. Originally developed as an account of stranger rape, the model emphasized the avoidance of risky behavior such as hitchhiking or going out alone after dark. When the victim precipitation model is applied to acquaintance rape, risky behaviors are expanded to include such things as drinking, wearing short skirts, and inviting a date into one's living space. Much of feminist theorizing about rape has attempted to refute this model with its associated victim-blaming (Brownmiller, 1975).

The *social structural* model views rape as a societal problem rather than in terms of women's individual or interpersonal actions. It emphasizes that rape can be seen as sexual terrorism and its prevalence tied to patriarchal aspects of cultures such as greater male status and social power. The model also implicates cultural justifications of inequality, such as the beliefs that women are the property of men, women's sexuality is inherently evil, and males are entitled to the sexual services of females (Sheffield, 1989). Although it does not blame women for their own victimization, this model does not offer specific individual strategies for avoiding or preventing rape.

The feminist movement and social science research have made overt victim-blaming less acceptable, at least to helping professionals and academics. However, the victim precipitation model has not been replaced by the social structural model, or by an emphasis on interactions between social structural and interpersonal factors. Perhaps a social structural analysis has failed to gain wide currency because 'it is a bit overwhelming to consider changing family, educational, legal, political and economic systems as rape prevention strategies' (Corcoran, 1992: 136).

I will illustrate the deployment of all three models in accounting for rape by analyzing a segment of a 1991 talk show in which four experts, a public radio host, and several callers discuss 'date rape.' The immediate impetus for the program came from two alleged rapes. The first was a gang rape of a woman student at a large US university (Urban U) by six fraternity members. The second, reported to authorities only four days later, was the rape of another Urban student by an acquaintance in her campus apartment. Taken together, these two events generated a great deal of negative publicity for Urban U and fostered public discussion of the causes of date rape.

The host begins the one-hour program by introducing the experts. One is the Provost of Urban U as well as a sociologist whose research is on gender relationships. Another is a Professor of health education at Urban. The third, assistant district Attorney in the city where Urban is located, has prosecuted rapists for four years. Provost, Professor, Attorney, and Host are women. The fourth guest, a man, is a Psychiatrist who treats rapists and rape victims at an institute for sexual offenders. The session has begun with a discussion of similarities and differences among gang rape, stranger rape, and acquaintance rape. The following segment occurs about five minutes into the program, when Host introduces the question of why rape seems to be so prevalent on college and university campuses:

Date Rape

(1)   *Host*: Let's let's talk about (.) ahm (.) for a moment, the (.) the factors perhaps on a college campus that contribute towards making rape perhaps more prevalent in in this situation, and I would think they'd have to do with a number of social factors, they're young

(5)   adults away from home for the first time? (.) living together? (.) and there's a certain amount of peer pressure (.) to (.) to (.) perform (.) sexually or or to succeed sexually, and I've also read that the beginning of the fall term is described as rape season. Maybe you could comment on that.

(10)   *Professor*: .hh Well I would like to, ahm, it definitely is rape season (.) and (.) I think it happens to the young freshmen because they are very unaware. I had a Master of Public Health student placed (.) in a student health service ah doing a survey a few years ago, and she discovered that most of the freshmen surveyed (.) had no idea that

(15)   rape was a problem on that campus. The sophomores, a larger proportion knew (..) the juniors most knew (..) and by the time (.) she was talking to seniors, they all knew, this is a big problem. So, (.) the beginning of the term is the time young men take advantage of unaware young women. This is not lost on the young men. That

(20)   they're there, and they're vulnerable and they can do it. And:: there is a peer culture that gives men credit for, in quotes, taking women.
Host: At taking freshmen, they–
Professor: [Yes
Host: [They count them, I -
(25)   *Professor*:   [Yes, yes
?:   m-hm
.
.
.
(30)   .

Provost: . . . There are a lo:t of pressures about (.) being popular, about being liked, about being cool, and and also not knowing the rules. So young women come into this situation, they don't really

(35)   know what the rules are, but they do:: know that it, that somehow if they get a reputation for being, (.) I'm probably using the wrong word but uncool, they, they ah, that's, that's going to be social

problem for them, and ah there are tremendous pressures on them at that point, and I also suspect tremendous pressures on young
(40) men too, to be successful, to be able to score, to talk tough, to not have sent- not be sentimental, not be caring, not be concerned, those things seem to come later, but at that age (..) it seems to me when you talk to young men and young women the sexism is still really rampant.
(45) *Host*: What, what role do you think that alcohol plays and drinking on campus, (.) and (.) and from the look of a some of the ads I was looking at student newspapers (.) um, (.) and billboards around campus, and and banners at football games, it seems that students are (.) are being told that that the message is drink and and you'll
(50) get sex.
Psychiatrist: I think beer particularly, is very important on campuses, and important generally in rape. Ah, I think (.) with the older rapists that drugs often are very important too. Ah, not, I think, the hard drugs on college campuses, but ah (.) marijuana (.) I think
(55) is a (.) significant ah factor. I think ah lo:sing the inhibition that ah alcohol can uh can cause, can cause a a loosening of social inhibition for both males and females a:nd permit men to do things they ordinarily wouldn't do. And permit women to do things they wouldn't do, to, to miss signals, ah to to get sloppy in their reading
(60) (.) of the signals so that it's (..) Ah, I, (..) many of the men I talk with (.) feel and seem sincere (.) in their (.) not recognizing the fact that they were raping, that they don't get the signals from the women.
Host: Well if you, if if you're drunk=
(65) *Psychiatrist*: =Yeah!=
Host: =And it's late and you're tired=
Psychiatrist: =Right!=
Host: =And and you did invite ah or or or you've consented to have someone in your room or or even in your bed ? to sleep ? I can see
(70) how things can get confusing, which is part of uh of of of or seems to be the nature of a lot of of date rape, that it almost goes beyond communication.
Psychiatrist: I think for for a lot of the the women who get involved in this as well as the men, having the (.) the (.) responsibility for the
(75) sex sort of being diffuse. So that she doesn't cle:arly say,(.) Okay, or it's not okay, and he doesn't clearly say, I'm gonna rape you (.) or If you say no, I'll stop. Neither of, none of that communication goes on (.) and I think both parties often are pleased that it doesn't go on, that it leaves things more vague.
(80) *Host*:   [Vague
Psychiatrist: And–
Host: Well you don't write a contract before you sleep with someone.
Psychiatrist: Right.
Provost: Now and this is an area right, ah one of the things I think
(85) you have to add to this is that this is an area where nonverbal communication becomes particularly important. Ahm, (.) there is quite a bit of research showing that people really do misread

nonverbal cues all the time, in all sorts of situations, that we're not very good at– we have a difficult enough time when we talk to one
(90)   another, knowing what we mean to say. When we don't talk and we do it in a nonverbal way, it's very very difficult to understand what the other person means. And it's precisely those areas that are hard to talk about of course. (..) .hh that become the areas at where nonverbal communication takes place,

(95)   *Psychiatrist*: Yes

Provost: and sex is a prime example of that.

Host: ((Attorney)), we don't want to leave you out of, out of the conversation, that must be very im– important in a, in a trial, what exactly gets said, as–

(100)   *Attorney*: Absolutely, and what I was going to say i::s what everybody is touching on right now I have to deal with constantly in court and I have to present to the jury or argue to the jury repeatedly she was not asking to be raped, what she did was stupid, she shouldn't have had so much alcohol, or she shouldn't, shouldn't of been alone with
(105)   this man, or y'know, so on and so forth, took a ride with somebody she had just met.(.) Ahm (.) But I constantly have to (.) ahm (.) argue to them .hhh even though she did x, y, and z (.) or whatever put herself in this situation, she wasn't asking to be raped because the statute's very clear, it doesn't have a footnote .hh that says,
(110)   y'know, the statute doesn't apply if the woman doesn't use good common sense and take care of herself at all times. Ahm.

Host: ((Reintroduces guests to radio audience))

.
.
(115)   .

Host: I think what ((Attorney)) was talking about was (.) terribly (.) important and so many people you hear them (.) say it, you hear it in in the newspapers, so many people reacted to the situation of ah (.) uh date the date rape at ((Urban)) in this way. That she brought
(120)   this guy up to her room she barely knew,(..) ah they were drinking, (.) she let him sleep in her bed, what did she expect?

Psychiatrist: Well what she, (.) that may have been very poor judgment on her part, because she may not have been able to read (.) this (.) guy very well and know (.) what he had in mind. But her poor
(125)   judgment, I agree uh with (..) ((Attorney)), her poor judgment doesn't justify his doing anything she didn't want done. However, it's important that HE KNOW that she not want it done. It's important that SHE SAY (.) she DOESN'T WANT (.) what's happening. Otherwise it leaves him in limbo as to what's expected.

(130)   *Provost*: Let let me add another complicating factor, ((slight laughter)) I did a study some years ago on how people met their spouse. And one of the things that I found was that a very significant proportion of people, this is the person they were currently married to, had in fact picked their spouse up. And I think that we have to add that to
(135)   this scenario. One of the factors of modern life (.) is that if you don't take risks you can be safe and you can be alone and safe, and one one of the problems that happens in modern society is that

people do have to take risks with strangers in order (.) to have
relationships because it's extraordinarily difficult for young adults
(140)   in modern urban society to meet people in safe (...) settings where
the other person is absolutely guaranteed to be safe, now, of course,
that makes it more difficult for women than for men, because
women are taking more risks so, I think that probably there isn't a,
there isn't a woman, (...) naa, I shouldn't say there isn't a woman,
(145)   but I suspect that most women in their lives, have, in fact, taken
these kinds of risks. And that of course makes it more complicated.
Host: Let's hear what our callers have to, say about this. Hi, you're on
the air.
Caller 1: Yeah, I think that lady just (.) never got any when she was in
(150)   school (.) and ah that's what her problem is. hh
Host: Excuse me? (..) Hello? (..) .hh, that's certainly a point of view,
let's take another call. ((Slight laughter)) Hi, you're on the air. (...)
Hi.
Caller 2: Hello.
(155)   *Host*: Hello.
Caller 2: Yes, I'm sorry I didn't realize I was comin' on. Ahm, ah, the
last call was ridiculous=
Host: =mmh
Caller 2: ahm, the thing is I just graduated from college a year ago, I
(160)   was a rugby player, so you can tell, that I was an idiot in college
and I I did drink, drink a lot of times and go to parties, but I have
to, ah, question the subtlety of communication that was brought up
a minute ago. Ahm, (..) the fact is, (.) that I mean, it shouldn't be
hard for anybody regardless of the amount of alcohol they've taken
(165)   in to tell the difference between a ah, you know, a coy no and a, and
a giggle (..) and begging, pleading, and screaming. Ahm (..) that is
the crime we're talking about right, I mean–
Host: Although, although, I think the issue in in a lot of these cases, is
that there might not be screaming, there might be struggling, there
(170)   might be someone who's so afraid, or intimidated that she's afraid
to to strike out or scream, ah I I think it it could become very
subtle in that way, which is the point that you're (..) that our guests
are making, and and ah ((Professor)) would like to reply to that.
Professor: I I would hope that the communication would be clear the
(175)   way you:: suggest it should be and that any reasonable person could
read it. Unfortunately, young women are too often socialized to be
very passive ? to not speak up ? to be seen as sexually desirable only
if they are somewhat passive, it makes it difficult in situations
sometimes too, to really speak up and say No, get off. Women are
(180)   taught that that's not how you're supposed to speak to others. So,
many women have more difficulty with this than I think some men
realize. .hh I–
Host: [I don't think we can deny either that that there are still,
there are certainly men who think that a no might mean yes?
(185)   *Provost*:   I was going to add that, I think
Psychiatrist: [OH, YES!
Professor: [YES!

Provost: [in lots and lots of
situations, that a, that a coy no and the giggle that you described,
(190)   gets interpreted as having been a coy no and a giggle, when in fact it
was closer to a scream. There's a certain social definition that goes
on in .hh in what those two things mean and I think for many men,
(.) and that first caller was not totally ridiculous as a matter of fact,
I think he represents how a lot of people feel, that women really
(195)   secretly want to be raped. So if anybody is sitting up here talking
about date rape as having been something bad, it isn't really
something bad because it's what what women want to be chased.
And that feeling is very predominant still in this society.

Host: Does that start to answer your question?

(200) *Caller 2*: Yes, absolutely, I'd if I could say um,(.) that the issue of date
rape, which was something I wasn't exposed to until I was at school
(.) where it did happen a bit,(.) ah has given me a (.) a n-nhew
respect for women, it must be very difficult to face (.) obstacles that
a that a, a guy never has to deal with. (And a)

(205) *Psychiatrist*:   [I think for both men and
women the, the communication is difficult. There are a lot of
women who do have fantasies of being coerced (.) and forced and
they're exciting, there are a lot of men who have

Host: [And they must be ashamed of, of them too,

(210) *Psychiatrist*:   [YES,]
Host: [I
mean some of them...

Psychiatrist: [a lot of them are, and a lot of men have fantasies in
which they are not the prime mover of the sexual encounter, where
(215)   the women is, women- woman is, where they are seduced and so, I
think both genders like to diffuse that so that they don't feel all the
responsibility for initiating the sex themselves and that makes it
difficult for both:: to read the signals from the other.

Host: Thank you for your call, and thank thank you for your honesty
(220)   too. .hhh I think, eh, I I find this hard to believe and I'd and I'd like
you to comment on it ((...Provost)), that um, I think there is a
significant number of men (.) out there and, and perhaps college
students in particular who who are just thinking about these things,
who grow up knowing that stealing is wrong, that murder is wrong,
(225)   that ah (.) sneaking up on a strange woman and dragging her
into the bushes to rape her is wrong, but that having sex with a
woman who might (.) not (.) really want you to do it or has said no
or you definitely know she doesn't want to do it, while on a date,
that isn't wrong, and that it might be something that you're entitled
(230)   to.

Provost: Wa-well, there are there are different definitions in how men
and women, and what men and women believe are going on in
those relationships. Um, if you ask young men and young women
for example, if you date someone who's slept around a lot and
(235)   everybody knows she slept around a lot, does that mean that she's
probably agreed to have sex with you when you ask her out and
spend money on her. And young men will say yes and young

women will say no. Ahm, if you've been out going out with
someone for a while and you've been sleeping together before, and
(240) you've broken up and then you go out on a date again, does that
mean she's consented to have sex with you? Young men will
typically say yes and young women will typically say no. Because
they have different definitions. And so, that I I think that one of the
areas that we're trying to t-talk about here, is what is the definition
(245) of consent. It's very difficult to determine when when when consent
has occurred when men and women have such a diff-different
understanding of the meaning. And if I may add, I think until
recent(ly), I think one of the things we're seeing now, is that young
women ARE coming to have a different definition, because for a
(250) very long time, I believe that young women have felt guilty and
responsible when these date rapes occur, and have taken on male
definition and haven't said anything about it. I think what's going
on more recently is that young women are say(ing), Hey I didn't say
yes to this, I didn't want it to happen, it wasn't all right, and I didn't
(255) agree, and I'm not to blame.

Host: ((Attorney)), what does a court of law eh ah, what does the law
say about the definition of consent and how do you see it changing
as more women are reporting ah rape, and apparently, I I think
those statistics last year were that only about 10 percent of all date
(260) rape is reported.

Attorney: Well, ahm, first of all I'd have to say, that as far as all the
cases that I've, that I've a handled, it's been very clear, the woman if
it's a young woman, in this sort of um drinking fraternity house ah
sort of situation that gets raped, has been very clear about saying
(265) no, or in the alternative, I mean, meaning there, I haven't
experienced, I haven't had a woman come to me and say well I just
giggled and kind of pushed him away gently I mean, they've usually
been real clear about it and really been physically forced or in the
alternative they've been unconscious because of the amount of
(270) alcohol, and that's really very common. So, um that's been, that's
been my experience. As far as ahm the consent issue though, there's
ahm (..) a lot of cases, a case law now that we argue that that ah
ahm is very clear, in other words, um, the relative sizes, you know,
of the victim compared to the defendant, ahm is taken into
(275) account, whether or not it's daylight, night time, ahm, words that
are used, in other words, all those things are taken into
consideration or the jury's instructed to take into consideration as
well as what she said. In other words, whether she said no.

Host: [So did]
(280) *Attorney*: I mean in other words, if she didn't scream no, you can still
though look at other circumstances, you know, look at other

Psychiatrist: [The]

Attorney: factors.

Psychiatrist: The rapists we work with at the ((Therapy)) Institute
(285) very often are excellent at getting women into situations where
they're confus::ed, where they don't have the supports they
ordinarily have, where ah they are afraid to resist, ah and the rape

(290) doesn't occur occur <u>instantly</u>, it may occur two or three or four hours into the relati<u>on</u>ship after they really intimidated her so that (.) from their point of view she has agreed. She stayed around, from her point of view she's been <u>terrified</u> and afraid to resist, and so it's <u>it's</u> it's not (.) typical in in our <u>clinical</u> situations that a man will grab a woman at a bus stop, pull her into the bushes and rape her. I mean that happens, and and we work with men who get convicted

(295) of that, but that's not a typical rapist. The kind of thing we're talking about today is, is the typical rapist today.

Attorney: That's absolutely right, I think the majority of rapes are are what we're talking about today and not the stranger drag off the street those are very <u>clear cut</u> cases.

(300) *Host*: Although what ... ((Psychiatrist)) is describing and I wd think some of our, someone listening would say, but that sounds like the <u>criminal</u> (.) <u>mind</u>. And we're talking about these boys at football games at co<u>llege</u>, at college, th-th-that you draw a distinction there.

Psychiatrist: But the guys in the fraternity <u>probably</u> supported each

(305) other in this, <u>probably</u> created an atmosphere in which it was difficult for her to re<u>sist</u> and that probably went on for several hours I don't know the details of that case, so, I m–, ah, but in general that's the way it goes.

Accounting for Rape

The participants in 'Date Rape' draw on all three models in accounting for rape. However, the three models are presented and supported in different ways. I will look at how participants call on each model in turn.

Victim Precipitation   Women who are raped by men are blamed or seen as complicit in the rape. They are blamed for being naive (10–19), using alcohol (55–60), not understanding the rules of social interaction (32–8), inviting dates to their rooms (68–72), taking risks in order to meet men (135–46), and so on. More subtly, women and men are presented as *equally* invested in vague communication even when the vagueness results in the man raping the woman:

Psychiatrist: I think for for a lot of the the women who get involved in this as well as the men, having the (.) the (.) <u>responsibility</u> for the

(75) sex sort of being diffuse. So that she doesn't <u>cle:arly</u> say,(.) Okay, or it's not okay, and he doesn't clearly say, I'm gonna rape you (.) *or* If you say no, I'll stop. Neither of, none of that communication goes on (.) and I think both parties often are pleased that it <u>doesn't</u> go on, that it leaves things more vague.

(80) *Host*:   [Vague

Psychiatrist: And–

Host: Well you don't write a contract before you sleep with someone.

Psychiatrist: Right.

However, the victim precipitation model is presented as an *unacceptable* account of date rape. This is achieved by presenting the model in exaggerated fashion and attributing its endorsement to others, not the participants. Those who endorse the model, first jurors (100–12) then an unspecified 'so many people,' (116–21) are depicted as needing to be convinced that it is false. In lines 100–21, Attorney effectively rebuts the notion that women cause their own rapes by reminding listeners of her status as an attorney who argues cases in front of juries, and by asserting her knowledge of the rape statute. She draws upon the authority of the law to define rape as a crime that exists independently of whether the victim has used poor judgment. However, Host deflects the force of her rebuttal by immediately changing the topic, and then reintroduces a victim-blaming account, attributing it to 'so many people.' This time it is Psychiatrist who rebuts the victim-blaming, asserting his agreement with Attorney that a woman's poor judgment does not justify rape (122–6). However, Psychiatrist then continues his turn (126–9) by moving to a miscommunication model and placing responsibility for clear communication on the woman. It is important that men know women's intentions, and it is women's responsibility to insure that men obtain this knowledge, 'It's important that SHE SAY (.) she DOESN'T WANT (.) what's happening.' Provost follows with an empiricist justification ('I did a study some years ago') for the view that women's risk-taking contributes to rape. This view is consistent with the earlier (contested) view attributed to jurors and others, that women's poor judgment is a cause of rape.

The victim precipitation model is a contested account in this conversation among experts, given voice largely by being attributed to other people. However, although participants seem to be taking great pains to dispel the notion that women are to blame for men raping them, victim-blame reasserts itself in their explanations. And, if women are not to be blamed for poor judgment, they can still be blamed for failing to communicate.

Societal Forces   In contrast to the victim precipitation model, endorsement of a social structural model is unproblematic. Host introduces the topic of causation, and participants agree that there is a peer culture that encourages men to treat women as prey (1–10), creating a 'rape season' on campus. They speak of men 'taking' and 'counting' vulnerable sexual partners (19–26). They note pressures on both sexes to comply with social norms, and sexism is named as a problem by one speaker (32–44).

Miscommunication   There is much talk of miscommunication throughout this segment. People talk about 'signals' that are missed by the intended recipient. They discuss factors that impede accuracy of communication. Alcohol loosens inhibitions so that both men and women 'get sloppy' in reading their partner's signals. People communicate poorly when they are 'tired.' Both actors *prefer* vague communication. And nonverbal cues are inherently confusing (55–96). Moreover, women are socialized not to speak up, and men may misinterpret their cues (174–95). Even sexual fantasies are enlisted as a factor that 'makes it difficult for both:: to read the signals from the other' (205–18).

In a general sense, the miscommunication model underlies much of the accounting for rape by the speakers in this group. However, the notion that miscommunication occurs because women and men have divergent conversational goals and styles is not voiced at all. The closest participants come to a two-cultures model is in lines 231–83, where Provost introduces the notion that women and men have 'different definitions' of consent. However, participants quickly reject a 'different-but-equal' account, maintaining that whose interpretation prevails when definitions conflict is determined by social structural factors. The importance of social power is emphasized by Provost's point that women in the past accepted 'male definitions;' this did not, however, prevent them from being raped, but only from feeling entitled to seek redress.

How do participants hold to a miscommunication model while they are also endorsing social structural factors such as greater male power? They make the claim that different-but-equal interpretations of the same events are unlikely, given that men's interpretations are given more weight in a patriarchal society, yet they also maintain that sexual negotiations are fraught with well-intentioned miscommunication. If miscommunication is not due to different-but-equal conversational styles, what is its cause? It must be due to one of two things: either someone is not good at sending messages, or someone is not good at receiving them. At times, both sexes are said to have these communication problems, due to the unique nature of sexual communication (68–96). At other times women are highlighted or singled out as the senders of vague, inconsistent, or weak messages (174–82). Men are never singled out as deficient senders of messages, and only once are they cited as culpable in their reading of messages, when Host rather tentatively suggests 'I don't think we can deny either that that there are still, there are certainly men who think that a no might mean yes?,' eliciting agreement from others (183–87).

Men, but not women, are portrayed as *justified* in their misunderstandings, thus implying that it is some inadequacy in women's speech that is the source of the miscommunication. It is not that men are poor at 'getting' signals; only women are singled out as 'sloppy' in this regard. The use of vocal emphasis and pauses in lines 55–63 convey the honest bewilderment of men who rape women without noticing that they are doing so:

(55)   *Psychiatrist*:   I think ah lo:sing the inhibition that ah
       alcohol can uh can cause, can cause a a <u>loosening</u> of social
       inhibition for both males and females a:nd permit men to do things
       they ordinarily wouldn't do. And permit <u>women</u> to do things they
       wouldn't do, to, to <u>miss signals</u>, ah to to <u>get sloppy</u> in their reading
(60)   (.) of the signals so <u>that it's</u> (..) Ah, I, (..) many of the men I talk
       with (.) <u>feel</u> and <u>seem sincere</u> (.) in their (.) <u>not recognizing</u> the fact
       that <u>they were</u> raping, that they don't <u>get</u> the <u>signals</u> from the
       women.

Men's misunderstanding of women's intent is again justified by
Psychiatrist when he posits an asymmetrical responsibility for direct
communication. Women are enjoined to *say* what they do not want,
but men are not enjoined to say what they intend or check to make sure
they have obtained consent. Men are 'in limbo' because of women's
speech acts, not their own:

(126)   *Psychiatrist*:   However,
            it's important that HE KNOW that she not want it done. It's
            important that SHE SAY (.) she DOESN'T WANT (.) what's happening.
            Otherwise it leaves him in limbo as to what's expected.

When Caller 2 expresses empathy and respect for women, noting the
'obstacles that a that a, a guy never has to deal with,' Psychiatrist
abruptly shifts the topic to women's sexual fantasies of being raped
(200–18), thus deflecting the opportunity to present justifications of
women's misunderstandings. Yet later, Psychiatrist notes that the
rapists he has worked with in therapy are 'excellent at getting women
into situations where they're confus::ed, where they don't have the supports they ordinarily have, where ah they are afraid to resist, (285–7).'
  Within the miscommunication framework, tensions exist. Men are
portrayed both as innocent victims of justifiable misunderstanding and
as manipulative, clever abusers. However, they are not taken to task for
failing to communicate. Women are fleetingly portrayed as being in a
difficult social position, but more often are positioned as the *source* and
cause of miscommunication. The miscommunication model, as it is
deployed in accounting for date rape, is not a model of separate-but-
equal styles. Rather, it is a deficiency model, and the deficiency is more
often women's than men's.

Missing Agency: Where is the Rapist?
Throughout the discussion, rape is presented not as the action of an
agent but as something that 'happens.' Moreover, it is euphemized
rather than presented as an act of coerced sexual penetration, and participants do not contest the use of euphemisms. The agency of men
who rape is disguised through use of the passive voice. Women *get*
raped; 'it happens' (11, 202). Although it is acknowledged that men use

physical force to rape, men are described only in terms of 'situations' where 'rape occurs' (261–4, 284–8). Alternatively, when the actor is named, the action is euphemized. Men rather quaintly 'take advantage of' women and 'do things.'

> *Professor*:   ... this is a big problem. So,
> (.) the beginning of the term is the time young men take advantage
> of unaware young women. (17–19)
> *Psychiatrist*:   I think ah lo:sing the inhibition that ah
> alcohol can uh can cause, can cause a a <u>loosening</u> of social
> inhibition for both males and females a:nd permit men to do things
> they ordinarily wouldn't do. (55–8)
> *Psychiatrist*:   But her poor
> judgment, I agree uh with (..) ((Attorney)), her poor judgment
> doesn't justify his doing anything she didn't want done. (124–6)

There are only two places in the segment where rape is described as a violent and coercive act by a man. The first is when Host presents the actions described *in explicit contrast to what occurs in date rape* (220–30):

> *Host*:   I'd like
> you to comment on it ((...Provost)), that um, I think there is a
> significant number of men (.) out there and, and perhaps college
> students in particular who who are just <u>thinking</u> about these things,
> who grow up knowing that stealing is <u>wrong</u>, that murder is wrong,
> that ah (.) sneaking up on on a <u>strange</u> woman and dragging her
> into the bushes to rape her is wrong, but that having sex with a
> woman who <u>might</u> (.) <u>not</u> (.) really want you to do it or has said no
> or you definitely <u>know</u> she doesn't want to do it, <u>while on a date,</u>
> that <u>isn't</u> wrong, and that it might be something that you're entitled
> to.

The effect is to distance date rape from acts of physical coercion in which men are intentionally and culpably assaulting women. She uses the word 'rape' to describe the latter, and likens it with stealing and murder; in contrast, she uses 'having sex' to describe the former. By implication, date rape is not as serious, does not involve (as much) coercion and men are not as responsible for it. Discursively, she achieves a distinction between date rape and what we might call 'real rape,' a distinction that functions to relieve men of their agency in date rape. However, the view that date rape and real rape ought to be perceived differently is attributed to others, 'a significant number of men out there and perhaps students in particular,' not to herself or the other participants.

The only place in the segment in which rape is described in the form 'X rapes Y' is lines 284–303. When Psychiatrist describes a man grabbing and raping a woman the act is described in explicit contrast to 'typical' rapes, once more achieving the real rape/date rape distinction, and eliciting agreement from Attorney. Host's next statement seems to attempt a further distinction, this time between good men and bad men. The rapists treated at the psychiatrist's clinic have 'criminal minds,' in contrast to 'these boys at football games at college.' The active agency of the rapist, whether it is expressed in 'grabbing a woman at a bus stop' or in maneuvering women into intimidating, terrifying and confusing situations, cannot be attributed to college boys. As with her earlier distinction between real rape and date rape, she distances herself from this view by attributing it to others. However, Psychiatrist rejects the further distinction and asserts the similarity between his clinical patients and 'the guys in the fraternity' (304–8).

Accountability

Host's distinction between college boys and men with criminal minds, had it been accepted by the other participants, would have functioned to excuse college boys from responsibility for raping women they know, on the grounds that they are not the sort of people who would deliberately intimidate and coerce women. Thus, if a college boy does coerce a woman, it must be the result of a misunderstanding. Although participants did not endorse this view, at other times they offer reasons why men who rape their dates and acquaintances should not be held fully responsible. Students learn from billboards and banners that if they drink they will 'get sex' (45–50); alcohol loosens their inhibitions; men rape without realizing it because women give inadequate 'signals' (55–63); actors are tired (66); people in general misread nonverbal cues (84–96); men are 'in limbo' because women don't *say* they would rather not be raped (127–9), and so on. The underlying model for each of these justifications is the miscommunication model. Earlier, I showed how the model is deployed to blame women for not communicating directly and clearly. In these extracts, the model is deployed to excuse men from responsibility for obtaining the consent of a prospective sexual partner.

Crises and Resolutions

As we have seen, the participants in this public discussion of date rape disown the victim precipitation model. They acknowledge, but do not elaborate on, social structural influences. For the most part, they rely on the notion of miscommunication, but they do it in an asymmetrical fashion. Although a two-cultures model could be deployed to ask, *why don't women and men communicate sexual and relational intentions directly and responsibly?* And, *how can both groups be educated to do so?*, the model is not used in this gender-neutral fashion. Rather, it is used to deflect men's accountability for rape. In order to achieve this, men who rape must be portrayed as *well meaning* (not hostile or sexually aggressive); thus Host's distinction between college boys and those with criminal minds. Men who rape must also be portrayed as *honestly confused* and unable to decipher women's messages to stop assaulting them. This is done in two ways: by positioning women as poor communicators and by calling on external factors (alcohol, fatigue) to explain why communication is impeded.

Two male callers disrupt this account, creating crises for the participants (147–82). The first caller is verbally sexually aggressive, claiming that the views of an (unspecified) woman speaker are due to sexual deprivation. His violation of the norms of public discourse undercuts the presentation of men as essentially well meaning and cooperative in their interactions with women. The participants do not immediately respond to this violation, except for Host's embarrassed slight laugh, but the second caller labels it 'ridiculous.' He then situates himself as entitled to speak about campus violence against women by virtue of his credentials as a former college student, rugby player, and alcohol user. He disputes men's inability to recognize when they are raping women, claiming that it is in fact very easy to tell the difference between coyness and resistance. Moreover, he names rape as a *crime*.

Rather than accept Caller 2's expert status and the threat his account makes to the miscommunication model, Host and Professor reassert the model. They claim that communication in date rape situations is 'very subtle' and they introduce a social learning explanation: women are socialized to be passive, and this learned passivity makes it difficult for them to communicate clearly. As I discussed earlier, socialization explanations for women's speech styles have the effect of siting the causes for women's supposed deficiencies in the distant past and obscuring the influence of current interactional and social structural factors. In this instance the deployment of a socialization explanation serves to deflect the focus on men and their accountability which has occurred as a result of the callers' comments. It is not until the sixth conversational turn after Caller 1's verbal aggression that a participant, Provost, enlists his behavior to reintroduce social structural factors in rape (191–8).

A crisis occurs for participants when Caller 1 and Caller 2 enter the discussion. In distinct ways, these two male callers assert male agency in violence against women. Caller 1 insults a woman participant. His allegation that she is engaging in a public forum on rape because she 'never got any when she was in school (.) and ah that's what *her* problem is' is bizarre and aggressive – and also cowardly, since he is protected by anonymity. Caller 2 positions himself as a past member of the social group the speakers are analyzing: he drank, played rugby, and went to parties. The miscommunication model provides him with a justification for coercive sexual acts he or his friends may have committed. Yet he challenges the notion that men rape women without realizing it. *As* men, both these callers have a privileged status in this discussion; they are members of the class (potential rapists) that the experts are trying to understand. Yet the opportunity to enlist these callers' behavior in naming male agency is lost. Although Provost attempts to connect Caller 1's insult to larger cultural conceptions of women's sexuality (191–8), the discussion soon turns in other directions, and the crisis is resolved by a return to the miscommunication model.

Implications of a Miscommunication Account of Rape

The miscommunication model has been regarded as a progressive alternative to the victim precipitation model with its associated victim-blaming. It has gained ascendancy over a sociocultural model as well, perhaps because it seems to lead to more specific recommendations through which individuals can prevent rape. Indeed, the miscommunication framework has become the culturally dominant explanation for acquaintance rape among helping professionals, educators, and the college students whose behavior the model seeks to explain (Corcoran, 1992). What are the consequences of the widespread acceptance of miscommunication as a causal explanation for relationship violence? I will discuss evidence for three consequences: that women are encouraged to accept sole responsibility for rape prevention; that they are blamed (and encouraged to blame themselves) if rape prevention strategies fail; and that power issues in the interpretation of relationship violence are obscured.

Rape Prevention: a Woman's Job   It can be seen from the talk of the radio panel analyzed above that, even in the hands of helping professionals, the miscommunication model does not eliminate victim-blaming. In addition to being blamed for drinking or inviting dates to their living spaces, women are blamed for failing to say no clearly and unambiguously. If miscommunication is a woman's problem – and there are few suggestions by proponents of the model that men communicate poorly – then preventing rape remains a woman's responsibility.

The majority of campus rape education efforts are aimed at women. Within them, very little is said about men:

> If you were unfamiliar with our culture and you happened to attend a typical college date rape program, you might have a hard time figuring out that men have any responsibility for rape or rape prevention. It is impolite to say that men rape and outrageous to point out that the only way to change the incidence of rape and eliminate rape is for men to stop raping. (Corcoran, 1992: 137)

The prevention strategies recommended in campus rape education programs emphasize *self-empowerment* for women. They include self-defense training and verbal assertiveness training. In this extract from a female student's evaluation of such a program, the student has accepted the responsibility for protecting herself from rape by improving her communication style:

> [W]hat I got out of the whole program was that date rape happens a lot because there is a communication gap between two people and a preventative measure may be to bridge this gap . . . I was reminded that although rape is the attacker's fault, I can help protect myself by being more aggressive, giving firm answers, clear signals, and by communicating with the male. (Corcoran, 1992: 135)

In Chapter 3 I criticized the notion that through assertiveness training women could empower themselves and end discrimination. The self-empowerment model is stretched even further when applied to rape. Although there is some evidence that *physical* resistance may deter rapists, there is little evidence that *verbal* resistance has the same effect. It is misleading and potentially harmful to women to emphasize assertive communication as a rape avoidance strategy when there is no evidence that a man whose goal it is to have sexual intercourse (with or without consent) will be dissuaded by an assertive statement (Corcoran, 1992). A naive belief in the efficacy of individual prevention strategies is exemplified in this student's account of an acquaintance rape discussion in her college dorm:

> The group discussed teasing a man, and leading him on when you are not meaning to . . . I learned a lot about communication, to say no and explain yourself, and if you do communicate then you will not be forced to do anything you don't agree with, or feel comfortable with. (Corcoran, 1992: 136)

While the notion of empowerment has appeal because it makes people feel more in control of their fates, conceiving power as an internal possession of the individual encourages victim-blaming (Kitzinger, 1991). And the popular press is quick to pick up on the potential for holding women responsible for the violence enacted upon them. Celia Kitzinger (1991) cites a US women's magazine article that uses psychological research to assert that some women have a 'victim look' that attracts rapists. In this account, power is conceived as a mental set, a belief about oneself, not a relational construct. A woman becomes a victim because she does not believe in her own power.

It must have been my Fault: Self-blame   When educational programs emphasize the subtlety of communication, the inevitability of misunderstandings between women and men, and women's responsibility for communication clarity, their potential for fostering self-blame is great.

'If a woman does not employ self-empowerment strategies (or if they are not effective), there is the danger she will blame herself ("I must have miscommunicated or not communicated assertively enough")' (Corcoran, 1992: 135–6). Moreover, educational programs may lead women to believe that they have been giving out subtle cues of which they are unaware. As the student quoted above said, they may believe that they have 'led men on' even though their conscious intention was to refuse.

The individualistic notion of power encoded in violence prevention programs has been shown to increase self-blame. Jenny Kitzinger (1990, cited in C. Kitzinger, 1991) has analyzed the consequences of child abuse prevention programs that encourage young children to speak up and assert their rights. Adopting an individualistic concept of power, these programs focus on empowering children to reject the abuser's attempts by saying 'No.' In a follow-up study, children in one prevention program were *more* likely to blame themselves, believing that if a child is abused it is his/her own fault. In a participant observation study, women students perceived themselves as having significantly *less* right to resist an attack after taking a 14-week self-defense class (Kidder et al., 1983). Qualitative analyses suggested that this disturbing result was due to the instructor's emphasis on the student's power to maim or injure an attacker, combined with a more subtle message about the grave consequences of exercising one's rights injudiciously. The instructor often gave cautionary messages about over-reacting to a potential assault. In a comparison class, taught with a more feminist emphasis on a woman's right to control her own body, perceived changes were more positive. Thus, the psychological lessons learned by students in programs designed to 'empower' them may be quite unexpected.

Telling people that they have the right to say no is not enough. Unless this individualistic notion of rights and the power to exercise them is placed in a context that recognizes how those rights are constrained by social forces, the discourse of self-empowerment provides yet another rationale for blaming the victims of violence – one that people use even when they themselves are the victims.

Social science researchers seem to recognize the limits of self-empowerment when they write about their *own* experiences of power and powerlessness (Adcock and Newbigging, 1990; Kitzinger, 1990, 1991; Parlee, 1991; Tiefer, 1991; Unger, 1983; Wilkinson, 1990; Wilkinson and Burns, 1990; Yoder, 1985). Whether it is accounts of tenure battles by women faculty, efforts to mobilize women to achieve a place in the organizational structure of psychology, or encounters with tokenism, when women social scientists write about their own struggles with a power hierarchy they do not speak of communication deficiencies, lack of entitlement, fear of success, and so on. They do not recommend assertiveness training, communication seminars, or therapy. They do not blame themselves or believe that they are unconsciously causing their own problems by sending out 'mixed signals.' Rather, they focus on the structural and political barriers they confront, and they emphasize sociopolitical strategies for change.

Men: the Missing Agents   As I showed in the talk show analysis, men are rarely named directly as the agents of rape. Rather, women 'get (themselves) raped;' 'it does happen a bit.' In rape prevention programs, as Carole Corcoran suggested, it seems to be impolite to mention that rape is an act of physical and psychological coercion that one person *does* to another, let alone that these actors are men and that they bear some responsibility for their actions.

Recent work on dating violence suggests further troubling implications of the miscommunication model. Like acquaintance rape, dating violence has become a recognized social issue only within the last decade. Two models have typically been used to explain it: the miscommunication model and a dominance model. In a novel analogue study, Roger Chaffin and Deborah Mahlstedt (1994) examined whether a focus on one or the other of these two models influences perceptions of who is responsible for an incident of dating violence.

College student participants read either a paragraph justifying greater male power in relationships on traditional grounds (women should look up to the significant men in their lives, men should be heads of households, men should be the leaders in initiating dating relationships) or a paragraph emphasizing effective communication in relationships (both sexes should clearly and directly communicate feelings and intentions, family decisions should be discussed and agreed upon, open communication facilitates mutual understanding, and so on). They then read a dating scenario in which a heterosexual couple's disagreement escalates into shouting (by both partners), then pushing and slapping (by the male). Finally, participants rated the extent to which each character was responsible for the violence, failed to communicate, and felt they could intimidate the other.

The dominance and miscommunication frameworks did not lead to different evaluations of the male character's behavior. Both sexes saw him as more culpable on all three measures (responsibility, communication, and intimidation) than his partner was. However, men who had read the miscommunication paragraph rated the *female* character as *more responsible* for being pushed and slapped in the face than those who had read the dominance paragraph. When violent behavior is placed in a miscommunication context, college students place more responsibility on the victim of violence.

The Social Construction of Miscommunication

Representing the talk of women and men in Venusian/Martian dichotomies or opposing 'genderlects' takes researchers full circle back to 1975 (DeFrancisco, 1992). Moreover, the dichotomies are being extended to new realms, including explanations of violence against women. The regression is made more palatable by downplaying the working of power: 'report talk' and 'rapport talk' are less disturbing than 'powerful' and 'powerless' language. Although the 1970s search for sex-differentiated features and the subsequent assertiveness training fad have not entirely faded away, miscommunication is the bandwagon of the 1990s. It is interesting to speculate why.

In an analysis of (heterosexual) couples' advice books of the late 1970s, Ellen Ross (1980) noted that there is a genuine 'love crisis' at this point in history – a transformation of family forms and social life, along with a paucity of material resources for coping with it. Heterosexual feminists, she argues, have focused largely on issues of workplace equity and political/economic change, leaving their intimate relationships with men 'unreformed.' Indeed, feminists are just beginning to theorize heterosexuality (Wilkinson and Kitzinger, 1993). The contradictory message about speech style aimed at women in the 1990s – pay for assertiveness training to help you get ahead at work, but accommodate to your Martian at home – is a powerful form of backlash against the social transformation of the family and feminist theorizing about it.

Janis Bohan (1993) has spelled out the 'chilling scenario' of 1990s backlash with respect to the belief that women are more caring and relationally oriented than men. Her scenario is equally chilling with respect to the two-cultures debate:

> Imagine a scenario where women have begun to recognize their marginalization and to assert their personal and collective right to self-worth. Imagine that women are making notable if limited strides both in improved quality of life and personal autonomy and in raising the consciousness of their society to their oppression and the need for redress. Imagine, further, that the lingering product of that oppression is women's distinctive 'way of being,' a more relational, caring approach to others.
>
> If you were a member of the long-dominant male power structure in this society, a group that wished to retain its hegemonic position, how might you proceed in the face of such challenges? First, no conscious conspiracy need direct such an undertaking; socially constructed understandings of what gender is and should be, what women are and should be, will suffice to guide both your traditionally empowered group and the response of the public at large. It will seem clear that your agenda is self-evidently right . . .
>
> Here are some suggested strategies for retaining power. You should call public attention to instances where the proposal for a return to traditional roles comes not from you but from among women's own numbers. At the

same time, you should be vocal in your personal admiration for these qualities. Women will welcome your praise for qualities now seen as inherently
theirs and inherently valuable, and it will offer no threat to your power to
grant such acclaim, for these are traits of the disenfranchised.

You should employ and encourage public and political discourse that
support your agenda . . . You should encourage media coverage that blazons
across the front page commentary highlighting sex differences and support-
ing 'traditional' values. Serious scholarly and political criticism must be
relegated to academic journals where it will go largely unnoticed.

If effective, this strategy should result in a populace convinced of the
merit of separate spheres and comfortable with their own place in such a system. Critics will be largely unheard; those who are heard will appear
resistant to the truth of common experience and hostile to the natural order.
(1993: 9–10)

Viewed in this way, the conclusion reached by Nancy Henley and
Cheris Kramarae (1991) gains added force: the construction of miscommunication between the sexes is a powerful tool, perhaps even a
necessity, for maintaining the structure of male supremacy.

5

On Conversational Humor

In previous chapters I have described three important approaches to gender-and-language research and offered a feminist critique of each in light of the social constructionist perspective introduced in Chapter 1. Most often, talk – and research on talk – has functioned to enact, re-create, and maintain the gender system. This chapter is different. In it, I will look at a particular kind of talk, a mode of speech that is indirect, ambiguous, fraught with multiple interpretations, and potentially subversive of the social order.

In humorous discourse, many of the issues addressed earlier in this book are played out in interesting ways. We will see further evidence that women's and men's speech is best conceptualized as a collaborative social activity rather than being grounded in essential individual traits. The individualist approach, widely used in humor research, has served only to confirm cultural stereotypes that women lack a sense of humor.

In examining conversational humor, we will once again come upon issues of *difference* and *dominance*. Although humor is often viewed as trivial, it is an important site for gender-and-language research because the relationship between gender and humor can be analyzed at all levels of the gender system. At the individual level, we speak of *having* a *sense of humor*, essentializing it as a stable trait (and one that women are often said to lack). At the interactional level, conversational humor can function to maintain gender relations, and, under some conditions, to subvert them. At the social structural level, mediated humor (published collections, comic routines) and conceptualizations of humor in psychological research reflect dominant views of gender. On the other hand, the political uses of humor by feminists indicate the potential of the humor mode to infiltrate and disrupt dominant meanings.

If women's talk is to disrupt relations of inequality, women must privilege talk with each other above talk with men (Cameron, 1985). It is exceedingly difficult for gender-and-language researchers to privilege the study of women's talk with women. As we have seen in earlier chapters, the rhetoric of difference influences what questions seem worth asking, what groups are compared, and what results are read as meaningful. In this chapter, there are, to be sure, further examples of man-as-norm and woman-as-problem research. But much of the work described here is woman-centered. I analyze women's accounts of what it means to have a sense of humor. Perhaps most important from a social constructionist perspective is the re-emergence of a distinctively feminist humor. At this historical moment, women's feminist humor can be a powerful agent of social change.

In this chapter, then, I analyze the contrasting views of humor that stem from essentialist and social constructionist conceptualizations. Next, I examine how difference and dominance are constructed and enacted as women and men create humor in both same- and mixed-sex groups. Finally, I will document the emergence and potential of a distinctively feminist women's humor. In Chapter 1, I noted that there is a need to better theorize power. Although feminist researchers have reason to be concerned with power and its workings, it has been little developed as an explanatory concept, especially within psychology. The dominance approach, while important, has sometimes been used naively, as though men always use talk to dominate, and women are always dominated by talk. This approach can lead to dilemmas of circularity: are women dominated in talk because they lack social power, or do they lack social power because they are dominated in talk? Following the lead of Celia Kitzinger (1991), I called for a more textured conception of power, one that recognizes different kinds of power at different levels of the gender system, and within differing kinds of discourse. In research on humor I see the beginnings of that more textured conception of power and some possible ways out of difference-versus-dominance dilemmas.

Humor as Collaborative Activity

Imagine that you and I are having a conversation. For you to be able to tell a joke, I have to give you the floor and signal in subtle (usually non-verbal) ways that I'm willing to let you be funny. Then I have to pay attention to your witticism – let you hold the floor. And then I have to let you know I 'got it' – and know you meant it as a joke – by laughing, giving nonverbal responses such as rolling my eyes, or by adding a witticism of my own. If this delicate interpersonal transaction goes awry, your wit may fall flat, or I may be shocked or offended rather than amused. The need for conceptualizing language as social process is nowhere more apparent than when we start to think about how people use conversational humor and wit.

People signal their intention to make humor nonverbally, with a wink, a shift in posture, or a laugh. They use other paralinguistic devices as well. To repeat an example from Chapter 3, the ironic sense of the following exchange depends on intonation and vocal emphasis:

Have you met the new Provost?
A *charming* man.

Speakers signal their use of humor verbally, too, by using standard joke-prefacing devices ('Did you hear the one about . . .?') or opening a wedge for their telling of a humorous anecdote ('You won't believe what just happened to me!') (Cashion et al., 1987). Whatever the signalling devices (and they are usually multiple), they are inherently ambiguous and subtle. Direct statements and clear-cut, one-dimensional cues would be characteristic of serious, not humorous, discourse.

When an individual signals her/his intent to introduce humor into an ongoing conversation, others can either choose to collaborate or resist (Long and Graesser, 1988; Mulkay, 1988). They can facilitate and participate in humor, or they can respond with a serious counter. This process is worth examining in more detail for its implications about gender and conversational humor. Among Michael Mulkay's (1988) examples of informal collaboration in humor initiation are two conversational sequences that are relevant to gender issues. The first is taken from Mulkay's own recording of adolescent girls talking together:

Madeleine's Joke

A: Have you heard the one with the woman at the doctor's?
B: Might have. I dunno till you tell us.
C: Go on tell us anyway, it don't matter if we've heard it.
A: Right. At the doctor's
C: Don't tell me, there was this woman.
A: Oh shut up.
C: All right, all right.
A: At the doctor's there was this woman with a baby ...
(Mulkay, 1988: 58)

In this sequence, A offers a formulaic joke-prefacing device, 'Have you heard . . .?'; B and C offer verbal encouragement to continue with 'I dunno till you tell us' and 'Go on tell us anyway.' Moreover, C makes fun of the formulaic nature of the incipient joke with 'Don't tell me, there was this woman.' Thus, potential recipients of a joke are helping the prospective joke-teller to create conversational 'space' for her humor; indeed, they respond to her gambit in ways that carry them into the humor episode together (Mulkay, 1988). I find this example interesting partly because it provides a counter-example to the claims of some researchers that girls and women do not initiate humor, do not like or remember jokes, and lack a sense of humor. This sort of collaboration in the production of a joke has also been recorded among adolescent boys (for example, Sacks, 1978).

The second sequence (Mulkay, 1988: 59–61) is taken from Deborah

Tannen's close analysis of conversation among a mixed-sex group of
friends at a Thanksgiving dinner party (Tannen, 1984: 88–9). In it,
Peter tries to insert a joke into the conversation as people are engaged
in the serious-mode activity of gathering around the table and deciding
where each will sit.

Smoking after Sex

(1) *Steve*: So should we do that? Should we start
    Deborah: Sure
    Steve: with the white?
(2) *Peter*: Didju hear about the –lady, who was asked,
(3) *Deborah*:   I'm gonna get in there, right?
(4) *Chad*: Okay.
(5) *Peter*: Didju?
(6) *David*: We have to sit boy girl boy.
(7) *Chad*: Boy girl boy?
(8) *Peter*: Didju hear about the lady who was asked,
(9) *Chad*:   There's only two girls.
(10) *Deborah*: What?
(11) *Peter*: Did you hear about the lady who was asked . . . Do you
     Chad: Boy girl boy
     Peter: smoke after sex?
(12) *David*: I don't know I never looked. (nasal tone)
(13) *Deborah*: And she said? What?
(14) *Peter*: I don't *know* I never *looked*
(15) *Deborah*:   Oh (chuckles)

As the group decides where people will sit, Deborah says, 'I'm gonna
get in there, right?' and Chad replies 'Okay.' David contributes (line 6)
'We have to sit boy girl boy.' This conversation continues in lines 7
and 9. Meanwhile, Peter tries to tell a joke. His first attempt is in line 2,
with the formulaic 'Didju hear . . .' but he is interrupted. Undaunted,
he tries again in line 5, with the same opening. And again in line 8.
Finally, on his fourth attempt, he overrides Chad's interruption and
manages to get his set-up line out: 'Did you hear about the lady who
was asked 'Do you smoke after sex?' (line 11). However, the punch
line is delivered not by Peter but by David (line 12).

In his analysis of this episode, Mulkay emphasizes that, while collaboration is initially lacking (Peter tries three times before he gets a
chance to tell his joke), it eventually is forthcoming: 'David, for example, intervenes halfway through the joke and pronounces the punch line
in a funny tone of voice, whilst Deborah first provides a response which
allows Peter to restate the punch line and then supplies the terminal
chuckles which are needed to complete the humorous exchange.' Thus,
what originated as a solo becomes a 'joint accomplishment of the
group's members' (1988: 60).

Looking at the episode through a gender lens, however, I would emphasize somewhat different aspects. It is true that Peter has had to work hard to get the group's permission to tell his joke – he persists through three failed attempts. Despite his efforts, David steals his punch line, in a status-enhancing move against another male. Yet, with Deborah's help, Peter achieves his moment in the limelight and retrieves his status position in the group. Deborah comes to his rescue by giving him an opportunity to say his punch line after all (line 13) and to get his reward – the ritual chuckle that signifies that he has successfully told a joke (line 15).

Episodes such as this, Mulkay argues, are examples of pure humor or social play, and unrelated to gender. The dinner party is an informal social occasion, and the only two relevant roles are (gender-neutral) host and guest. However, I would argue that expectations and roles associated with gender may be in operation at any time and in any social setting, depending on group composition and purpose, sex ratio within the group, and many other factors (Unger and Crawford, 1992). Thus, I read gender into the ways that Peter is supported and enabled in his intrusive joke-telling, while Mulkay does not.

Women are expected to provide conversational support to men. As research on topic control, minimal responses, and interruption suggests, there are powerful norms that shape the ways men are provided with the limelight, sometimes through the efforts of both sexes. (In an old *New Yorker* cartoon, an intellectual-looking man and woman sit across a café table gazing into each other's eyes. 'But enough about me,' he says. 'What did *you* think of my last book?')

It can be funny (at least to women) to see these norms violated. A Sidney Harris cartoon in the *Chronicle of Higher Education* depicts a man and a woman in conversation at a party. The man's gambit, 'Wasn't it Kierkegaard who said "We perceive life through the filter of our lives, and though the world remains virtually unchanged, we see it changing continually?"' receives the deadpan reply 'No, Kierkegaard never said anything like that.' This humor is gendered in that it would not be as funny if the sexes of the actors were reversed. Applying the gender reversal test shows us that the humor in this interaction rests on implicit assumptions about what is conversationally appropriate for women and men. Feminist humorist Nicole Hollander often creates humor by mocking expectations of supportive conversational 'stroking' from women. In a panel from a *Sylvia* strip, a man strikes up a conversation in a bar with the line, 'You know the kind of woman I could really go for?' Sylvia responds, 'Is there anything I can say to prevent you from sharing these thoughts with me?'

Researchers need to analyze many more examples of girls' and women's humor in conversation, along with others' responses. We need to look at how and whether people collaborate with women when they initiate humor. As David and Deborah and their friends illustrate in 'Smoking after Sex,' in order for an individual to make humor he or she must be given the floor. Others must signal that they know the speaker is initiating humor and that they are willing to join the play. 'Madeleine's Joke' gives us one example of collaboration among girls. But what happens in mixed-sex groups? Are women's signals of a shift to humor ignored, just like their topic shifts (cf. Fishman, 1978)? Do their potential contributions go unrecognized? How often do they get the sort of support that Deborah gave Peter so that he could have his little moment in the spotlight? Is Peter's persistence in intruding his set-piece joke into the conversation a sort of behavior that is tolerated from men but not women?

Just Kidding: the Advantages of Indirectness

If 'serious' and 'humorous' can be thought of as distinct modes of discourse, the humor mode is clearly a subordinate mode (Mulkay, 1988). We're expected to (and do) operate in the serious mode most of the time, with only occasional flights into the humor mode. (One piece of evidence for this claim is that we can say in conversation, 'Hey, I was just kidding' but not 'Hey, I was just being serious.') Yet, although it's subordinate, every culture has a humor mode. And just because it's not serious doesn't mean it's trivial. On the contrary, humor can be used to accomplish very serious conversational work.

The key to understanding how people accomplish serious interactional goals through this subordinate mode of discourse is the recognition that people can use humor to convey messages that they can then deny, or develop further, depending on how the message is received by the hearer. Because it is indirect and allusive, the humor mode protects the joker from the consequences that his or her statement would have if conveyed directly in the serious mode. Hospital humor, for example, enables staff and patients to interact around the taboo topic of death. When old Mr Jones says jokingly to the nurse, 'I won't be wearing out those shoes,' and the nurses reply, 'Oh, Mr Jones, you'll be wearing your dancing shoes by next month' everyone involved can deny that the patient's impending death was mentioned. When the taboo topic is framed as a joke it does not become part of the 'real' discourse. Other examples include teasing, in which criticism is expressed indirectly and in deniable form, and the sort of sexual joking that allows participants to determine sexual availability without direct interrogation (Mulkay, 1988). As I discussed in the context of indirect requests (Chapter 3) and sexual communication (Chapter 4), people choose indirect modes in delicate situations. Indirect modes can save face, minimize accountability for one's actions, and slip taboo topics into conversation. And humor is perhaps the most flexible and powerful of indirect modes.

When someone sends the message 'I consider women to be less than full human beings' framed as humor, it is difficult for others to reject or even directly address the message. After all, sexist intention can easily be denied. 'I was only joking.' 'Can't you take a joke?' 'Lighten up.' 'Just kidding.' One simple reason women as a group may appear less humorous is that they are unwilling to participate in their own denigration. For example, Christine Griffin (1989) recorded a conversation in a train in which three women were discussing their work as reference librarians. The male companion of one interrupted with the following joke:

'What's the difference between a feminist and a bin liner?
A bin liner gets taken out once a week.'

The joke, which was totally unrelated to the women's topic, was greeted by silence, not laughter. Having interrupted the flow of conversation, the man then introduced a different, unrelated topic, and took an active part in the conversation.

Designed for Difference: Research on Humor

Why Women have No Sense of Humor
The stereotype of the humorless female has been embedded in Western culture for at least the past century (Sheppard, 1986; Walker, 1988). Men's accusations that women lack a sense of humor appear to be one of the firmest and most enduring of speech stereotypes (Kramarae, 1981). When Nancy Walker (1988) set out to study American women's humorous writing, she recalls that

> I felt as though I had ventured into uncharted territory. Studies of American humor abounded, but, as is the case in so much traditional scholarship, the women were left out or relegated to footnotes . . . At first I assumed that the virtual absence of women's humor from anthologies and critical studies was caused by the same myopic perspective that had made us think for so long that there had been no female composers or scientists. And this is certainly part of it. But as I continued to investigate, I discovered an even more basic reason: women aren't supposed to have a sense of humor. Time and again, in sources from the mid-nineteenth century to very recently, I encountered writers (male) commenting – and sometimes lamenting – that women were incapable of humor, and other writers (female) explaining that they knew women weren't supposed to have a sense of humor and then proceeding to be very funny indeed. (1988: ix–x)

Feminists in particular are charged with lacking or having 'lost' a sense of humor (Weisstein, 1973) although it is not clear how we can have lost what women were never believed to have.

Women as a Muted Group

Cheris Kramarae (1981) has applied the theory of muted groups (Ardener, 1975) to issues of gender-related difference in language use. This theory proposes that in every culture there is a dominant social group that determines the culture's ways of thinking and perceiving. The perceptions of other, less powerful, groups in the culture are imperfectly coded into language and less well represented in public modes of discourse. Although members of muted groups do develop their own models of the world, they must openly subscribe to the values of the dominant group.

In a chapter devoted to humor, Kramarae (1981) shows how lack of knowledge about gender and humor has stemmed from many factors, including the scarcity of research that involves women participants, the customary focus on measuring responses to ready-made humor, the lack of attention to spontaneous wit and its appreciation, and the paucity of studies in naturalistic settings. All these practices reflect the encoding of dominant group views in social science practice – a point that I will further document below.

Women's Language, Assertiveness Training, and Humor

Robin Lakoff's work provides an example of the sort of androcentric practices named by Kramarae. Lakoff (1975) claimed that joke-telling and humor are among the crucial stylistic differences between the sexes. Moreover, the difference was conceptualized entirely in terms of women's failure to meet a standard based on public performance. Women can't tell jokes. Moreover, they don't 'get' jokes. In short, women have no sense of humor. As I discussed in Chapter 2, Lakoff's model equated form with function. Therefore, it could not readily encompass conversational humor. When Mandy Rice-Davies ironically used the tag question 'Well, he would, wouldn't he?' she used a form Lakoff characterized as deferent. However, she used it for humorous effect and in the service of a very serious conversational goal.

The behaviorist-influenced assertiveness training movement conceptualized ideal speech as direct speech, based on stereotypes of dominant group behavior. There was no room in this formula for allusive, indirect speech modes, veiled meanings, or word play – indeed, no mention of the use of humor in conversation. In retrospect, it is astonishing that a model of ideal speech that omitted conversational humor could have gained such popularity.

Muted group theory provides a framework for understanding why the implicit norm for speech style is the (perceived) style of white upper-class men, and why even feminist-influenced theorists such as Robin Lakoff and the feminist therapists of the assertiveness training movement sometimes find themselves reading 'difference' as 'female deficiency.' It also helps us to understand why an androcentric defini-tion of humor has been encoded into cultural productions such as the humor anthologies Nancy Walker examined.

Reading the Experimental Results: the Social Construction of Women's Deficiency

My own review and analysis of psychological research on humor con-vinces me that Kramarae's claims about male bias are justified. There is a very large empirical literature on the psychology of humor (cf. Chapman and Foot, 1976; Goldstein and McGhee, 1972; McGhee and Goldstein, 1983a, b). Unfortunately, much of the older literature rep-resents the typical female as a person who lacks both the ability to appreciate others' humor and the desire or ability to create humor her-self (Crawford, 1989b). For the most part, social science research appears to have reproduced and reinforced the stereotype of the humorless female rather than challenged it.

Psychological research on humor has typically examined the *appre-ciation* of humor by presenting humorous 'stimuli' and trying to identify the characteristics of the stimuli or the participants that influ-ence perceptions of funniness. A typical experiment has participants rate the funniness of jokes or cartoons that have been preselected on a dimension of interest to the experimenter, such as hostility. Participants' ratings are sometimes correlated with scores on person-ality measures such as extroversion, and then inferences are made from these correlations. The *creation* of humor has rarely been studied (Marlowe, 1989). The social uses of humor have been examined pri-marily by dividing people into social reference groups (blacks versus whites, liberals versus conservatives) and comparing average ratings of funniness for supposedly relevant jokes.

Sex of subject is the most frequently analyzed 'group' variable in the literature, probably because both male and female participants have often been included routinely and differences have been documented where they occurred (McGhee and Goldstein, 1983a, b). Testing for group differences in the absence of clear theoretical reasons is a com-mon way that 'difference' gets encoded in research literature (Jacklin, 1981). However, gender has rarely been the central focus of research projects on humor. Although many studies have used both male and female participants, the majority of single-sex experiments have used males (Goldstein and McGhee, 1972). Occasionally, researchers in psy-chology, anthropology, and linguistics have concluded that only males appreciate sexual humor after choosing to study it only in all-male groups (Thorne et al., 1983). In the past, some experimenters have gone so far as to recommend using only males because females are 'inconsistent' (Middleton and Moland, 1959). Older anthologies frequently omitted women's humor. More recently they may contain a separate chapter on women's humor, while index listings make no mention of gender, sex differences, or any aspect of women's humor elsewhere in the book (for example, Mintz, 1988).

Bias in sampling is compounded by biases in the materials chosen for research. Humor created by women has been largely ignored in psychological research materials as well as by historians and literary critics (Dresner, 1988; Sheppard, 1986; Walker, 1988). Women are more likely to be the 'butt' of the public humor from which humor researchers draw their exemplars. For example, one analysis of jokes about old people found that twice as many jokes about men were positive in tone than jokes about women; three-quarters of all jokes about old women were negative (Palmore, 1986). Humor researchers studying hostile or sexist humor have frequently failed to control for sex of the initiator/recipient of aggression or the butt of sexual humor (McGhee, 1979). Women and minorities appear in jokes not as representatives of humanity in general but only when they are to be explicitly disparaged:

> It is rare to find the image of a woman in a mainstream joke used to symbolize universal human attributes. The reason for this could be that our society does not find images of women to be neutral. Mentioning a woman in a joke is frequently done so as to make some kind of statement about the nature and motivations of women. And the most effective way to make this statement is to have women function as the butts of jokes rather than as the subjects or heroes. (LeBell, 1983: 15)

There are whole categories of jokes about women for which there are no male parallels: prostitute jokes, mother-in-law jokes, dumb blonde jokes, woman driver jokes, Jewish mother jokes. Cartoons and jokes used in humor research have frequently used sexist or sexually suggestive stimuli which may well have different meanings for women and men (Love and Deckers, 1989). Only very recently have nonsexist or feminist cartoons or jokes been used in humor research. When nonsexist and/or nonaggressive materials are used, sex differences in humor appreciation have been few, although, not surprisingly, women tend to appreciate feminist humor (Chapman and Gadfield, 1976; Henkin and Fish, 1986; Stillion and White, 1987).

Researchers have recently tried to remedy gender bias in humor experiments by systematically varying the sex of the recipient of hostile behavior (Losco and Epstein, 1975) or the butt of sexual humor (Chapman and Gadfield, 1976) and by including the humor of female comedians in stimulus materials (Levine, 1976). If the problems with humor research were simply that it has incorporated the sorts of biases I have described, it could probably gain in ecological validity if such changes became the norm. However, like the analogue research on assertion discussed in Chapter 3, humor research has had more fundamental problems with ecological validity. Perhaps the most important of these is its decontextualization of humor phenomena. Just as analogue research on assertion decontextualized an 'assertive statement' by defining it operationally in terms of a scenario constructed by the experimenter, humor researchers decontextualized 'sense of humor' by defining it operationally in terms of ratings of experimenter-selected jokes in a laboratory setting. In both cases, they neglected the social context in which speech actions are usually embedded.

Researchers' definitions may have little relationship to participants' own meaning of 'sense of humor.' Goldstein and McGhee (1972) pointed out that less than 10 percent of the studies they found in preparing their extensive bibliography were on humor creation or production. Spontaneous wit has been virtually ignored as a source of stimuli in humor research (Goodchilds, 1972). As early as 1930, researchers had access to diary studies in which people were asked to keep logs of the occasions and topics of their spontaneous humor. Kambouropoulou's (1930) study is notable for the detail and care of its design and analysis and also for its use of only women participants (perhaps the latter was a factor in its neglect). This and later diary studies (Graeven and Morris, 1975; Mannell and McMahon, 1982) showed that reported humor events do not map onto classification schemes used by researchers. Moreover, the diary studies showed that set-piece jokes formed a very small part of most people's lived experience of humor; most reported humor was spontaneous and context-embedded. All these differences between people's experience of humor and researcher's definitions contribute to a lack of ecological validity for this research.

Having established sex differences in humor appreciation through the use of male-biased research materials, samples, and settings, researchers needed to account for those differences. Taking the accounts produced by humor researchers as texts, I completed an analysis of a representative sample of pre-feminist research on gender and humor (Crawford, 1990). With a student, Diane Gressley, I looked at the use of generic masculine language, justifications for studying sex differences, explanations for obtained differences, and other aspects of the written discourse. Perhaps the most striking feature of these accounts is the absence of explanation. Although they had chosen to compare the sexes, researchers typically included only a few, very vague lines, invoking the words 'societal expectations' for the sex differences they found. Because researchers' choices were based on their own pre-scientific and unexamined assumptions about sex differences and gender roles, their results both reflected and helped to legitimate sex-biased assumptions about human nature.

All the features of the empirical research that I have described – male-oriented stimuli, androcentric biases in research design and sampling, decontextualized settings, and an individualistic focus – had produced a deeply flawed literature on the psychology of humor. In accounting for the differences thus obtained, researchers constructed a discourse that naturalized and essentialized them by treating them as not in need of explanation. In much of the pre-feminist research, psychology has participated in the social construction of women as a deviant and deficient group with neither the wit to create humor nor the 'sense of humor' to appreciate it (Crawford, 1989b).

Gender and Conversational Humor: New Approaches to Difference and Dominance

Women's and Men's Accounts

Because psychology's understanding of how social meanings of humor are gendered is based largely on a deficiency model, I decided to explore people's accounts of their own humor and their definitions of what it means to have a sense of humor (Crawford and Gressley, 1991). Instead of imposing experimenter-defined 'humor stimuli' on participants in a laboratory, I chose to elicit their judgments about how much they create and appreciate a variety of humor types. In addition, I asked participants to create and justify their own definition of a sense of humor, and to assess their sense of humor in comparison with others, by rating themselves. By working in a less-structured situation than the traditional humor experiment, I hoped to allow aspects of humor to emerge that are not readily expressed in such experiments. Using these exploratory techniques, I hoped to develop a potentially more ecologically valid picture of gender similarities and differences in perceptions of one's own and others' sense of humor.

My students and I asked over 200 diverse people to participate in the study. Because this was an exploratory and descriptive study, we conceptualized variability as richness, not 'noise.' We asked participants to write a paragraph as follows:

> Think of a person you know who has an excellent sense of humor. Without using the person's name, describe his or her sense of humor and why it is outstanding.

We also asked participants to respond to a humor questionnaire that we had developed by observing humorous interaction in our own social groups before generating items. The 68-item questionnaire represented a wide variety of humor media (cartoon, familiar jokes, story-telling), topics (sexual humor, ethnic jokes) and types (slapstick, sarcasm, puns). Because previous research had stressed appreciation of humor and paid little attention to its creation, we chose to balance items on this dimension. Therefore, approximately half the items assessed the creation of humor (e.g., 'Do you tell funny stories about things that have happened to your friends and acquaintances?') and half assessed the appreciation of humor (e.g., 'Do you enjoy ethnic jokes?').

Our results gave a rich picture of our participants' understanding of what it means to have a sense of humor. The social value of a sense of humor was evident: they considered themselves to have a better sense of humor than the typical person of their sex. Moreover, males evaluated their sense of humor more positively than did females. Their responses also revealed 10 distinct factors in humor when factor analyzed (see Table 5.1). On the whole, women and men were more alike than different; sex differences occurred on only four of the 10 factors. Women scored higher on story-telling. Men scored higher on hostile humor, jokes, and slapstick comedy.

Five themes emerged from the narratives that people wrote about someone with an outstanding sense of humor: creativity, caring, real life (anecdotes, story-telling), hostility, and jokes. The caring dimension is particularly interesting because it had not been captured on the questionnaire. Respondents frequently wrote about a sense of humor that was employed to ease social tension, to 'cheer up' other people, and to reduce others' stress or anxiety.

As shown in Table 5.2, the rank order of the top three dimensions used was identical for male and female participants. Men used the creativity dimension significantly more. There were no differences in frequency of use for any other dimension.

In thinking of someone with an outstanding sense of humor, women preferred male models by 2:1 and men preferred male models by 5:1. People used the same dimensions in about the same proportions, except that when respondents chose to write about a male model, they were more likely to employ the creativity dimension.

In sum, women and men agreed that the most important characteristics of a good sense of humor are creativity, caring, and a basis in real-life events. The only difference in their views was one of degree rather than kind: men were more likely to use the creativity dimension than were women. Women's responses were more evenly spread among the top three dimensions. Creativity seems to be a relatively more important dimension to the men in this sample, while the women value creativity, caring and real-life humor more equally.

Our participants provided a wide variety of idiosyncratic descriptions of humor's functions in their lives. For the most part, the picture that emerged from these descriptions is not a gendered one, either in

Table 5.1   *Sex similarities and differences on the humor questionnaire*

Factor name	Sample item	Factor score Males	Females	t	p
Hostility	Are you likely to enjoy a joke even if it makes fun of a racial or minority group?	0.407	−0.223	4.86	< 0.0001
Joking	How often do you tell jokes?	0.355	−0.195	4.11	< 0.0001
Creativity	Do you make spontaneous or 'off the cuff' witty remarks?	0.040	0.022	0.46	n.s.
Laugh at self	How likely are you to be offended when others make fun of you?	0.054	−0.030	0.65	n.s.
Cartoons and comics	How often do you read the comics in the newspaper?	0.013	−0.007	0.16	n.s.
Female *v.* male	Do you think that men (women), on average, have a sense of humor?	0.052	−0.029	−0.64	n.s.
Slapstick	Do you enjoy slapstick humor?	0.187	−0.103	2.35	< 0.02
Anecdotal humor	Do you tell funny stories about things that happen to you and your acquaintances?	−0.209	0.115	−2.59	< 0.01
Sexual humor	Would you make a quip or witticism about sex in mixed company?	−0.016	0.009	−0.19	n.s.
Missing the point	Are you likely to miss the point of a joke?	0.066	0.037	0.08	n.s.

Factor scores are expressed as Z scores. $N = 72$ males and 131 females for each comparison; degrees of freedom for each t test = 201.
Source: Crawford and Gressley, 1991

terms of the dimensions important to female and male respondents or in terms of the dimensions they attribute to their self-chosen female and male models. Gender does enter the picture in that both female and male respondents were far more likely to choose a male model as embodying a good sense of humor and more likely to describe males as creative. Like the narratives, the structured questionnaire revealed more gender-related similarities than differences. In addition to documenting

Table 5.2 *Sex comparisons in the dimensions used to characterize an 'outstanding sense of humor'*

Dimension	Male (%)	Female (%)	χ^2
Creativity	73.47	56.52	3.91[1]
Caring	26.53	40.22	2.61
Real life	20.41	27.17	0.78
Jokes	12.24	18.48	0.91
Hostility	16.33	5.43	3.32
None	10.20	11.96	0.10

Each cell shows percentage of 49 male and 92 female respondents who used the dimension in their description.
[1] $p < 0.05$
Source: Crawford and Gressley, 1991

sex differences in appreciation, questionnaire responses suggest that males also *use* more hostile humor and formulaic joke-telling. Women preferred anecdotes and stories more than men did. In these respects, both women's and men's accounts are congruent with observational studies stemming from the two-cultures model (Jenkins, 1985; Tannen, 1990).

Humor research in psychology has rarely considered the importance of anecdotes and stories, although the accounts of our participants suggest that they are an important form, especially in women's humor. Like the diary studies, our qualitative data suggested that the folk definition of a sense of humor is at odds with the definition often imposed in psychological experiments. In the traditional experiment, sense of humor is operationally defined as ratings of jokes and cartoons that are very often hostile. But our participants told us that to them, these have very little to do with a good sense of humor. Instead caring, contextual (real-life), and creative aspects of humor were valued by both sexes. These dimensions frequently have been muted or overlooked in empirical research on humor.

One reason psychology has been blind to contextualized humor is that it has essentialized humor, regarding it as a property of individuals. For example, sex differences in joke ratings have sometimes been taken as evidence that women are more inhibited, more conventional, or lacking in self-esteem – all of which are internal, stable (trait) attributions. Humor has rarely been conceptualized as socially produced and embedded in social hierarchies.

Humor and Hierarchy: Ethnographic Studies
A few researchers have been attentive to the workings of gender and how they are played out in humorous interaction in mixed-sex, often

hierarchical settings. One of the earliest is Ruth Laub Coser's (1960) deservedly classic ethnography of joke-telling in a psychiatric work group. Coser wrote that, although female staff members demonstrated a capacity for humor, they deferred to males, who made 99 of 103 witticisms at staff meetings. Humor followed the staff hierarchy of rank and prestige, with those at the top making more humor and directing it downward. Men made more jokes; women laughed harder. More recently, Franca Pizzini (1991) analyzed humor generated in 100 observations of conversations surrounding childbirth in the maternity wards of five Milan hospitals. Pizzini noted the topic of humor, its initiators and targets, and the social functions it served in these medical settings. Like Coser, Pizzini found that the initiators and the targets of humor mirror the hospital hierarchy. Nurses who joked among themselves failed to do so in the presence of doctors. Interestingly, she noted that on the rare occasions when humorously intended remarks were initiated by someone low on the hierarchy, the intended recipients 'let them fall in silence without laughing,' thus preventing the humor attempt from disrupting the status quo (1991: 482).

Pizzini found that most humor in the childbirth setting functions to introduce the two taboo topics related to birth: pain and sex. Even as they work on the sexual parts of a woman's body, the staff are not permitted to openly connect what is happening to her with sexual activity. Nor are they taught to openly acknowledge her pain. Therefore, both topics are dealt with in the humor mode, where the talk 'need not become part of the history of the encounter, nor need it be . . . built into the meaning of subsequent acts. Because humor officially does not count, persons are induced to risk sending messages that would be unacceptable if stated seriously' (1991: 481).

In the birth episodes, there were many jokes about the woman's vagina, with medical staff interpreting suturing of an episiotomy as 'making it new again' or 'tailoring.' Pain was sexualized in remarks that encoded both taboo topics:

> A woman became taut with pain during post-partum cleaning and the nurse said with a smile: 'Do you act this way when your husband touches you too?' The patient shook her head in disagreement. A nurse said: 'Naughty girl, when her husband touches her she's all relaxed, but when we touch her she gets tense!' (1991: 481)

Sexual Humor and Male Dominance

Hierarchies of rank and achieved status are often confounded with hierarchy based on gender. How is gender hierarchy reflected in humor when other hierarchies are less salient? One way to ask this question is to examine informal sexual humor. The assumptions underlying men's sexual humor, and the ways in which it represents male–female relationships, may function both to express male dominance and to support and strengthen it. Michael Mulkay (1988) has examined the representation of women in men's sexual humor, using as data two interesting types of mediated humor: collections of 'dirty jokes' made by folklore researchers and observations of comic routines in British pubs. There appear to be four basic principles in men's sexual humor:

1 The primacy of intercourse – all men want is sex.
2 The availability of women – all women are sexually available to all men even when they pretend not to be.
3 The objectification of women – women exist to meet men's needs, and are, or should be, passive.
4 The subordination of women's discourse: women must be silenced.

It is easy to find examples of male sexual humor based on these four principles. Currently, a popular format for sexual humor is 'beer is better than women' one-liners. To my knowledge, they first appeared in mimeographed form on North American college campuses, but soon moved to T-shirts, bumper stickers, and formal publication. Examples from a recent book include 'Beer is better than women because . . .

> . . . beer doesn't expect an hour of foreplay before satisfying you.
> . . . you can try dark beers and lite [sic] beers without upsetting your parents.
> . . . a beer doesn't change its mind after you've taken off its top.
> . . . a beer never wants to stay up afterwards talking about respect. (Brooks et al., 1988)

In this humor, the male voice always triumphs over the female. 'In men's dirty jokes, it is not only women's bodies and services that are at men's disposal, but also women's language' (Mulkay, 1988: 137).

The same principles operate in humor use as in representation. Humor in conversation can be used by men to silence women, negate their personhood, and maintain conversational control. Mulkay analyzes humor use by drawing on James Spradley and Brenda Mann's classic ethnographic study of cocktail waitresses. In the bar under study, all the cocktail servers were women and all the bartenders were men. The bartenders had legitimate authority over the waitresses, but were also dependent on them. Men initiated and benefited from joking in this situation. They used it to reinforce their control over the women and deal with problems in maintaining their authority (for example, when they had made a mistake in an order). They made fun of the women's bodies with remarks like 'It'd look better if you had some tits. Who wants to pull down a zipper just to see two fried eggs thrown against a wall?' (Mulkay, 1988: 148).

For women, humor was a source of frustration because it was asymmetrical – women had much less latitude in what they could say, and they knew it, as illustrated by the following reconstruction of a conversation among waitresses:

> Rob made some reference about my chest.
> Same here. But I don't know what we can do to get him back.
> Maybe we could all get together and try grabbing him.
> That's silly, we aren't strong enough and they would just make a joke about it.
> We could all ignore him, but that wouldn't work because he would just pick at us until we responded. If we ignore him, we're admitting defeat.
> There's no way we can get them back. We can't get on their level. The only way to get them back is to get on their level and you can't do that. You can't counter with some remark about the size of his penis or something without making yourself look really cheap. (Mulkay, 1988: 145)

Mulkay concludes from his analysis of 'bar talk' that 'men's informal humor constantly denigrates women's bodies and stresses their inferiority as social beings' (1988: 149). Lest we think that only bartenders do this sort of thing, it is worth noting that in a recent sex discrimination case against the Wall Street investment firm Goldman Sachs, an employee, Kristine Utley, testified that the office humor was a source of sexual harassment. Memos introducing new female employees were illustrated with nude Playboy pin-ups, and other company memos contained 'beer is better than women' jokes, for example 'because a beer always goes down easy' (Kocol, 1989).

If the discourse of men's informal humor is an attempt to control women's meanings, are there effective strategies for reasserting control? Cocktail waitresses and investment bankers alike can be effectively silenced when those who denigrate them have institutionalized power over their employment. But there are other situations in which power relations are less constraining. Street remarks from strangers, often a source of embarrassment and shame to women, serve to remind their targets that men control public spaces and that women's bodies are acceptable objects for public denigration (Gardner, 1980). But what if women respond not with shame but with counter-attacks? Regina Barreca (1991) has argued that returning hostility with its like is a legitimate form of self-defense. She suggests that when a construction worker yells, 'I'd like to get into your pants, baby!' a woman should feel free to yell back, 'No thanks, I've already got one asshole in there!' or 'The bigger the mouth, the smaller the dick!'

Like the strategies women learn in physical self-defense classes, verbal strategies for self-defense turn the aggressor's energies back onto the aggressor. Like physical strategies, they are not 'natural' but must be learned through practice. Women taught to interpret their own behavior in essentialist terms may believe that they lack creativity, a sense of humor or the ability to take center stage in conversation, and that these 'deficiencies' are uniquely theirs. It is important for women to recognize that what may seem like *women's* deficiencies actually reflect *situations* in which anyone, female or male, might find it difficult to deliver a witty riposte. When I was a graduate student, the area of psychology in which I then specialized (learning theory and animal behavior) was almost entirely dominated by men, both numerically and in terms of holding positions of power. There were many occasions on which I became the target of sexual verbal aggression. Specialized conferences in particular were troublesome because men were over-represented by perhaps 10:1. At one such conference I found myself on an elevator with six men: four friends and colleagues and two strangers. I recognized one of the latter because, earlier in the day, I had attended his paper presentation on inducing tonic immobility (a response that can be seen in birds and some mammals in which they go limp, and 'play dead' when attacked).

Turning to this man, I remarked that I had enjoyed his paper. He proceeded to go into a lengthy routine about how his technique worked with women, too: just grab 'em by the back of the neck and hold tight and they go glassy-eyed and stop resisting. It was an excruciating moment: between floors on an elevator, with no possibility of a digni-fied withdrawal, and surrounded by watching males. The effrontery of a man who publicly would make a joke of rape, and so totally without provocation (other than the presence of a lone woman), rendered me speechless. After an eternity, the elevator doors opened and we parted. My colleagues and I walked a few feet. I was red-faced and near tears with shame and humiliation. But when I finally looked up at my friends I saw that they too were red-faced and shamed. Unlike me, they had not been directly attacked, but they had been witnesses to clearly out-of-bounds behavior and had not spoken up. Finally, one mumbled, 'You didn't do anything to deserve that.' Like me, they had been unable to come up with a response – dignified, witty, or any other – in response to unwelcome, hostile, and aggressive humor.

In Chapter 3, I discussed an implicit male norm of assertive speech that implies that normal people (a.k.a. white males) typically respond swiftly and assertively to infringements of their rights. I also reviewed field studies and other research showing that such direct assertion is not nearly as prevalent as the standard implies. Like the notion of uni-versal male assertiveness, the idea that men have a universal ability to top insults or squelch another's verbal aggression is a myth. Women's 'deficiencies' in this regard are socially constructed in part by repre-senting stereotypes of men's abilities as actualities to which women should aspire. Moreover, as I argued with respect to the sorts of rights infringements addressed in assertiveness training courses, women and members of other subordinated groups live in different social worlds than white men of privilege. Other sites of subordination overlap with gender (color, sexual orientation, disability, age) and the assaults on subordinated people are much more frequent and intense. One can hardly imagine a situation comparable to rape jokes in an elevator which could be aimed at a white man *as white man*. If privileged men were presented with similar situations at a similar rate as other people, their limitations would become more evident.

Humor in Women's Talk with Women

From Deficiency to Difference   A central assumption of the two-cultures model is that, for women, the primary goal of conversation is intimacy and, for men, the goal is positive self-presentation. Because of these gender-linked conversational goals, the interaction climates in all-female and all-male groups are very different, and the humor generated differs too. The most extensive discussion of humor in the context of the two-cultures model is by Mercilee Jenkins (1985). Her work is an attempt to decenter men and male humor by considering the model's implications for women in their social groups. As Jenkins (1985: 10) puts it, 'Men in their groups seem to be saying, "I'm great." "I'm great, too." "Gee we're a great bunch of guys."' In contrast, women seem to be saying, '"Did this ever happen to you?" "Yeah." "Oh, good, I'm not crazy."'

Assuming the differences in women and men's goals for friendly conversation, Jenkins proposes that their humor can be expected to serve different functions. Women's humor supports a goal of greater intimacy by being supportive and healing, while men's humor reinforces performance goals of competition, the establishment of hierarchical relationships, and self-aggrandizement. Jenkins studied gender differences in humor style through participant observation, and her results fit the two-cultures model well. She characterizes the women's humor she observed as follows:

> much more context-bound [than men's]. It is more often created out of the ongoing talk to satisfy the needs of [a] particular group of women. Since the goal of interaction is intimacy, there is not the same need to compete for performance points . . . [women's] humor includes and supports group members by demonstrating what they have in common. (Jenkins, 1985: 6)

As I discussed in some detail in Chapter 4, differences between men and women in conversational goals is a relatively uncontroversial interpretation. According to this view, men and women are just different. They speak in different voices (quite literally) because they seek to gain different things from talk. Women just want to be friends and men just want to look good in front of other men. A related but distinct (and less benign) explanation is related to muted group theory and emphasizes conversational dominance. Men control conversation and dominate discourse in order to control and dominate the meanings that women can give voice to. Women are literally silenced by men's appropriation of conversational time and topics and aggressive use of humor. Perhaps the most compelling evidence for this framework comes from Mulkay's analysis of the content and function of men's sexual humor about women. However, it is important to remember that humor is a flexible speech strategy that can be brought to bear in the service of many conversational goals (Long and Graesser, 1988; Mulkay, 1988). Any model that dichotomizes humor strategies and goals by sex is surely oversimplified.

The two-cultures model suggests that women's humor is best studied in same-sex groups. If women's predominant style is cooperative and communal, and men's competitive and hierarchical, the male style would predominate in mixed-sex groups, and women's humor would remain unarticulated. In Jenkins's study of a group of mothers of young children who met weekly at a neighborhood church, she found examples of humor that gently mocked unrealistic expectations of mothers (One mother to another: 'I don't know about you, but my children are perfect.'). She also noted a collaborative story-telling style. Instead of a single speaker holding the floor and leading up to the climax or punch line of a story in linear fashion, speakers told stories of their own experiences by first presenting the main point and then recounting the tale with the encouragement and participation of the other group members. Susan Kalcik (1975) observed a similar dynamic in women's rap groups, in which the 'kernel' of a story would be told first so that hearers could participate in the telling, knowing the direction and point of the story all along in collaboration with the teller.

Women's reputation for telling jokes badly (forgetting punch lines, violating story sequencing rules, etc.) may reflect a male norm that does not recognize the value of cooperative story-telling (Jenkins, 1985). While the collaborative style of story-telling is not unique to women it may serve their interests better than more individualistic styles when they are in all-woman groups. However, the study of humor in women's groups creates an interpretive problem for the two-cultures model. Many of the groups to which researchers have had access are support groups of one kind or another – rap groups, consciousness-raising groups, mothers' clubs. It is impossible to decide whether the cooperative, supportive speech styles observed occur because the participants are women or because the norms of support groups call for cooperation. As so often happens, local context and norms are confounded with speaker sex. As I noted in Chapter 4, nonhierarchical, supportive speech styles were not 'natural' in feminist groups but were laboriously developed to meet ideological goals (Cameron, 1985). One approach to the problem of separating sex from context is to study one's own social groups, where group norms and goals are understood from the inside by the researcher (Jenkins, 1985).

In a unique account of women's humor in spontaneous social groups, folklorist Rayna Green (1977) has described the sexual humor of US Southern women based on her own (white, lower-middle-class) social network. Like Jenkins, Green suggests that much of women's humor is private, not public, and distanced study is neither appropriate nor rewarding. Most of the humor she describes occurred at family gatherings at which men congregate outdoors while women and children are in the kitchen. Many of the most outspoken of the bawdy humorists were old women. Like many traditional cultures, the US South allows increasing license to old women, and Green notes that the women she observed took full advantage in presenting themselves as wicked: 'Once, when my grandmother stepped out of the bathtub, and my sister commented that the hair on her "privates" was getting rather sparse, Granny retorted that "grass don't grow on a racetrack"' (Green, 1977: 31).

Green collected many examples of sexual jokes. Often the source of humor was men's boasts, failures, or sexual inadequacies – what one woman termed 'comeuppance for lack of upcomance.' Preachers were the butt of many jokes, reflecting the rigid control of women's lives by evangelical Christian traditions. However, there was a marked absence of racism and hostility in humor about sexuality. Instead, these women engaged in creative word play, inventing comic names for genitals that mocked the euphemism expected of them. Thus, children were told to 'Wash up as far as possible, down as far as possible, and then wash possible.' Women's pubic areas were affectionately called 'Chore Girl' (after a bristly scrubbing pad) or 'wooly booger;' male genitals were 'tallywhackers.'

The functions of humor were several. First, the story-teller gained respect and admiration as an inventive and entertaining user of language. 'The ability to evoke laughter with bawdy material is important to these women's positive images of themselves' (1977: 33). Secondly, the sexual humor of these family gatherings is educational. Green suggests that the sexual information children gleaned from stories of lustful young married couples, cynical prostitutes, rowdy preachers, impotent drunks and wicked old ladies was at least as accurate as a parental lecture on where babies come from, and much more creative and fun. Finally, women's bawdy humor was educational in subversive ways. The bawdy tales 'debunk and defy' the cultural rules controlling women's sexuality. 'The very telling defies the rules . . . Women are not supposed to know or repeat such stuff. But they do and when they do, they speak ill of all that is sacred – men, the church, marriage, home, family, parents' (1977: 33). Green speculates that in their humor the women vent their anger at men, offer alternative modes of understanding to their female hearers, and, by including the ever-present children in the circle of listeners, perform 'tiny act(s) of revenge' on the men who have power over their lives.

Just such a 'tiny act of revenge' in a more public setting occurs in the story-telling of Bessie Eldreth. Eldreth is a renowned Appalachian story-teller in a tradition largely dominated by males. To succeed in this genre, Eldreth must negotiate norms that women should be subordinate and silent in public. Patricia Sawin, who has studied Eldreth and the functions of her stories, shows how Eldreth manages her role incongruity and achieves public acclaim and status within her community by positioning herself as the 'good woman,' telling stories of 'bad women' whose sins and transgressions wreak havoc. However, Eldreth also takes advantage of the role of the story-teller to offer commentary on her own life, which included an oppressive marriage to a man who was unable or unwilling to help provide for his large family. In the following 'ghost story,' Eldreth describes to Sawin how she told the story of a 'haunting,' a popular form of Appalachian folktale, and simultaneously managed a public criticism of her late husband's inadequacies. In the last line of this transcript ('I had them all laughing') Eldreth indicates the positive effect of her own transgression:

BE:You know, I've thought about that, about / when my husband died, he / they was / about that light, you know, that would flash up in my bedroom so much.
Did I ever tell you about it?
PS: I think so.
BE: And, uh, it was / for a long time it would kindly / it'd dashed me, you know.
But I got 'til I, when I'd turn the light off I'd close my eyes right tight.
But now, honestly, that light would go down in under the cover with me.
It did.
That light'd / when I'd turn that cover down and after the light was turned off, that light'd go down under that cover as pretty as I ever saw a light in my life
And, uh, I had a quilt on my bed that I thought might be the cause of it, that / that was on *his* bed when / before he died.
And I rolled that quilt up and sent it to the dump.
Because I felt like that maybe that's the reason.
But I still saw the light.
It didn't make / it didn't change a thing.
But the light . . . / for a long time, well, for two or three year or longer . . . probably than that, that light would flash up.
But I've not seen it now in a good while.
I told this / I was talking to somebody about this where I'd went to sing

one time, and these people said, 'Well, you know, maybe,' said, 'maybe
it was the Good Lord watching over you.'

I said, 'Well, I've thought of that, 'cause,' I said, 'it was / it was as bright a
light as I ever saw.'

And, I said, 'I / a few times I've thought, well, it might be my husband.'

And I thought / and then I said, 'But he wasn't that protective over me
when he's living' [laughs].

I had them all laughing, those people, I said that. (Sawin, 1993)

The Power of Humor

What, then, do people do with humor? The answer seems to be – virtually anything. Humor is a flexible conversational strategy. People
collaborate in creating and sustaining interaction in the humor mode.
With it, they can introduce taboo topics, silence and subordinate individuals, create group solidarity, express hostility, educate, save face,
ingratiate, and express caring for others. The power and flexibility of
conversational humor is related to its indirectness. It allows the
unspeakable to enter the discourse.

Yet humor has been characterized as conservative; that is, it may
release tension but it does not disrupt the social hierarchy. Much of the
research on humor in hierarchical social settings confirms this view;
humor moves largely down the hierarchy. Moreover, the degree of
structure in the social setting is an important determinant of the kind
and amount of humor generated (Mulkay, 1988). Highly structured situations generate less humor. Less formal settings lead to less obvious
structural constraints on participants' discourse and therefore more
humor. (For example, joking during a wedding ceremony is extremely
rare; joking during a wedding reception is common.) While informal
settings may generate more humor, it tends to be 'pure' humor, or play,
unlikely to have the biting edge of subversion. At best, it may permit
'tiny acts of revenge.' However, I suspect that much of women's self-
aware humor in informal social groups *is* critical and disruptive and
does challenge social structures.

At this historical moment, women have arrived at a group consciousness that had been absent since the dissipation of the last wave of
feminism in the 1920s (Weisstein, 1973). Gender is both a highly salient
and highly unstable social category. As women began to question
received wisdom about gender roles and relations in the consciousness-raising groups and political organizations of the 1970s, they
evolved a distinctive humor that is expressed in public and private settings and is a powerful tool of political activism.

Humor as a Feminist Strategy

Feminist Humor Goes Public

As I noted earlier, the stereotype of the humorless woman has long been a part of Western culture. There is an interesting paradox in this stereotype. If we accept the argument that humor is a subordinate mode of discourse that rarely disrupts social hierarchies, there seems to be no reason for the culture to represent women as lacking a sense of humor. Much as we enjoy the wit or the clown, we award public power to those who can perform competently in the serious mode (with a few exceptions, of course – Dan Quayle leaps to mind). The general rule cross-culturally is that any behavior or task that is low status is assigned to women (and any task assigned to women becomes low status). Humor should be the specialty of women. Just as women have been allowed to specialize in the devalued forms of visual art (quilts, ceramics, watercolors, lace making), writing (diaries and domestic novels), and the low status, underpaid work of industrialized societies (caring for children, the ill, and the elderly; serving food and cleaning up), women should get assigned that most trivial, low-status form of creativity, spontaneous humor. Racist stereotypes of African-American people traditionally portrayed them as smiling and laughing, joking, and telling tales – as exaggeratedly comic. Why, then, the cultural representation of women as humorless?

The answer may lie in the subversive potential of humor. Feminists have noted that women are the only subordinated group that is fully integrated with the dominant group. Perhaps women's humor poses more of a threat than the humor of other subordinated groups because of the social proximity of women and men. Humor can be used in ordinary social interaction to introduce and develop topics that would be taboo in the serious mode, while protecting the speaker from the serious consequences of having broken a taboo. This provides a unique opportunity for members of a subordinate group. Perhaps creating humor is culturally specified to be something that women cannot and must not do precisely because women's humor undermines the social order. And perhaps this danger is the source of the even more strongly made claim that feminists in particular lack a sense of humor. When a charge is directed against a political and social movement, it is wise to examine the politics behind the charge (Weisstein, 1973).

Mary Douglas (1975) offered the intriguing analysis that humor occurs when there is 'a joke in the social structure.' For women, there are very many jokes embedded in the social structure. The Big Joke is not only that women are second-class citizens but that *their subordination is culturally represented as apolitical, natural, or even as privilege.* Thus, the fact that women are judged by a harsh standard of youth and

beauty is presented as an opportunity for women to 'express their individuality' through fashion, starvation dieting and cosmetic surgery
(Wolf, 1991). The discourse of the romance novel represents male indif-
ference and brutality as evidence of love, and promises women that
their endurance in abusive relationships will be rewarded with their
men's transformation (Unger and Crawford, 1992). Social conservatives argue that women belong in the home in patriarchal marriages,
and indeed that they can find happiness and fulfillment in no other way
(Faludi, 1991). Motherhood is idealized in ways that have changed little in the past half-century (Silverstein, 1991; Unger and Crawford,
1992). Women are asked to believe that arrangements of inequality are
all for the best: women and men are just naturally different and one is
lucky to be a woman. And, if women are unhappy, we are told that it is
not current social practices but feminism that is to blame (Faludi,
1991). Feminist humor exposes these jokes in the social structure (cf.
Merrill, 1988).

Much of women's humor subverts aspects of The Big Joke – for
example, the premise that women are less competent than men and
cannot wield power. A feminist aphorism on T-shirts and lapel buttons
in the 1970s stated that 'To be seen as equal, a woman has to be twice
as good as a man. Fortunately, that isn't difficult.' A more subtle message about the ways women may wield power, even in constrained roles,
is encoded in the following joke:

> The mayor and his wife were strolling down Main Street when they came
> upon some men digging a ditch. One of the men gave a cheery hello to the
> mayor's wife, who replied, 'Why, hello, Frank, how are you?' They engaged
> in friendly talk for a few minutes and then the couple moved on. After a
> while, the mayor asked his wife, 'How do you know that guy?' She replied,
> 'We went to high school together. In fact, we dated for a while before I met
> you.'
> The couple walked on in silence. Then the mayor said, 'Isn't fate strange.
> Just think – if you'd married Frank you'd be married to a ditchdigger instead
> of to a mayor.' His wife smiled and replied gently, 'No dear, I'd still be mar-
> ried to a mayor.'

This is a curious and quite atypical joke. It was told to me by a woman.
When I have told it in mixed-sex groups, men often fail to comprehend
it. (The mayor's wife is implying that it is her influence that has led to
her husband's success.) It violates formulaic joke patterns in which
women appear only when they are to be the butt of aggression or sexual innuendo. Therefore, to men who hear and tell many formulaic
jokes, the married-couple-meets-other-man set-up in this joke may lead
to false expectations (a revelation about the wife's sexual promiscuity,
perhaps). While we cannot know whether it originated with a woman,
women seem not only quicker to comprehend it but more likely to

appreciate it. An updated version of this joke, current in 1993 and circulated on a feminist electronic mail network, has Bill and Hillary Clinton in place of the mayor and his unnamed wife.

Just as the sexual humor of some men expresses the premise that all women are sexually available at all times even when they profess not to be, feminist humor mocks the idea that women need men to fulfill their sexual and emotional needs and cannot survive without them. Another 1970s feminist aphorism is 'A woman without a man is like a fish without a bicycle.' A current example of feminist humor that pokes fun at women's presumed obsession with men is Nicole Hollander's two-panel cartoon seen on T-shirts and calendars. The first panel, titled 'What men hope women are saying when they go to the washroom together,' depicts two women bragging about the skill of their lovers. The second, 'What they're really saying,' shows the women's actual conversation: 'Do you think cake is better than sex?' 'What kind of cake?' (Hollander, 1994).

In an interview, Hollander noted that 'Men are frightened by women's humor because they think that when women are alone they're making fun of men. This is perfectly true, but they think we're making fun of their equipment when in fact there are so many more interesting things to make fun of – such as their value systems' (quoted in Barreca, 1991: 198).

Feminist humor deconstructs the ideology that the roles and activities designated for women are fulfilling and sufficient. In Walker's study of 150 years of women's written humor, she concludes that a common theme is 'how it feels to be a member of a subordinate group in a culture that prides itself on equality, what it is like to try to meet standards for behavior that are based on stereotypes rather than on human beings' (Walker, 1988: 10). In a long tradition of domestic humor, middle-class white American women writers have catalogued the frustrations and complexities of their unpaid work: out-of-control children, rampaging dogs, exploding appliances, dense husbands, boring tasks, crazy relatives. However, this writing is much more than a catalog of housewives' failures. Rather, the writers manage to convey through wit and humor that the real failure is a social system that makes women solely responsible for the functioning of the household and sets impossibly high standards for their performance. Comedian Rosanne Barr, as an independent-minded working-class housewife, talks back with 'Hey, I figure if the kids are still alive when he gets home at night, I've done my job' and 'I'll do the vacuuming when they invent a ride-on vacuum cleaner.'

As Mulkay noted, the silencing of women and the suppression of their views of the world is frequently played out in men's humor. In a comic postcard, a man is depicted driving a car while a woman sits blank-eyed beside him with a large auto muffler protruding from her mouth. The man is saying cheerfully, 'New muffler really keeps the car quiet, eh honey?' Even this sort of humor, in which men control the discourse of gender and can silence women, can be turned on the aggressor: a feminist friend sent me this postcard for my collection, with the note, 'How about the air bag in the driver's seat?'

A great deal of feminist humor can be thought of as the humor of a muted group in that it acknowledges men's ability to define reality in ways that meet their needs. Yet, in making that acknowledgment public, it subverts men's reality by exposing its social construction. As Florynce Kennedy said, 'If men could get pregnant, abortion would be a sacrament.' Gloria Steinem's (1983) essay, 'If Men could Menstruate' describes how 'menstruation would become an enviable, boast-worthy, masculine event' and 'sanitary supplies would be federally funded and free.' Women would, of course, suffer from acute cases of 'menses envy.' Another much-reprinted feminist classic applies the blame-the-victim logic of the dominant culture's assessment of rape victims to male robbery victims. An exchange between the investigator and the robbery victim in 'The Rape of Mr Smith' illustrates the absurdity of the questions posed to victims of rape:

'Have you ever given money away?'
    'Yes, of course—'
'And did you do so willingly?'
    'What are you getting at?'
'Well, let's put it like this, Mr Smith. You've given away money in the past – in fact, you have quite a reputation for philanthropy. How can we be sure that you weren't *contriving* to have your money taken from you by force?'
    'Listen, if I wanted–'
'Never mind . . .'

And later:

'What were you wearing at the time, Mr Smith?'
    'Let's see. A suit. Yes, a suit.'
'An *expensive* suit?'
    'Well, – yes.'
'In other words, Mr Smith, you were walking around the streets late at night in a suit that practically *advertised* the fact that you might be a good target for some easy money, isn't that so? I mean, if we didn't know better, Mr Smith, we might even think you were *asking* for this to happen, mightn't we?' (Unknown, 1990)

In the following joke, which was told to me in conversation, a man learns about the social construction of women's reality the hard way:

Joe used to spend many evenings at his neighborhood bar with his friends, having a beer and socializing. Then, inexplicably, he was absent for over a year. One evening, a beautiful woman came into the bar, sat down, and said, 'Hello everybody. Do you remember me? I used to be Joe, but I had a sex change operation, and now I'm Debbie.' His/her friends were astounded. They gathered around to hear the story.

'What was it like? Did you have to take hormones?'

'Yes, I took hormones for a year, but it wasn't too bad.'

'Did you have to learn how to dress and walk like a woman? And wear high heels?'

'Yes, but that's okay, I liked it actually.'

'But . . . the operation! You know . . . Wasn't it horrible? I mean, when they cut . . .'

'Yes, I know what you mean. No, that part wasn't too bad, it was all done by medical experts.'

'Well, then, what was the *worst part* about becoming a woman?'

Joe/Debbie replied slowly and thoughtfully, 'I guess it was when I woke up from the operation and found out that they'd cut my paycheck by forty percent.'

With the re-emergence of a feminist sensibility and culture since the late 1960s, there has been increasing attention given to feminist humor. Several anthologies have been published (Kaufman, 1991; Kaufman and Blakely, 1980; Stillman and Beatts, 1976). Researchers in the empiricist tradition have measured appreciation of nonsexist and feminist jokes, cartoons, and slogans in women and men with different degrees of allegiance to feminism. While they have been valuable in naming and claiming women's humor, anthologies of feminist humor should not be taken as necessarily representative of feminist humor; nor should we assume that all feminists will find them funny. Moreover, research projects on humor appreciation do not analyze the functions of feminist humor within a feminist culture. In addition to studies and collections of mediated humor, there is a need to analyze feminist humor in natural settings among feminist participants (White, 1988).

Humor and Feminist Identity

There has been almost no research on women's humor in informal groups. However, there are compelling reasons for doing such studies. The work of Michael Mulkay, Rose Coser, and Franca Pizzini all suggest that highly structured situations lead to humor that functions to maintain the structure. If humor tends to maintain social structures in formally structured settings, we might expect that less formal situations, such as women's groups, would generate more subversive humor. This might be especially true in those groupings where women are gathered as women – where the purpose of the group is gender-related or feminist issues, such as in a consciousness-raising group. Of course, it is important to attend to other aspects of subjectivity and context as well, to avoid the Generic Woman fallacy.

In an early study of discourse in feminist consciousness-raising groups, Susan Kalcik (1975) noted that humor was used supportively to increase group cohesion. The women in these groups frequently mocked themselves. When one woman had difficulty expressing herself, she apologized with, 'Well, you know how we women are; our hormones get up in our brains and fuck up our thinking.' This superficially self-denigrating humor (also noted by Jenkins in her groups) seems to echo the strategies of the post-war domestic humor writers: by pointing out the stereotypes of women and their own failures to meet patriarchal standards, these women mock the norms and standards. Like Jenkins, Kalcik also observed a collaborative storytelling style in which 'kernel stories' emerge, become part of the group repertoire, and are repeated or mentioned to support another story with a similar point.

Mary Jo Neitz (1980) reports an impressionistic study of humorous interaction in a group she describes as radical feminists tending toward separatism who met on a college campus over a two-year period (1971–72). According to Neitz, set-piece jokes were rare; most humor consisted of spontaneous witticisms. The two most common themes for conversational humor were self-denigration and hostility toward males. Like Jenkins and Kalcik, Neitz speculates that apparently self-denigrating remarks (for example, a group of women climbed into a car and the driver remarked, 'Do you think you can be safe with a woman driver?') functioned to help women manage role incongruities and to affirm group values in opposition to the dominant culture. Remarks denigrating women and their roles generated no laughter when they were contributed by outsiders. Hostile humor, much of which consisted of castration themes, functioned to overcome two taboos for women, sexuality and aggression. Moreover, 'These jokes gloried in women's strength rather than colluding to hide it' (1980: 221). The group used hostile humor in mixed-sex as well as same-sex settings, but used woman-denigrating humor only among themselves.

These studies are but first attempts to examine feminists' talk in context. Kalcik's study focuses on narrative structures and styles, with little direct examination of humor. Neitz's report is sketchy, and provides no details of how the humor episodes were collected or analyzed. There is a need for methods that permit connections between a distinctive feminist culture and the specific humor generated (White, 1988).

What values are expressed in feminist humor? How do feminists differentiate themselves as feminists in and through their humor? And what functions does humor serve in the creation of a feminist culture? To address these questions, Cindy White (1988) asked self-identified feminists to keep diaries of feminist humor in mundane settings over an eight-week period. From an analysis of three diaries, White concluded that the values expressed were generalized positive evaluation of women, celebration of women's experiences, affirmation of women's strengths and capabilities, and autonomy and self-definition for women.The rarity of anti-male humor suggested to White that these diary-writers also valued men, and that they made a distinction between men as individuals and patriarchal culture.

One reported witticism that reflects some of these values is the following:

> At a staff meeting at a college health center, the clinic director told a story about Harvard University's struggle with their health fee. Men objected to paying the same fee as women, since they couldn't get a Pap smear. So Harvard went through all this rigmarole to figure out what part of the health fee was attributable to the Pap smear. Finally, they notified the men that they could come pick up their 50-cent checks. K (. . . a feminist and therapist) says quietly, 'Pap smear envy.' (White, 1988: 82-3).

This example uses word play to ridicule the Freudian-based belief that women are more envious by nature than men due to penis envy. The feminists in the group were able to reverse the notion of penis envy to their own advantage. (Interestingly, the diary writer noted that the feminists were the only ones who laughed at this joke.) Moreover, the feminist speaker takes a routine gynecological test as the norm and celebrates it. The Pap smear becomes an enviable experience, one that men feel deprived of, and this explains their over-reaction to differential health fees.

The value of autonomy and self-definition for feminists is suggested by the following diary entry quoting a woman who presented a paper on lesbian sexuality at a conference:

> Politically correct sex lasts at least three hours, since everyone knows we're process-oriented and not goal-oriented. If we do have orgasms, those orgasms must be simultaneous. And we must lie side by side. Now I know that some people think that orgasms are patriarchal. But I've given up many things for feminism, and this isn't going to be one of them. (White, 1988: 83)

White notes that, just as feminist humor subverts the inflexible gender roles of the dominant culture, it mocks inflexibility in feminism. In the orgasm example, a feminist jokes about how the notion of political correctness can be coercive for women, and asserts her autonomy, placing limits on the influence she will allow to feminist doctrine in her own life.

White argues on the basis of the humor diaries she analyzed that the most important role for humor in the creation of a feminist culture is the articulation of common meanings. Feminists differentiate themselves as feminists through humor not by adhering to a doctrinaire or monolithic notion of feminism, but by expressing shared, in-group meanings. When a diarist records that one woman has referred to another as 'a witch in the patriarchal sense of the word,' she is acknowledging that the speaker and her hearers share another, more positive definition of 'witch' than the dominant group's. By creating and affirming their own meanings, feminists create a sense of community. When common meanings express in-group/out-group relationships, they help set the boundaries for feminist culture. These factors allow women to self-identify as feminists and re-create (enact) their feminism in everyday interaction.

Feminist Humor as Political Action

Kate Clinton (1982), a lesbian comedian, has described feminist humor as not just a string of jokes but a 'deeply radical analysis of the world and our being in the world because it, like the erotic, demands a commitment to joy. Feminist humor is a radical analysis because we are saying that we have the right to be happy, that we will not settle for less' (1982: 40). Because feminist humor allows its makers to enact their feminism in ongoing social interaction, it is readily used in the service of political activism. Interaction among feminists disrupts rather than reproduces gender. Instead of creating self-fulfilling prophecies in which women's 'deficiencies' are confirmed, feminist interaction opens the way to exposing gendered social structures. A core shared value of feminisms is the necessity for social change to benefit women, whether one identifies as a liberal, radical, socialist, separatist or any other variant. Indeed, there are many examples of feminists' use of humor and irony to gain a political voice. I will briefly describe four.

Activism in the Art World: the Guerrilla Girls
In 1985, a series of inflammatory posters began appearing in New York's SoHo art district. 'Do Women Have to be Naked to Get into the Met Museum?' asked one, which featured a nude woman in a gorilla mask with statistics on the Metropolitan Museum's modern artists (over 95 percent men) and depictions of nudes (85 percent women). Other posters listed galleries and critics that ignore women artists and proclaimed that only four galleries in the entire city show the work of black women artists. The posters were signed 'The Guerrilla Girls – Conscience of the Art World.'

The Guerrilla Girls is an anonymous group of women involved in the visual arts who have used ironic public humor so effectively that they have become national spokespersons for gender equity in the creative arts. Group members use the names of women artists of the past as 'covers,' and encourage supporters to sign gallery visitors' books 'Guerrilla Girl' to increase their visibility. Anonymity protects them from reprisals, allows them to focus on issues rather than individual fame or personality, and, most important, gets press coverage. In response to charges that anonymity is cowardly, they reply, 'No one accuses the Lone Ranger or Batman of being cowardly.'

I had heard about the Guerrilla Girls but I did not expect to see their activism celebrated in *Mirabella*, a large-circulation fashion magazine aimed at affluent midlife women (Carr, 1992). It seems that the group's use of humor to highlight the taboo topic of sexism made it palatable to a mass audience of women (who may or may not identify as feminists, but who are normally addressed largely as consumers of fashion in this magazine). The appearance of this article is potentially quite subversive. It plants the idea that women – as gallery visitors, buyers of art, arts administrators and volunteer workers – can and should engage in direct and indirect political tactics to make sure that women get a fair share of the art world's rewards.

The Guerrilla Girls were commissioned by *Mirabella* to design a new poster. In this poster, and other recent work, they have moved beyond arts equity to encompass other social issues. The *Mirabella* poster, *Guerrilla Girls Explain the Concept of Natural Law*, is shown in Figure 5.1. 'We wanted to have some fun with our anger. Then it snow-balled,' a founding member reported. After seven years and more than 40 posters, the Guerrilla Girls now travel the world for speaking engagements in which they appear in gorilla masks, often with fishnet stockings and mini skirts. Their unique form of feminist humor has been a significant force for change in the New York art world. They see the need to continue their guerrilla act because 'Making art is making the culture. If we aren't included in the culture-making process, all women are marginalized' (Carr, 1992: 34).

Critical Street Theorizing: Ladies Against Women
In an interview for *Socialist Review*, 'Virginia Cholesterol' and 'Edith Banks' talk about their political organization, the San Francisco Bay Area branch of Ladies Against Women:

> *Interviewer*: I think I would like to start out by asking a rather basic question, and that is: What do you see as the role of women in politics?
> *Edith Banks*: That's exactly the problem, we don't believe that anyone should be women at all; our organization is Ladies *Against* Women. We believe that ladies should be ladies; no one should be women, especially men.
> *Interviewer*: Let me rephrase the question: What is the role of Ladies in politics?
> *Virginia Cholesterol*: Preparing coffee cake, standing beside successful husband candidates on election night, giving fund raisers and bake sales.
> (Omi and Philipson, 1983: 10–11)

GUERRILLA GIRLS EXPLAIN THE CONCEPT OF NATURAL LAW.

1. Protecting the rights of the unborn means precisely that. Once you're born, you're on your own.

2. Sexual harassment is man's natural response to women on the job. Women who report it are uptight prudes. Women who don't are ambitious whores.

3. Women are paid less in the workplace because they have no business being there.

4. Anyone who is unemployed or homeless deserves it.

5. The people who have the most money are entitled to the best health care.

6. AIDS is a punishment for homosexuality and drug abuse. Only heterosexuals, celebrities, and children deserve a cure.

7. Life is beautiful. Artists, writers, or performers who want to inflict disgusting, homosexual, erotic, satirical or political images upon the public should have their grants cut off.

A PUBLIC SERVICE MESSAGE FROM

GUERRILLA GIRLS

A feminist comedy troupe, LAW uses street theater to satirize reactionary views of women. Wearing white gloves, fur coats, and ladylike hats, LAW members stage public demonstrations carrying signs such as 'Roses not Raises,' 'Sperm are People Too,' and 'Misterhood is Powerful.' At an appearance of arch-conservative Phyllis Schlafly, a LAW spokeswoman was quoted as saying, 'It's so thrilling to have a visit from someone like Mrs Schlafly, who represents everything that women should stand for – militarism, racism, true religion, and women's submission.' In response to Schlafly's speech opposing the Equal Rights Amendment to the US Constitution, which she titled 'Do We Want a Gender-Free Society,' a LAW member voiced her enthusiastic support: 'We can't just hand out genders free to anyone who wants them. The only thing that should be free in America is the market.'

While President Ronald Reagan held a prayer breakfast with conservative clergyman Jerry Falwell, LAW simultaneously held a bake sale 'for the (federal) deficit.' The group claimed wholehearted support for the 1984 Republican platform, except that they had hoped for a plank condemning the Democrats for nominating a 'girl' for vice-President, on the grounds that 'real ladies never run; they walk gracefully or are driven.' Among the group's other political policy tactics were a 'Reagan for Shah' campaign, the formation of Students for an Apathetic Society ('How can we invade El Salvador if no one is apathetic?') and a proposed revision of the US Criminal Code to include a Dress Code banning the 'feminist blight' of comfortable clothes and 'female facial nudity.' Who sponsors their demonstrations and press conferences? 'Another Mother for World Domination,' 'Future Fetuses of America,' and the 'National Association for the Advancement of Rich White Straight Men,' of course.

M. Nawal Lutfiyya (1992) (whose work provided the examples above) analyzes their humor as 'critical street theorizing.' By conducting 'nonserious' demonstrations, LAW disrupts the serious context of public conservative politics. Humor and satire open an avenue for questioning the social construction of women's second-class status, whether in the claims of anti-feminist speakers or the alliance of a US President and a right-wing evangelist. Lutfiyya notes that the binary opposition of left/right (in the political sense) is deconstructed when LAW parrot the rhetoric of the right in the protest style of the left. This tactic, which draws on the tolerance for ambiguity and incongruity characteristic of the humor mode, could only 'work' within that mode. Moreover,

> [T]he purpose of the demonstrations is to critique by challenging and making a comment on explicit opposing standpoints. The demonstrations not only make a comment on the debate, the lecture, or the breakfast in light of the contemporary situation of women in the United States, but because of

their fanciful essence which recontextualizes they encompass the scene and therefore momentarily *become* the political situation of women in the United States. As this happens, the binary opposition of acting/real life is deconstructed. (Lutfiyya, 1992: 38–9)

Ladies Against Women 'self-consciously and purposely demonstrate that the creation of meaning is a political activity occurring within language by historically situated actors' (Lutfiyya, 1992: 43). Their comedy is aimed at creating solidarity in a critical community of feminists and liberal activists and at educating people across the political spectrum. In an interview, one member noted that contradictions and inconsistencies about gender relations are part of most women's lives, and that humor which 'pushes things to the extreme' can help raise awareness of unexamined assumptions: 'I think it helps to keep the edge on people's commitment to change, to take the other side and exaggerate it so badly that they see the absurdity of the hypocrisy in their own lives' (Omi and Philipson, 1983: 22).

By adopting the dress and stereotypical speech style of privileged white women, Ladies Against Women play at being those in power. This humorous play shows their hearers that 'political policies and power structures are people acting and creating, and as we act and create we all participate in the structure of power. Accordingly, if people act and create *differently*, then different social and organizational structures will emerge' (Lutfiyya, 1992: 26).

The Politics of Labeling

Feminists have analyzed the pervasive sexism in psychiatry in many of its guises (Unger and Crawford, 1992). One of the most obvious is in the politics of diagnosis and labeling. Mental health practitioners rely on the *Diagnostic and Statistical Manual of Mental Disorders* (DSM), a 567-page tome that contains a list of diagnostic labels, descriptions of each disorder, and criteria for their application. The DSM is *the* standard diagnostic reference, and the 'bible of many mental health professionals' (Pantony and Caplan, 1991). Its categories are used not only in diagnosis but in much mental health research, and, in the US, to determine whether government agencies or private insurers pay for mental health services for a client.

The DSM is periodically updated by a panel of experts drawn primarily from among white male psychiatrists. When the most recent version of the manual was being revised, feminist therapists realized that several new and highly misogynistic categories of 'mental illness' were being considered for inclusion. Two of these, now termed 'Self-defeating Personality Disorder' and 'Late Luteal Phase Dysphoric Disorder,' correspond to popular notions of the masochistic personality and to premenstrual syndrome respectively.

Feminist psychologists marshalled empirical and theoretical arguments against these new diagnostic categories, which they viewed as codifications of the misogynistic opinions of privileged white men. They pointed out that the self-defeating personality classification pathologized women by ignoring sociocultural causes of apparently self-defeating behaviors. For example, the researchers who conducted the field trials in developing the self-defeating personality category never questioned the participants about their experiences of sexual, physical, or emotional abuse, although abuse may precipitate apparently self-defeating behaviors (Brown, 1986). Moreover, many of the behaviors that define the category disappear when a victimized person is removed from the abusive environment for even a short time (Committee on Women in Psychology, 1985). Instead of recognizing the social consequences of victimization, the self-defeating personality category essentializes behavior by treating it as internally driven, fixed, and enduring.

Ignoring a history of abuse, and the behavioral consequences of abuse, results in blaming the victim. The label self-defeating or masochistic allows both mental health practitioners and the larger society to blame women for their 'failures' without requiring anyone to question the effects of cultural and situational contexts on psychological functioning (Brown, 1986).

As for 'late luteal phase disorder,' this label establishes a mental disorder purportedly caused by a normal process unique to women. By targeting women's biology as the source of their problems, it adds another layer of taint to an already maligned physiology. Although DSM categories are expected to be based on empirical research, there is no empirical validation of such a disorder.

The arguments made by feminist psychologists enlisted all the standard rhetoric of the social sciences in discrediting the scientific basis of the sexist new categories. The lack of scientific justification for the new disorders, both theoretical and empirical, was strongly and persuasively presented (Caplan and Gans, 1991; Committee on Women in Psychology, 1985). Despite what may seem to be a compelling case, both 'disorders' were added to the revised DSM in 1987 in an appendix of labels deserving further study. Once a category is rendered official by DSM inclusion, it takes on a life of its own as a 'proven, valid and legitimate diagnostic category with a firm scientific foundation;' it becomes 'an existing, legitimate, clinical construct' (Caplan and Gans, 1991: 267).

The politics of the DSM illustrate yet again how masculine norms combined with sociostructural power vested in males lead to viewing women as deficient and problematic to others. However clear this might be to feminists, others have remained unconvinced. Using a classic role-reversal strategy, Paula Caplan and Margit Eichler (1989) exposed the social construction of female pathology by constructing another new diagnostic category, one they claimed is more characteristic of men: Delusional Dominating Personality Disorder. Its taxonomy includes the following:

> The presence of any one of the following delusions: (a) the delusion of personal entitlement to the services of (1) any woman with whom one is personally associated, (2) females in general for males in general, (3) both of the above; (b) the delusion that women like to suffer and be ordered around; (c) the delusion that physical force is the best method of solving interpersonal problems; (d) the delusion that sexual and aggressive impulses are uncontrollable in (1) oneself, (2) males in general, (3) both of the above; (e) the delusion that pornography and erotica are identical . . .
>
> A pathological need to affirm one's social importance by displaying oneself in the company of females who meet any three of the following criteria: (a) are conventionally physically attractive; (b) are younger than oneself; (c) are shorter in stature than oneself; (d) weigh less than oneself; (e) appear to be lower on socioeconomic criteria than oneself; (f) are more submissive than oneself.
>
> A distorted approach to sexuality, displaying itself in one or both of these ways: (a) a pathological need for flattery about one's sexual performance and/or the size of one's genitalia; (b) an infantile tendency to equate large breasts on women with their sexual attractiveness.
>
> A tendency to feel inordinately threatened by women who fail to disguise their intelligence. (Pantony and Caplan, 1991: 121)

Caplan and Eichler have said that Delusional Dominating Personality Disorder began as a consciousness-raising exercise. By pathologizing stereotypically male personality attributes they were able to show how judgments of 'pathological' behavior depend on who is doing the observing and labeling. By adopting the dry, pompous style and authoritative stance with which the North American psychiatric establishment presents its opinions in the DSM, they were able to question the fundamental authority of those opinions. When I talked with Paula Caplan about whether the category was intended to be no more than a humorous rendering of 'Macho Personality,' she noted that when she gives professional talks about the DSM and Delusional Dominating Personality Disorder, the audience's initial reaction is often laughter. However, this initial reaction changes to the recognition that they know people who meet the diagnostic criteria for DDPD. The new diagnostic category is now available to professional audiences as a perfectly serious psychological problem that has its own research literature, assessment instruments, and documented effects on those who interact with the disordered individual (Pantony and Caplan, 1991). Perhaps it will eventually be listed in the DSM.

The Ideology of Femininity: Making the Personal Political

In my own study of people's accounts of humor, both women and men defined an outstanding sense of humor as one that breaks social tension, eases another's unhappiness, cheers rather than wounds, and is sharp, clever, and spontaneous, but refrains from hurting others. In short, they viewed humor as 'social lubrication,' compassion, and connection. In a sense what my respondents told me was self-contradictory. Although they more likely thought of a male, the definition of humor they used – nonhostile, contextually sensitive, emerging spontaneously from the fabric of their lives – is much closer to the women's self-reported humor than the men's.

Can this sort of personal idiosyncratic humor be turned to activism? I believe that it can, and as an example I will describe the humor of feminist psychologist Nancy Datan. I came to know Nancy only near the end of her life, when I asked her to speak at a conference. At the time (1987) I was a visiting professor in a small psychology department that had never tenured a woman in its long and distinguished history. In fact, no woman had ever been hired in a tenure-track position until five years before. The first two women, both involved in studying women and gender, were about to come up for tenure. One of my goals in organizing the conference was to represent gender studies to the senior members of the department as a legitimate, rigorous area with its own highly developed body of knowledge, and thus to facilitate the evaluation of these two women's credentials. To that end, I invited only speakers with high national visibility and very distinguished reputations – and Nancy Datan was perhaps the most distinguished of the group.

I expected Datan to talk about her research. Instead, she decided to make the personal political by talking about the nonconscious ideology of femininity underlying advice to breast cancer patients, with an *n* of one – herself. Datan stood at the podium, pulled a large foam rubber prosthesis out of her tote bag, and began to wave it around. The effect on the audience was stunning. The effect on me was similar. My thoughts were that the scientific credibility of my conference was doomed – I had let a crazy woman into the room. But Datan pulled it off brilliantly. Her thesis was that

> Breast cancer is not a cosmetic disease, but it is embedded in a larger social and political context in which the cosmetic industry is itself a social and political phenomenon. Thus, if one rejects the *a priori* assumption that a missing breast demands an all-out cover-up, one finds oneself at war with the very material which is meant to promote healing. (Datan, 1989: 178)

Nancy took on this topic, so terrifying and so close to home for women, with grace and humor. She spoke of the problem of preventing one's breast prosthesis from riding up on the body:

> The Reach to Recovery solution: fill the form with birdseed, rice, barley, small plastic beads . . . drapery weights, fishing sinkers, gunshot or BBs. My first response to this suggestion was the cognitive equivalent of wound shock. Surely this represented a merger of Frederick's of Hollywood, Ace Hardware, and the American Cancer Society. (1989: 179)

She also spoke of the implied identity that the breast cancer patient should strive for, which she labeled as 'perpetual would-be cheerleader:' 'I've never been a cheerleader, and I couldn't see trying out for the part with falsies.'

But her humor was compassionate too. Because Nancy agreed with Audre Lorde (1980) that the cosmetic response to breast cancer leads to self-alienation, and scorned the life of perpetual disguise it implied, she refused breast reconstruction surgery. But she respected the different choices made by other women:

> If a hospital room is no place for a crash course in Total Womanhood, neither is it the place for retroactive consciousness-raising. Breast cancer is a trauma. If a woman feels she is entitled to *four* silicone breasts after a mastectomy, I applaud her originality. (1989: 181)

This humor was strong stuff. It achieved one of the classic functions of interactional humor, facilitating talk about taboo topics. In this case, the focus on the unspeakable gained additional impact and poignancy because the events were so clearly part of the fabric of the speaker's life. Datan's chemotherapy-induced baldness was covered by a scarf, and loose clothing softened but did not deny the physical evidence of mastectomy. Her personal, social, psychological and political analysis of the workings of the gender system in cancer treatment was moving and unforgettable.

Twenty years or so before the Guerrilla Girls, Ladies Against Women, Paula Caplan's DDPD and Nancy Datan's courageous humor, Naomi Weisstein wrote about the missing comic tradition of women. She noted that other oppressed groups – Jews, African–Americans – used humor as a survival strategy and a weapon against oppression. She could point to no comparable tradition in women's humor:

> By women's humor, I don't mean women being funny. I mean a humor which recognizes a common oppression, notices its source and the roles it requires, identifies the agents of that oppression . . . if such traditions existed or exist now, I have been denied them. I remember no redemptive or fighting humor about my condition. (Weisstein, 1973: 5)

Weisstein acknowledged that this conclusion was a very painful one for her. At the same time, she recognized that the seeds of change had already been planted with the re-emergence of the women's movement. Recently, she articulated again the power of humor in an interview with Celia Kitzinger (1993: 191):

I think that the uses of comedy and performance have not been explored enough by feminist academics. Comedy is a beautiful way of equalizing power in the most intimidating of circumstances, and it should be deliberately and consciously used by us. I've always tried to make my scientific presentations –well, *all* my talks – funny. When you're doing insurgent science, that is, you are dissenting from the reigning theories, you have to challenge them with more than just the truth of your findings if you're going to be heard. You have to challenge the theater of science, its authoritarian grandeur and elitist majesty.

Naomi Weisstein anticipated that women would reclaim humor. Her visionary description of the processes taking place has been realized in the feminist political humor I have described:

The women's movement is taking back what has been taken from us. We are reclaiming our autonomy and our history, our rights to self-expression and collective enjoyment. In this process, we are taking back our humor. The propitiating laughter, the fixed and charming smiles are over. When we laugh, things are going to be funny. And when we don't laugh, it's because we have a keen and clear sense of humor, and we know what's not funny ... we are constructing a women's culture with its own character, its fighting humor, its defiant celebration of our worth, a women's culture that will help get us through to that better world, that just and generous society. (1973: 9–10)

6

Toward a Feminist Theory of Gender and Communication

The quest for sex differences in speech features began in the context of the 1970s feminist social movement and gained credibility by connecting to deeply rooted stereotypes of women and their talk. The assertiveness training movement, grounded in Western individualism and liberal feminism, disguised an implicit male norm and encouraged women to believe that they could achieve equality one by one through transforming their speech. As researchers and activists began to focus on the systemic nature of sexism, the two-cultures model emerged with its apolitical account of how no-fault, universal differences complicate the talk of (always well-meaning) women and men.

Much of the research on women's talk of the past two decades has been characterized as 'normal science' in the Kuhnian sense: 'additional tests of one or another extant communication concept or theory using one or another timeworn research protocol with the added "twist" of gender as a variable' (Stanback, 1988–89: 188). The definitive differences between the sexes have proved elusive. Ahistorical, cross-situational differences have been impossible to pin down, and evidence of sex *similarities* in comparable situations continues to emerge. Yet beliefs in fundamental differences persist (Kessler and McKenna, 1978; Thorne et al., 1983), and continue to fuel the self-help industry. Deborah Tannen's latest trade book, *Talking from Nine to Five* (1994), is currently being touted in the mass media as the answer to women's powerlessness in the corporate world.

The emphasis on sex differences has had important consequences within the research community and among psychological practitioners. It has encouraged researchers to rely on a formal analysis of language, counting features such as tag questions. Therapists teach 'communication skills' by dictating specific forms such as 'I–me' sentence constructions. By equating form with function, and ignoring the interactive nature of talk, these approaches reach a conceptual and practical impasse.

Moreover, the discourse of difference supports existing institutions and reproduces existing power relations. Sex difference research is not generated apolitically, and ideas about difference cannot enter the public discourse neutrally. A great deal of popular psychology since the emergence of the contemporary women's movement can be seen as a form of 'backlash' in which women are pathologized, problems are invented, feminism is blamed, and 'solutions' involving a return to patriarchal control are advocated. Moreover, the backlash appropriates the language of both psychology and feminism:

> As many media-conscious therapists in the '80's discovered, feminist-bashing 'feminists' garnered the most airtime. Susan and Stephen Price, authors of the popular *No More Lonely Nights: Overcoming the Hidden Fears That Keep You from Getting Married*, were one such 'feminist' husband-and-wife therapy team who got a lot of press mileage plugging this backlash diagnosis of modern single women: 'androphobia.' This 'problem without a name,' they wrote, shamelessly stealing Friedan's phrase, was a 'deep-rooted intense fear of men' shared by most unmarried women over thirty, especially professional women. The cause: 'You have been deeply influenced by feminism.' (Faludi, 1991: 340)

Connections between the social science disciplines and the larger North American culture are multi-stranded *and reciprocal*. Many traditionally trained social scientists would acknowledge that their theories 'seep' out to the larger culture and affect it. A social constructionist perspective encourages a further analysis of how the larger culture contains particular distinct types of social theories that 'seep *into* and mold the discipline(s)' (Burman and Parker, 1993: 161).

How can the next generation of scholarship be made more sophisticated and useful? Throughout this book I have relied on a social constructionist perspective, conceptualizing gender as a system of social relations operating at individual, social structural, and interactional levels. My hope is that this model, used heuristically, will help keep social science research on gender and communication from collapsing into individualistic and essentialist modes of explanation.

Moreover, I have articulated and applied a social constructionist view of language. This view encourages research on interaction rather than isolated features of speech – a functional rather than a formal analysis. It opens the way for analyzing how social groupings, hierarchies, and power relations structure interaction, constrain speakers' options, and affect the kinds of social feedback speakers receive. It allows researchers to conceptualize not only the workings of the gender system but its interactions with other systems. '[R]acism, sexism, and classism are not just talk, but racist, sexist, and classist talk are forms of racist, sexist, and classist *action:* oppressive talk reinforces and re-creates oppression in human relationships' (Stanback, 1988–89: 192).

Theories and Methods: a Plurality

Within the broad epistemological framework of social constructionism, there is a need for the development of communication theories that can encompass social relations. I have critically analyzed applications of many promising approaches: muted group theory (Ardener, 1975; Kramarae, 1981); speech act theory (Austin, 1962; Gervasio and Crawford, 1989; Grice, 1975); modes of discourse (Mulkay, 1988); the two-cultures model (Jenkins, 1985; Maltz and Borker, 1982). Each has proved to be a useful approach in some ways. At this point, none seems ideal, and a theoretical plurality seems warranted.

Methodological plurality is equally important. I advocate the use of a variety of methods by feminist researchers. In my view, it is important not to hierarchize methods. Masculinist social science has developed a hierarchy of method with quantitative, experimental, and laboratory studies at the top (Sherif, 1979); feminist social science sometimes has responded by inverting the hierarchy, placing qualitative, experiential, and naturalistic studies at the top (Peplau and Conrad, 1989). This reaction is understandable, since many women are justifiably suspicious of experiments, surveys, and statistical manipulations done *on* them and *about* them but not *by*, *with* or *for* them. Mainstream (malestream) social science research continues to be used to misrepresent women's lives (Stanback, 1988–89). Yet increasingly, feminist social scientists and philosophers are arguing that there should be no single privileged 'feminist method' and that any method can be a tool for feminist inquiry (Harding, 1987; Peplau and Conrad, 1989; Reinharz, 1992). I endorse this view. Methods that did not originate in feminist inquiry, such as conversation analysis, can be made to serve feminist ends with a sensitive attention to interactional context (Duranti and Goodwin, 1992; Goodwin, 1990).

In this book, I have focused on the methods I know best, quantitative experimental designs and discourse analysis. However, while both can be useful, neither is a 'best' method for gender-and-language research, and both invite continued feminist critique. The ongoing feminist critique of experimental methods is quite well developed and sophisticated (Fine and Gordon, 1989, 1991; Grady, 1981; Parlee, 1975, 1979; Peplau and Conrad, 1989; Sherif, 1979) and I will not replicate it in detail here. Briefly, it has centered on two main objections: first, that experimental methods strip behavior of its social context, substituting an artificial environment that may have little generalizability; and secondly, that these methods are inherently hierarchical, with a powerful researcher observing, manipulating, and sometimes deceiving 'subjects' who are denied their subjectivity.

This has been a crucially necessary critique because one characteristic of these methods as they are ordinarily used is an almost total lack of reflexivity. That is, quantitative experimental methods stem from an empiricist tradition which holds no conceptual space for analyzing the researcher's social position, the experiment as a social situation, or the sociology of scientific communities. The language of this tradition implies that data exist independently of people; like nuts and berries, they lie waiting to be 'gathered' or 'collected.' Or, if data are not natural phenomena, they are produced mechanically: 'quick and dirty' research can be 'cranked out' equally well regardless of whose hand is on the crank. Moreover, the empiricist tradition conceptualizes social science inquiry as a search for 'truth' in the form of ahistorical, universal laws of behavior, a conceptualization that discourages plurality of method. (Recently, as a consultant to a psychology department, I advocated broadening the Experimental Methods course; a faculty member asked in apparently honest bewilderment, 'What other methods are there?')

Despite its limitations, quantitative experimental research has important advantages for feminist inquiry. Precisely because it is enshrined at the pinnacle of psychology's value system, it has rhetorical value. For example, in court cases on sex discrimination, such research can be used to show how processes of stereotyping, tokenism, gender attributions, and the devaluation of women's work take place. Another advantage is that it allows abstraction of variables from interaction. When people 'do gender,' they are simultaneously reacting to multiple cues, and naturalistic studies cannot easily untangle the influence of particular cues. When a woman is interrupted in conversation, is it because she is female, or has a soft voice, or has a lower status than her male partner, or is younger? Analogue research such as laboratory studies of conversational dominance can be very useful in untangling multiple influences.

With the burgeoning interest in discourse analysis, this way of going about social inquiry is beginning to generate evaluation and critique (Burman and Parker, 1993; Edwards and Potter, 1992; Parker, 1992; Potter and Wetherell, 1987). The approach is more open ended, qualitative, and situation specific than quantitative methods; it does not in fact constitute a 'method' (Parker, 1992; Potter and Wetherell, 1987), a characteristic which can diffuse criticism. On the other hand, reflexivity is a part of the discourse analytic approach and self-questioning is characteristic of its practice. Thus, a recent collection of discourse analytic research concludes with a chapter detailing 'Thirty-two Problems with Discourse Analysis' (Burman and Parker, 1993). In it, Ian Parker and Erica Burman persuasively argue against replacing 'empiricist imperialism' with 'discursive imperialism' and caution against using discourse analysis indiscriminately.

Although I have relied on the discourse analytic work of others frequently throughout this book and offered some discursive analyses of my own, I do not see discursive psychology as a panacea. Indeed, I agree with Burman and Parker that it presents researchers and activists with problems. I will discuss several that are particularly relevant to gender issues.

It is *difficult to quantify and generalize* from discourse analytic work. If we find that a speaker uses a particular speech strategy or rhetorical device in a transcript, we have little sense of how often that speaker uses that device or how common it is among others. While I am not pretending that we should be able to find universal laws of social behavior, psychologists like to be able to extend their results beyond the specific situation and people observed. A related problem is that discourse analytic work is *open to alternative readings* and thus implies a *lack of closure*. Of course, those who work with statistical methods learn many techniques for 'massaging the data' (eliminating 'outlying' scores, using mathematical transformations, and so on) to generate alternative readings of their own. And there is plenty of room for debate about the meaning of a statistically significant difference (Unger and Crawford, 1992). Discursive research should not be compared unfavorably to an idealized notion of 'hard data.'

A very different problem is the *role of psychoanalytic readings* in discourse analysis. Psychoanalytic methods and analyses are outside my own expertise. Like many North American feminists, I remain deeply skeptical of the Freudian origins of such approaches (and the androcentric origins of their more recent versions), and suspicious of psychoanalytically based theories as accounts of women's lives (Lerman, 1986). Yet some feminists rely on these approaches to do groundbreaking work (Hollway, 1989, 1994; Squire, 1989; Walkerdine, 1988). One project for feminist researchers might be to engage in dialogue (especially between British and North American feminists) about theoretical frameworks for feminist discursive research.

Equally relevant for feminist perspectives are questions about the relationship of discursive approaches to feminist politics. There are power issues within discursive practices analogous to those within experimental practices. Just as experimental psychology is inherently hierarchical, discourse analysis privileges an 'expert' researcher who interprets the talk of others. To what extent can the expert step outside her or his social position in analyzing gendered talk? Because researchers, like other members of their culture, learn to function within the gender system, they may share stereotypes of women's speech, interpret speech actions through a gendered lens and impose the same timeworn set of polarized categories that more traditional research has perpetuated.

Power issues are involved in the relationship between discursive research and political action, as well (Parker, 1992). Many feminist theorists are troubled by the seeming *relativism* of discursive psychology (and social contructionism in general). If speakers create their social worlds in interaction, and meanings are multiple and context-specific, how can we argue for the validity of one interpretation over another? This problem is most clear in competing explanations for rape. If women and men genuinely hold different systems of meanings about consent, 'miscommunication' is inevitable and no one is culpable for rape. I have shown how the miscommunication model collaborates in erasing male agency and blaming women for crimes of violence against them. Strictly speaking, a 'motivated, partisan political orientation' such as I adopted in my analysis of 'miscommunication' is proscribed within discourse analysis. Yet, without it, how can feminists organize for collective actions that intervene in existing power relations (Burman and Parker, 1993: 167)? Using discursive methods reflexively can be part of the solution to this dilemma, but it can also become part of the problem; 'wallowing in the researcher's interpretive assumptions and processes can detract from the importance of the topic and possible political interventions' (Burman and Parker, 1993: 168).

Fortunately, the use of discourse analysis by feminists is increasing (Burman, 1992; Gavey, 1989, 1992; Gilfoyle et al., 1992; Hollway, 1989; Todd and Fisher, 1988; Wilkinson and Kitzinger, 1995). With more researchers using the approach, the issues it raises for feminist research practice will be sharpened and clarified, and perhaps a distinctively feminist mode will emerge. The complex relationship between feminism and discourse analysis is interrogated in forthcoming work (Wilkinson and Kitzinger, 1995) that will address many of the issues I have raised: realism, relativism, interpretive readings, and the employment of a variety of feminist perspectives.

Toward a Political Feminist Psychology

Michelle Fine and Susan Gordon (1989: 159) have proposed a 'project of political, feminist psychology' that is 'knitted to the conditions, complexities, asymmetries, pleasures and dangers of women's lives'. They challenge researchers to employ four new ways of learning about women:

1 *Interrogate the stuff of relationships* by studying women in interactions with others rather than in isolation and by acknowledging that 'the *subject* is constructed as she constructs herself, in reflection, relation, and in resistance to the *other*.'

2 *Desilence women.* Because women are 'sworn to secrecy' about the

pressures and structures of racism, sexism, ageism, and heterosexism that they experience, desilencing is an important mode of learning. This approach 'calls for a moratorium on secret-keeping. It tells – through letters, diaries, and groups, in contexts of relative safety and risks, because women need to tell and because women – and girls – need to know.'

3 *Fuse theory, practice, politics and methods*: for example, by studying political decision-making within groups of women who are activists.

4 *Study what is not normally connected with gender.* 'In order to understand gender as a relational concept and one with elastic boundaries, we need to investigate not only what is represented and experienced as gender, but also what is not represented, what is not known, and what is not imaginable about gender and about women . . . to disrupt prevailing notions of what is inevitable and "natural"' (from Fine and Gordon, 1989: 157–64).

Now, with the lessons of two decades of research on gender and communication style to draw upon, how might we go about doing such work? Throughout this book I have suggested new approaches to old questions, framed new questions, and stressed the political and social frameworks of research. In what follows I will summarize some of these points in terms of Fine and Gordon's (1989) four ways of learning.

On Relationships   Whether one's method of choice is the experiment, discourse analysis, or whatever, it is crucial to study women in *interaction* and to analyze speech as socially situated. This means that the larger context of the *speech community* must be attended to (Nichols, 1980). To date, few studies of black women's talk have been done (Stanback, 1988–89), and little research on lesbian speech communities.

When women interact with men in the public and domestic spaces controlled by men, they are placed in double binds of incompatible femininity and competence. When they are sexually coerced they may be blamed for failing to communicate clearly. Feminist approaches must recognize, not obscure, those dilemmas of position and power. However, the workings of power are not monolithic. Researchers must recognize that status, power, and the salience of sex, class and ethnicity fluctuate (Berger, 1985). Whether we are studying the social consequences of assertive speech (Carli, 1990), the politics of turn-taking (O'Barr, 1984), or the uses of conversational humor, the *local* context of the talk is part of what forms its meaning.

On Desilencing   Researchers must turn to the study of women in spaces they create with other women (Rakow, 1986; Thorne et al.,

1983; Todd and Fisher, 1988). Only in all-women groups can women's talk and women's conversational goals become the norm. Feminist humor creates group solidarity and inverts sexist culture to expose its fallacies. Often, it is in those spaces that resistance and rebellion are voiced and strengthened (cf. Green, 1977; White, 1988).

When women are asked about communication problems, their chief complaint is of being ignored and silenced (Cameron, in press). Researchers who are aware that women are often silenced in talk with men will want to interrogate how this silencing is produced (DeFrancisco, 1991; Thorne et al., 1983) and how it can be prevented. Such study might include analyses of women's uses of humor and other indirect modes to speak the unspeakable in cross-sex interactions (Barreca, 1991).

Part of the task of desilencing is to recognize that when women use distinctive speech strategies they may well be highly adaptive and necessary to those women's social position. 'Nonassertive' speech may lead to more positive social consequences than emulating male norms. 'Rapport talk' and 'nagging' may be effective strategies for engaging a partner who uses withdrawal as a power tactic (Sattel, 1983), and 'gossip' a means of creating in-group solidarity (Tannen, 1990). Rather than judge such speech strategies from the outside, or intervene with attempts to change them to meet mythical male standards, researchers should investigate their meaning and function from within their social location. As Marsha Houston Stanback noted about women of color, 'many aspects of [their] talk are "survival skills" which should not be changed unless the social relationships that create them are changed' (1988–89: 192).

On Fusing Theory and Practice   In much of the research literature on women and language, women have been portrayed *only* as victims of misguided early socialization that renders their speech inadequate and deficient. More recently, the notion of dual cultures and cross-sex miscommunication has been employed to obscure power relations between women and men. Feminist researchers need to step back from the techniques and methods of their research and ask *whose needs do these models serve* and *what are their social consequences?* While most social scientists are trained in the intricacies of their discipline's preferred methods, few are taught to critique their discipline's assumptions and practices. This self-reflexive political critique is essential. Because social science is a culturally privileged form of knowledge, doing research is inevitably a political act (Crawford and Marecek, 1989).

In analyzing how women activists have used humor to achieve feminist political goals, I have attempted to expand the study of communication from what women have *traditionally* done to include what women are doing to *subvert* tradition – from *what has been* to *what is* and *what could be* (Fine and Gordon, 1989). In analyzing how educational programs on interpersonal violence and 'date rape' rely on a miscommunication model that leads to increased victim-blaming and the social construction of a difference between 'date rape' and 'real rape,' I have urged feminist researchers and educators to critically reconsider the limitations of their models. I view such strategies as important in fusing politics with theory and practice.

On Studying what is Not   Among feminist theorists, women of color have led the way in recognizing that systems of oppression are linked, that all are based upon hierarchy and dominance, and all are supported by similar social structures (Hooks, 1981, 1984; Stanback, 1988–89). Throughout this book I have insisted on relating social structural, interactional, and internalized aspects of gender and recognizing that they interact as a multi-level system. Such a conceptualization of gender is not yet the norm in gender-and-language research, nor is recognition of the interaction of gender with other oppressive systems of social classification.

When gender researchers adopt these perspectives, the way is opened to study why and how social injustice can persist with no evidence of unhappiness or rebellion – the 'social construction of quiescence' (Fine and Gordon, 1989: 165). One important area for study is women's relationship with self-help literature, popular psychology, and therapy (Kitzinger and Perkins, 1993). Feminist scholars and cultural critics are beginning to ask searching questions about why particular themes arise in self-help literature at particular moments in history (Faludi, 1991); how popular psychology and 'verbal hygiene' books position women as in need of self-improvement projects (Cameron, in press; Worell, 1988); how women read relationship narratives and how these narratives serve social functions (Radway, 1984; Simonds, 1992). In analyzing not only disciplinary voices but the voices of popular culture in this book, I have suggested ways in which the social science disciplines and popular culture form a mutually influencing loop and how they collude in the social construction of quiescence.

It is also important to name and examine women's resistance to these forms of social control. Women may use self-help books and seminars not to adjust to male norms, but to reassure themselves that their experiences of unfulfilling relationships are common, even 'normal' (Simonds, 1992). Reading themselves into the familiar, trite anecdotes of a self-help book or the role-playing exercises of an assertiveness training seminar, women may recognize their own realities and gain reassurance that they are coping with real problems. Moreover, they may create interpretations that compete with the self-help authors' own proselytizing. All attempts at control run the risk of engendering resistance, of provoking a critical response simply by making a particular issue salient.

Resistance to silencing can be studied in interactional contexts, too. To do this, researchers need to look beyond dichotomies of difference/dominance. Rather than compete for the floor, thus accepting and reconstructing dominance as a conversational norm, some speakers may create a more inclusive dynamic, one that has as yet no name:

> Mischa Adams (1980) provides an example of this process in a discussion of telling moments when women and men have transformed stereotyped interactions. She describes a graduate seminar in which women were rendered silent, while the professor and most of the male students monopolized talk, controlling the floor through eye contact, interruption, and throwing the floor only to one another. Those who were squeezed out analyzed these patterns and set out to change them, not by adopting the dominant discourse, but by empowering one another. They arrived early and sat in a way that diffused eye contact around the group; they built on one another's comments in the discussion, giving the mutual gift of 'interaction work'; they invited the silent to speak. Rather than overvaluing and imitating the dominant style . . . they used collaborative patterns to draw in, and empower, more participants. (Thorne et al., 1983: 19)

On Feminist Identity and Social Change

Throughout this book I have documented ways in which social scientists have classified, pathologized, and attempted to change women's speech. I have argued against such interventions. Paradoxically, however, the preoccupation with sex differences in speech style may have inadvertent advantages for feminist social change projects. By drawing attention to the way identity is created in everyday talk, sex difference research has opened ways for women to reflect on their current identities and to imagine alternatives (Cameron, in press).

Because of the rise of the feminist movement, women have become more aware of external constraints on their ability to meet personal goals (Unger and Crawford, 1992). Indeed, women's dissatisfaction with the status quo in gender relations and public life is what fuels the self-help industry. However, in order for feminism to realize its transformative potential, women must both become dissatisfied with the way things are *and* believe that they can change social structures by their own efforts. The quest for self-transformation encouraged by individualistic social science does, at least, give women the message that 'Your life is yours to control.' And this belief may be necessary and empowering for anyone committed to change (Cameron, in press).

Feminists are particularly likely to hold a social constructionist view of reality (Unger, 1989). They understand that gender-differentiated behavior is constructed in interaction; they do not see it as existing naturally. Moreover, feminist activists hold apparently contradictory beliefs that social structural factors are beyond the individual's control and also that individuals can change social systems. Such a contradictory belief pattern may be particularly adaptive for the contradictory realities of women's lives.

Those who want to understand how the gender system is recreated and maintained are wise to focus on language use. Attention to language practices can be a crucial way of unmasking the politics of everyday life. However, an uncritical and non-reflexive approach to language can only help perpetuate the gender system, as researchers (and those who turn to research for help in understanding their social worlds) get caught up in discourses that reproduce existing power relations. The critical perspectives of feminism, with its refusal of dominant meanings, provide ways to both study and change the gendered social order.

Appendix
Transcribing Conventions

Throughout the book, I have reproduced transcribed talk exactly as it was reproduced in the original sources cited. The only exceptions are two segments from Edwards and Potter (1992), which appear in slightly simplified form in Chapter 2.

In the 'Date Rape' segment in Chapter 4, the transcription is my own, and I have used the following simple conventions:

...	Ellipses indicate talk omitted. When entire lines are omitted, the ellipses appear vertically in place of the missing line numbers.
[ ]	Square brackets indicate the beginning and end of overlapping talk.
(.) (..) (...)	Dots enclosed in parentheses indicate pauses. The number of dots roughly categorizes the pause as short, medium, or long.
if you're drunk= =Yeah= =and it's late	Equal signs connecting two lines indicate that the talk on one line was followed immediately by the next speaker's talk without even a momentary pause.
<u>rape season</u>	Underlining indicates vocal emphasis.
that HE KNOW	Words or syllables in capital letters indicate extreme vocal emphasis and loudness.
u::sually	Colons indicate that a syllable was elongated or 'stretched.' The number of colons roughly categorizes the extent of elongation.
And–	A hyphen indicates a sudden breaking off of speech.
women are say(ing)	Parentheses around words or syllables indicate that the transcriber is in doubt about the exact word or syllable because it was virtually inaudible. Empty parentheses indicate that a segment of talk was totally inaudible.

((slight laughter)) ((Urban U.))	Double parentheses indicate transcriber comments. In this transcript, I have substituted titles when speakers referred to others by name and have changed place names.
? , . !	Punctuation indicates pitch changes. The question mark indicates rising pitch, the comma a slight fall, the period a marked drop, and the exclamation point an emphatic pitch.
.hhh	This notation indicates audible drawing in of breath. The number of hs roughly indicates the duration of the inbreath sound.
n-nhew I'm gonna rape you	Modified spelling is used to suggest pronunciation variants.

References

Adams, M. (1980) Communication and gender stereotype: an anthropological perspective. Unpublished PhD dissertation, University of California, Santa Cruz.

Adcock, C. and Newbigging, K. (1990) Women in the shadows: women, feminism and clinical psychology. In E. Burman (ed.), *Feminists and psychological practice* (pp. 172–188). London: Sage.

Alberti, R. E. (ed.) (1977) *Assertiveness: innovations, applications, issues.* San Luis Obispo, CA: Impact.

Amir, M. (1967) Victim precipitated forcible rape. *Journal of Criminal Law, Criminology, and Police Science*, 58, 493–502.

Ardener, S. (ed.) (1975) *Perceiving women.* London: Malaby Press.

Austin, J. L. (1962) *How to do things with words.* New York: Oxford University Press.

Barreca, R. (1991) *They used to call me Snow White . . . but I drifted.* New York: Viking.

Baumann, M. (1976) Two features of women's speech? In B. L. Dubois and I. Crouch (eds), *The sociology of the languages of American women* (pp. 33–40). San Antonio, TX: Trinity University.

Beattie, M. (1987) *Codependent no more.* New York: Harper Collins.

Beckwith, B. (1984) How magazines cover sex differences research. *Science for the People*, 16, 18–23.

Belenky, M. F., Clinchy, B. M., Goldberger, N. R., and Tarule, J. M. (1986) *Women's ways of knowing: the development of self, voice and mind.* New York: Basic Books.

Bem, S. (1974) The measurement of psychological androgyny. *Journal of Consulting and Clinical Psychology*, 42, 155–162.

Bem, S. (1993) *Lenses of gender.* New Haven: Yale University Press.

Berger, C. R. (1985) Social power and interpersonal communication. In M. Knapp and G. Miller (eds), *Handbook of interpersonal communication* (pp. 439–499). London: Sage.

Berger, P. L. and Luckmann, T. (1966) *The social construction of reality.* Harmondsworth: Penguin.

Bilous, F. R. and Krauss, R. M. (1988) Dominance and accommodation in the conversational behaviours of same- and mixed-gender dyads. *Language and Communication*, 8, 183–194.

Bloom, V., Coburn, K., and Perlman, J. (1975) *The new assertive woman.* New York: Delacorte.

Bloom, V., Coburn, K., and Perlman, J. (1980) *The new assertive woman*, 2nd edn. New York: Dell.

Boden, D. (1991) Postcards from the edge. *Contemporary Sociology*, 20, 848–851.

Bogen, D. and Lynch, M. (1989) Taking account of the hostile native: plausible deniability and the production of conventional history in the Iran-Contra hearings. *Social Problems*, 36, 197–224.

Bohan, J. (1993) Regarding gender: essentialism, constructionism and feminist psychology. *Psychology of Women Quarterly*, 17, 5–22.

Booraem, C. D. and Flowers, J. V. (1978) A procedural model for training of assertive behavior. In J. M. Whitely and J. V. Flowers (eds), *Approaches to assertion training* (pp. 15–46). Monterey, CA: Brooks/Cole.

Bormann, E. H., Pratt, J., and Putman, L. (1978) Power, authority, and sex: male response to female leadership. *Communication Monographs*, 45, 119–155.

Brooks, M. L., Hanbery, D. E., Matz, I., Westover, T., and Westover, C. (1988) *Beer is better than women because . . .* Watertown, MA: Ivory Tower.

Broverman, J. K., Broverman, D. M., Clarkson, F. E., Rosenkrantz, P. S., and Vogel, S. R. (1970) Sex role stereotypes and clinical judgments of mental health. *Journal of Consulting and Clinical Psychology*, 34, 1–7.

Brown, L. S. (1986) Diagnosis and the Zeitgeist: the politics of masochism in the DSM-III-R. Paper presented at the meeting of the American Psychological Association, Washington, DC.

Brown, L. S. (1990) What's addiction got to do with it? A feminist critique of codependence. *Psychology of Women Newsletter*, 17, 1–4.

Brown, P. and Levinson, S. (1978) Universals in language usage: politeness phenomena. In E. N. Goody (ed.), *Questions and politeness: strategies in social interaction* (pp. 56–310). Cambridge: Cambridge University Press.

Brown, S. D. and Brown, L. W. (1980) Trends in assertion training research and practice: a content analysis of the published literature. *Journal of Clinical Psychology*, 36, 263–269.

Brownmiller, S. (1975) *Against our will: men, women, and rape*. New York: Simon and Schuster.

Burman, E. (1990) Differing with deconstruction: A feminist critique. In I. Parker and J. Shotter (eds), *Deconstructing social psychology* (pp. 208–220). London: Routledge.

Burman, E. (1992) Feminism and discourse in developmental psychology: power, subjectivity and interpretation. *Feminism and Psychology*, 2, 45–60.

Burman, E. and Parker, I. (eds) (1993) *Discourse analytic research*. New York: Routledge.

Butler, P. (1976) *Self assertion for women*. San Francisco: Canfield.

Butler, P. (1981) *Self assertion for women*, 2nd edn. San Francisco: Harper and Row.

Callahan, B. (1980) *Workshop models for family life education: assertiveness training*. Boston: Resource Communications.

Cameron, D. (1985) *Feminism and linguistic theory*. London: Macmillan.

Cameron, D. (1992) Review of Deborah Tannen's *You just don't understand. Feminism and Psychology*, 2, 465–468.

Cameron, D. (in press) *Verbal hygiene*. London: Routledge.

Cameron, D., McAlinden, F., and O'Leary, K. (1989) Lakoff in context: the social and linguistic functions of tag questions. In J. Coates and D. Cameron (eds), *Women in their speech communities: New perspectives on language and sex* (pp. 74–93). New York: Longman.

Caplan, P. (1993) *Lifting a ton of feathers: a woman's guide to surviving in the academic world*. Toronto: University of Toronto Press.

Caplan, P. and Eichler, M. (1989) *A proposal for the Delusional Dominating Personality Disorder*. Toronto: Authors.

Caplan, P. and Gans, H. (1991) Is there empirical justification for the category of 'Self-Defeating Personality Disorder'? *Feminism and Psychology*, 1, 263–278.

Carli, L. L. (1990) Gender, language, and influence. *Journal of Personality and Social Psychology*, 59, 941–951.

Carr, C. (1992) Guerrilla girls: combat in the art zone. *Mirabella*, 38, 32–35.

Cashion, J., Cody, M., and Erickson, K. (1987) 'You'll love this one . . .' An exploration into joke-prefacing devices. *Journal of Language and Social Psychology*, 5, 303–312.

Chaffin, R. and Mahlstedt, D. (1994) Perceptions of responsibility for dating violence among US undergraduates. In J. W. White (Chair), *The role of perceptions in relationship violence: a constructionist view*. Symposium presented at the meeting of the Southeastern Psychological Association, New Orleans.

Chapman, A. and Foot, H. (1976) *Humor and laughter: theory, research, and applications*. New York: Wiley.

Chapman, A. and Gadfield, N. (1976) Is sexual humor sexist? *Journal of Communication*, 26, 141–153.

Cheek, D. K. (1976) *Assertive black, puzzled white*. San Luis Obispo, CA: Impact.

Chipman, S. F. and Wilson, D. M. (1985) Understanding mathematics course enrollment and mathematics achievement: a synthesis of the research. In S. F. Chipman, L. R. Brush, and D. M. Wilson (eds), *Women and mathematics: balancing the equation* (pp. 275–328). Hillsdale, NJ: Erlbaum.

Cianni-Surridge, M. and Horan, J. J. (1983) On the wisdom of assertive job-seeking behavior. *Journal of Consulting Psychology*, 30, 209–214.

Clark, H. (1992) *Arenas of language use*. Chicago: University of Chicago Press.

Clark, H. and Clark, E. (1977) *Psychology and language: An introduction to psycholinguistics*. New York: Harcourt Brace Jovanovich.

Clinton, K. (1982) Making light: another dimension. *Trivia*, 1, 37–42.

Coates, J. and Cameron, D. (eds) (1988) *Women in their speech communities*. New York: Longman.

Cohen, S. L., Bunker, K. A., Burton, A. L., and McManus, P. D. (1978) Reactions of male subordinates to the sex-role congruency of immediate supervision. *Sex Roles*, 4, 297–311.

Comas-Diaz, L. (1985) Cognitive and behavioral group therapy with Puerto Rican women: a comparison of content themes. *Hispanic Journal of Behavioral Sciences*, 7, 273–283.

Committee on Women in Psychology (1985) *Statement on proposed diagnostic categories for DSM-III-R*. Washington, DC: American Psychological Association.

Corcoran, C. (1992) From victim control to social change: a feminist perspective on campus rape prevention programs. In J. Chrisler and D. Howard (eds), *New directions in feminist psychology* (pp. 130–140). New York: Springer.

Coser, R. (1960) Laughter among colleagues. *Psychiatry*, 23, 81–95.

Costrich, N., Feinstein, J., Kidder, L., Marecek, J., and Pascale, L. (1975) When stereotypes hurt: three studies of penalties for sex-role reversals. *Journal of Experimental Social Psychology*, 11, 520–530.

Cotler, S. (1978) Assertion training: a road leading where? In J. M. Whiteley and J. V. Flowers (eds), *Approaches to assertion training* (pp. 84–100). Monterey, CA: Brooks/Cole.

Cowan, C. and Kinder, M. (1986) *Smart women, foolish choices*. New York: Signet.

Cowan, G. and Koziej, J. (1979) Perception of sex-inconsistent behavior. *Sex Roles*, 5, 1–10.

Crawford, M. (1981) Emmy Noether: she did Einstein's math. *Ms*, 10, 86–89.

Crawford, M. (1982) In pursuit of the well-rounded life: women scholars and family concerns. In M. Kehoe (ed.), *Handbook for women scholars* (pp. 89–96). San Francisco: Americas Behavior Research Corporation.

Crawford, M. (1988) Gender, age, and the social evaluation of assertion. *Behavior Modification*, 12, 549–564.

Crawford, M. (1989a) Agreeing to differ: feminist epistemologies and women's ways of knowing. In M. Crawford and M. Gentry (eds), *Gender and thought* (pp. 128–145). New York: Springer-Verlag.

Crawford, M. (1989b) Humor in conversational contexts: beyond biases in the study of gender and humor. In R. K. Unger (ed.), *Representations: social constructions of gender* (pp. 155–166). Amityville, NY: Baywood.

Crawford, M. (1990) The discourse of humor: two levels. Paper presented at the annual meeting of the American Psychological Association, Boston.

Crawford, M. and Gressley, D. (1991) Creativity, caring, and context: women's and men's accounts of humor preferences and practices. *Psychology of Women Quarterly*, 15, 217–232.

Crawford, M. and MacLeod, M. (1990) Gender in the college classroom: an assessment of the 'chilly climate' for women. *Sex Roles*, 23, 101–122.

Crawford, M. and Marecek, J. (1989) Psychology reconstructs the female. *Psychology of Women Quarterly*, 13, 147–166.

Crawford, M. and Unger, R. K. (1990) Hearing voices, seeing differences. (Review of *Mapping the Moral Domain*.) *Contemporary Psychology*, 35, 950–952.

Crosby, F. (1982) *Relative deprivation and working women*. New York: Oxford University Press.

Crosby, F. and Nyquist, L. (1977) The female register: an empirical study of Lakoff's hypothesis. *Language in Society*, 6, 313–322.

Datan, N. (1989) Illness and imagery: feminist cognition, socialization, and gender identity. In M. Crawford and M. Gentry (eds), *Gender and thought* (pp. 175–188). New York: Springer-Verlag.

Deaux, K. (1993) Commentary: Sorry, wrong number – a reply to Gentile's call. *Psychological Science*, 4, 125–126.

DeFrancisco, V. (1991) The sounds of silence: how men silence women in marital relations. *Discourse and Society*, 2, 413–423.

DeFrancisco, V. (1992) Review of Deborah Tannen's *You just don't Understand*. *Language in Society*, 21, 319–324.

Dion, K. K., Berscheid, E., and Walster, E. (1972) What is beautiful is good. *Journal of Personality and Social Psychology*, 24, 285–290.

Douglas, M. (1975) *Implicit meanings*. London: Routledge and Kegan Paul.

Dowling, C. (1981) *The Cinderella complex*. New York: Pocket Books.

Dresner, Z. (1988) Women's humor. In L. Mintz (ed.), *Humor in America: a research guide to genres and topics*. New York: Greenwood.

Dubois, B. L. and Crouch, I. (1975) The question of tag questions in women's speech: they don't really use more of them, do they? *Language in Society*, 4, 289–294.

Duranti, A. and Goodwin, C. (1992) *Rethinking context: language as an interactive phenomenon*. Cambridge: Cambridge University Press.

Eagly, A. (1994) On comparing women and men. *Feminism and Psychology*, 4, 513–522.

Eakins, B. and Eakins, G. (1976) Verbal turn-taking and exchanges in faculty dialogue. In B. L. Dubois and I. Crouch (eds), *The sociology of the languages of American women*. San Antonio, TX: Trinity University.

Eccles, J. (1989) Bringing young women to math and science. In M. Crawford and M. Gentry (eds), *Gender and thought* (pp. 36–58). New York: Springer-Verlag.

Eccles, J. , Adler, T. F., Futterman, R., Goff, S. B., Kaczala, C. M., Meece, J. L., and Midgley, C. (1985) Self-perceptions, socializing influences, and the decision to enroll in mathematics. In S. F. Chipman, L. R. Brush, and D. M. Wilson (eds), *Women and mathematics: balancing the equation* (pp. 95–122). Hillsdale, NJ: Erlbaum.

Eccles, J. and Jacobs, J. (1986) Social forces shape math attitudes and performance. *Signs*, 11, 367–389.

Edwards, D. and Potter, J. (1992) *Discursive psychology*. London: Sage.

Egidio, R. K. and Pope, S. L. (1977) *Becoming assertive: a trainer's manual*. East Lansing, MI: Michigan State University Press.

Erwin, E. (1978) *Behavior therapy: scientific, philosophical, and moral foundations*. Cambridge: Cambridge University Press.

Eyer, D. E. (1993) *Mother–infant bonding: a scientific fiction*. New Haven: Yale University Press.

Falbo, T. (1982) PAQ types and power strategies used in intimate relationships. *Psychology of Women Quarterly*, 6, 399–405.

Falbo, T., Hazen, M. D., and Linimon, D. (1982) The costs of selecting power bases or messages associated with the opposite sex. *Sex Roles*, 8, 147–157.

Falbo, T. and Peplau, L. A. (1980) Power strategies in intimate relationships. *Journal of Personality and Social Psychology*, 38, 618–628.

Faludi, S. (1991) *Backlash: the undeclared war against American women*. New York: Doubleday.

Fine, M. (1985) Reflections on a feminist psychology of women: paradoxes and prospects. *Psychology of Women Quarterly*, 9, 167–183.

Fine, M. and Asch, A. (1988) *Women with disabilities: essays in psychology, culture, and politics*. Philadelphia: Temple University Press.

Fine, M. and Gordon, S. M. (1989) Feminist transformations of/despite psychology. In M. Crawford and M. Gentry (eds), *Gender and thought: Psychological perspectives* (pp. 146–174). New York: Springer-Verlag.

Fine, M. and Gordon, S. M. (1991) Effacing the centre and the margins: life at the inter-section of psychology and feminism. *Feminism and Psychology*, 1, 19–28.

Fishman, P. (1978) Interaction: the work women do. *Social Problems*, 25, 397–406.

Fishman, P. (1980) Conversational insecurity. In H. Giles, W. P. Robinson, and P. M. Smith (eds), *Language: social psychological perspectives* (pp. 127–132). New York: Pergamon.

Fiske, S. T. (1993) Controlling other people: the impact of power on stereotyping. *American Psychologist*, 48, 621–628.

Flowers, J. V., Whiteley, J. M., and Cooper, C. (1978) Assertion training: A general overview. In J. M. Whiteley and J. V. Flowers (eds), *Approaches to assertion training* (pp. 1–15). Monterey, CA: Brooks/Cole.

Fodor, I. G. (1985) Assertiveness training for the eighties: moving beyond the personal. In L.B. Rosewater and L.E.A. Walker (eds), *Handbook of feminist therapy* (pp. 257–265). New York: Springer.

Fodor, I. G. (ed.) (1992) *Adolescent assertiveness and social skills: a clinical handbook*. New York: Springer.

Fodor, I. G. and Epstein, R. C. (1983) Assertiveness training for women: where are we failing? In P. Emmelkamp and E. Foa (eds), *Failures in behavior therapy* (pp. 132–154). New York: Wiley.

Frank, F. W. (1978) Women's language in America. In D. Butturff and E. L. Epstein (eds), *Women's language and style* (pp. 47–61). Akron, OH: University of Akron.

Franks, V. and Rothblum, E. D. (eds) (1983) *The stereotyping of women: its effects on mental health*. New York: Springer.

Freed, A. (1992) We understand perfectly: a critique of Tannen's view of cross-sex communication. Paper presented at the Berkeley Women and Language Conference.

Galassi, J. P., DeLo, J. S., Galassi, M. D., and Bastien, S. (1974) The college self-expression scale: a measure of assertiveness. *Behavior Therapy*, 5, 165–171.

Galassi, M. D. and Galassi, J. P. (1978) Assertion: a critical review. *Psychotherapy: Theory, Research, and Practice*, 15, 16–29.

Gardner, C. B. (1980) Passing by: Street remarks, address rights, and the urban female. *Language and Social Interaction*, 50, 328–356.

Garfinkel, H. (1967) *Studies in ethnomethodology*. Englewood Cliffs, NJ: Prentice-Hall.

Gavey, N. (1989) Feminist poststructuralism and discourse analysis: contributions to a feminist psychology. *Psychology of Women Quarterly*, 13, 459–475.

Gavey, N. (1992) Technologies and effects of heterosexual coercion. *Feminism and Psychology*, 2, 325–352.

Gentile, D. (1993) Just what are sex and gender, anyway? A call for a new terminological standard. *Psychological Science*, 4, 120–122.

Gergen, K. J. (1985) The social constructionist movement in modern psychology. *American Psychologist*, 40, 266–275.

Gervasio, A. H. (1987) Assertiveness techniques as speech acts. *Clinical Psychology Review*, 7, 105–119.

Gervasio, A. H. (1988) Linguistic analysis of an assertiveness training film. *Psychotherapy: Theory, Research and Practice*, 25, 294–304.

Gervasio, A. H. and Crawford, M. (1989) Social evaluations of assertiveness: a critique and speech act reformulation. *Psychology of Women Quarterly*, 13, 1–25.

Gervasio, A. H., Pepinsky, H. B., and Schwebel, A. I. (1983) Stylistic complexity and verb usage in assertive and passive speech. *Journal of Counseling Psychology*, 30, 546–556.

Gilfoyle, J., Wilson, J., and Brown (1992) Sex, organs and audiotape: a discourse analytic approach to talking about heterosexual sex and relationships. *Feminism and Psychology*, 2, 209–230.

Gilligan, C. (1982) *In a different voice*. Cambridge, MA: Harvard University Press.

Goldstein, J. and McGhee, P. (1972) An annotated bibliography of published papers on humor in the research literature and an analysis of trends: 1900–1971. In J. Goldstein and P. McGhee (eds), *The psychology of humor* (pp. 263–284). New York: Academic Press.

Goodchilds, J. (1972) On being witty: causes, correlates, and consequences. In J. Goldstein and P. McGhee (eds), *The psychology of humor* (pp. 173–194). New York: Academic Press.

Goodwin, M. (1990) *He-said-she-said: talk as social organization among black children*. Indianapolis, IN: Indianapolis University Press.

Graddol, D. and Swann, J. (1989) *Gender voices*. Oxford: Basil Blackwell.

Grady, K. E. (1981) Sex bias in research design. *Psychology of Women Quarterly*, 5, 628–636.

Graeven, P. B. and Morris, S. J. (1975) College humor in 1930 and 1972: an investigation using the humor diary. *Sociological and Social Research*, 59, 406–410.

Gray, J. (1992) *Men are from Mars, women are from Venus*. New York: Harper Collins.

Green, R. (1977) Magnolias grow in dirt: the bawdy lore of Southern women. *Southern Exposure*, 4, 29–33.

Grice, H. P. (1975) Logic and conversation. In P. Cole and J. L. Morgan (eds), *Syntax and semantics: Speech acts*, Vol. 3 (pp. 41–58). New York: Seminar Press.

Griffin, C. (1989) 'I'm not a women's libber but . . .': feminism, consciousness, and identity. In S. Skevington and D. Baker (eds), *The social identity of women* (pp. 173–193). London: Sage.

Griscom, J. (1992) Women and power: definition, dualism, and difference. *Psychology of Women Quarterly*, 16, 389–414.

Gumperz, J. (1982a) *Discourse strategies*. Cambridge: Cambridge University Press.

Gumperz, J. (ed.) (1982b) *Language and social identity*. Cambridge: Cambridge University Press.

Gumperz, J. (1992) Contextualization and understanding. In A. Duranti and C. Goodwin (eds), *Rethinking context: language as an interactive phenomenon* (pp. 229–252). Cambridge: Cambridge University Press.

Gutek, B. A. (1985) *Sex and the workplace*. San Francisco: Jossey-Bass.

Hall, J. A. (1978) Gender effects in decoding nonverbal cues. *Psychological Bulletin*, 85, 845–857.

Hall, J. A. (1984) *Nonverbal sex differences: communicative accuracy and expressive style*. Baltimore: Johns Hopkins University Press.

Halpern, D. (1994) Stereotypes, science, censorship, and the study of sex differences. *Feminism and Psychology*, 4, 523–530.

Harding, S. (ed.) (1987) *Feminism and methodology*. Bloomington, IN: Indiana University Press.

Hare-Mustin, R. and Marecek, J. (1988) The meaning of difference: gender theory, post-modernism, and psychology. *American Psychologist*, 43, 455–464.

Hare-Mustin, R. and Marecek, J. (eds) (1990) *Making a difference: psychology and the construction of gender*. New Haven: Yale.

Hare-Mustin, R. and Marecek, J. (1994) Asking the right questions: feminist psychology and sex differences. *Feminism and Psychology*, 4, 531–537.

Harris, M. B. (1974) Mediators between frustration and aggression in a field experiment. *Journal of Experimental Social Psychology*, 10, 561–571.

Hartmann, M. (1976) A descriptive study of the language of men and women born in Maine around 1900 as it reflects the Lakoff hypotheses in *Language and Woman's Place*. In B. L. Dubois and I. Crouch (eds), *The sociology of the languages of American women* (pp. 81–90). San Antonio, TX: Trinity University.

Hassan, R. (1973) Code, register and social dialect. In B. B. Bernstein (ed.), *Class, codes, and control*, Vol. 2 (pp. 253–292). London: Routledge and Kegan Paul.

Heimberg, R. C., Montgomery, D., Madsen, C. H., and Heimberg, J. (1977) Assertion training: a review of the literature. *Behavior Therapy*, 8, 953–971.

Henkin, B. and Fish, J. (1986) Gender and personality differences in the appreciation of cartoon humor. *Journal of Psychology*, 120, 157–175.

Henley, N. M. (1977) *Body politics*. Englewood Cliffs, NJ: Prentice Hall.

Henley, N. M. (1980) Assertiveness training in the social context. *Assert*, 30, 1–2.

Henley, N. M. and Kramarae, C. (1988) Miscommunication – issues of gender and power. Paper presented at the meetings of the National Women's Studies Association, Minneapolis, June.

Henley, N. M. and Kramarae, C. (1991) Gender, power, and miscommunication. In N. Coupland, H. Giles, and J.M. Wiemann (eds), *'Miscommunication' and problematic talk* (pp. 18–43). Newbury Park, CA: Sage.

Heritage, J. (1984) *Garfinkel and ethnomethodology*. Cambridge: Polity Press.

Hesse-Biber, S. (1989) Eating patterns and disorders in a college population: are college women's eating problems a new phenomenon? *Sex Roles*, 20, 71–89.

Hill, A. O. (1986) *Mother tongue, father time: a decade of linguistic revolt*. Bloomington, IN: Indiana University Press.

Holland, D. and Eisenhart, M. (1990) *Educated in romance: women, achievement, and college culture*. Chicago: University of Chicago Press.

Hollander, N. (1994) T-shirt advertisement. *Funny Times*, 9, 22.

Hollandsworth, J. G. and Wall, K. E. (1977) Sex differences in assertive behavior: an empirical investigation. *Journal of Counseling Psychology*, 24, 217–222.

Hollway, W. (1989) *Subjectivity and method in psychology*. London: Sage.

Hollway, W. (1994) Beyond sex differences: a project for feminist psychology. *Feminism and Psychology*, 4, 538–546.

Hooks, B. (1981) *Ain't I a woman? Black women and feminism*. Rowley, MA: South End Press.

Hooks, B. (1984) *Feminist theory: from margin to center*. Boston: South End Press.

Horner, M. S. (1970) Femininity and successful achievement: a basic inconsistency. In J. M. Bardwick, E. Douvan, M. S. Horner, and D. Gutman (eds), *Feminine personality and conflict* (pp. 45–74). Belmont, CA: Brooks/Cole.

Hyde, J. (1992) Can meta-analysis make feminist transformations in psychology? In C. Etaugh (Chair), *Transformations: Reconceptualizing theory and method in research with women*. Symposium presented at the American Psychological Association, August.

Hyde, J. (1994) Should psychologists study gender differences? Yes, with some guidelines. *Feminism and Psychology*, 4, 507–512.

Hyde, J., Fennema, E., and Lamon, S. J. (1990) Gender differences in mathematics performance: a meta-analysis. *Psychological Bulletin*, 107, 139–155.

Hyde, J. and Linn, M. C. (1988) Gender differences in verbal ability: a meta-analysis. *Psychological Bulletin*, 104, 53–69.

Jacklin, C. (1981) Methodological issues in the study of sex-related differences. *Developmental Review*, 1, 266–273.

Jakubowski, P. (1977) Assertive behavior and clinical problems of women. In R. E. Alberti (ed.), *Assertiveness: innovations, applications, issues* (p. 163). San Luis Obispo, CA: Impact.

Jakubowski, P. (1978) *The assertive option: your rights and responsibilities*. Champaign, IL: Research Press Co.

Jenkins, M. (1985) What's so funny? Joking among women. In S. Bremner, N. Caskey, and B. Moonwomon (eds), *Proceedings of the First Berkeley Women and Language Conference*. Berkeley, CA: Berkeley Women and Language Group.

Jesperson, O. (1922) *Language: its nature, development, and origin*. London: Allen and Unwin.

Johnson, J. L. (1980) Questions and role responsibility in four professional meetings. *Anthropological Linguistics*, 22, 66–76.

Kahn, L. S. (1984) Group process and sex differences. *Psychology of Women Quarterly*, 8, 261–281.

Kalcik, S. (1975) '. . . like Ann's gynecologist or the time I was almost raped.' Personal narratives in women's rap groups. *Journal of American Folklore*, 88, 3–11.

Kambouropoulou, P. (1930) Individual differences in the sense of humor and their relation to temperamental differences. *Archives of Psychology*, 19, 1–83.

Kaplan, A. and Surrey, J. L. (1984) The relational self in women: developmental theory and public policy. In L. E. Walker (ed.), *Women and mental health policy* (pp. 79–94). Beverly Hills, CA: Sage.

Kaufman, G. (1991) *In stitches: a patchwork of feminist humor and satire*. Indianapolis: Indiana University Press.

Kaufman, G. and Blakely, M. K. (eds) (1980) *Pulling our own strings*. Bloomington, IN: Indiana University Press.

Keane, T. M., Wedding, D., and Kelly, J. A. (1983) Assessing subjective responses to assertive behavior. *Behavior Modification*, 7, 317–330.

Kelley, H. H., Cunningham, J. D., Grisham, J. A., Lefebvre, L. M., Sink, C. R., and Yablon, G. (1978) Sex differences in comments made during conflict within close heterosexual pairs. *Sex Roles*, 4, 473–491.

Kelly, J. A., Kern, J. M., Kirkley, B. G., Patterson, J. N., and Keane, T. M. (1980) Reactions to assertive versus unassertive behavior: Differential effects for males and females and implications for assertiveness training. *Behavior Therapy*, 11, 670–682.

Kessler, S. and McKenna, W. (1978) *Gender: an ethnomethodological approach*. New York: Wiley.

Kidder, L., Boell, J., and Moyer, M. (1983) Rights consciousness and victimization prevention: personal defense and assertiveness training. *Journal of Social Issues*, 39, 155–170.

Kitzinger, C. (1987) *The social construction of lesbianism*. London: Sage.

Kitzinger, C. (1990) Resisting the discipline. In E. Burman (ed.), *Feminists and psychological practice* (pp. 119–139). London: Sage.

Kitzinger, C. (1991) Feminism, psychology, and the paradox of power. *Feminism and Psychology*, 1, 111–129.

Kitzinger, C. (1993) 'Psychology constructs the female': a reappraisal. *Feminism and Psychology*, 3, 189–194.

Kitzinger, C. (ed.) (1994) Should psychologists study sex differences? *Feminism and Psychology*, 4, 501–546.

Kitzinger, C. and Perkins, R. (1993) *Changing our minds: lesbian feminism and psychology*. New York and London: New York University Press and Onlywomen Press.

Kocol, C. (1989) Taking responsibility. *The Humanist*, 49, 33–34.

Kohlberg, L. (1966) A cognitive-developmental analysis of children's sex role concepts and attitudes. In E. E. Maccoby (ed.), *The development of sex differences*. Stanford, CA: Stanford University Press.

Kramarae, C. (1981) *Women and men speaking*. Rowley, MA: Newbury House.

Kramer, C. (1974a) Stereotypes of women's speech: the word from cartoons. *Journal of Popular Culture*, 8, 624–630.

Kramer, C. (1974b) Women's speech: separate but unequal? *Quarterly Journal of Speech*, 60, 14–24.

Kramer, C. (1977) Perceptions of female and male speech. *Language and Speech*, 20, 151–161.

Labov, W. and Fanshel, D. (1977) *Therapeutic discourse: psychotherapy as conversation*. New York: Academic Press.

Lakoff, R. (1973) Language and woman's place. *Language in Society*, 2, 45–79.

Lakoff, R. (1975) *Language and woman's place*. New York: Harper and Row.

Lakoff, R. (1978) Women's language. In D. Butturff and E. L. Epstein (eds), *Women's language and style* (pp. 139–158). Akron, OH: University of Akron.

Lakoff, R. (1990) *Talking power: the politics of language in our lives*. New York: Basic Books.

Lange, A. J. and Jakubowski, P. (1976) *Responsible assertive behavior: cognitive-behavioral procedures for trainers*. Champaign, IL: Research Press.

Lapadat, J. and Seesahal, M. (1978) Male versus female codes in informal contexts. *Sociolinguistics Newsletter*, 8, 7–8.

LaPlante, M. N., McCormick, N., and Brannigan, G. G. (1980) Living the sexual script: college students' views of influence in sexual encounters. *Journal of Sex Research*, 16, 338–355.

Lazarus, A. A. (1973) On assertive behavior: a brief note. *Behavior Therapy*, 4, 697–699.

LeBell, S. (1983) Properties of the feminist joke. Cited in N. Levidow, When women are people too: a look at the new feminist comedians. In A. Nilsen (ed.), *The language of humor, the humor of language: proceedings of the 1982 WHIM (Western Humor and Irony Membership) conference* (pp. 212–214). Tempe, AZ: Arizona State University.

Leet-Pellegrini, H. M. (1980) Conversational dominance as a function of gender and expertise. In H. Giles, W. P. Robinson, and P. M. Smith (eds), *Language: social psychological perspectives*. Oxford: Pergamon.

Lerman, H. (1986) From Freud to feminist personality theory: Getting there from here. *Psychology of Women Quarterly*, 10, 1–18.

Levine, J. B. (1976) The feminine routine. *Journal of Communication*, 26, 173–175.

Levinson, S. (1983) *Pragmatics*. Cambridge: Cambridge University Press.

Lewin, M. (1984) Psychology measures femininity and masculinity. In M. Lewin (ed.), *In the shadow of the past: psychology portrays the sexes* (pp. 179–204). New York: Columbia University Press.

Linehan, M. M. and Seifert, R. F. (1983) Sex and contextual differences in the appropriateness of assertive behavior. *Psychology of Women Quarterly*, 8, 79–88.

Locksley, A., Borgida, E., Brekke, N., and Hepburn, C. (1980) Sex stereotypes and social judgment. *Journal of Personality and Social Psychology*, 39, 821–831.

Long, D. and Graesser, A. (1988) Wit and humor in discourse processing. *Discourse Processes*, 11, 35–60.

Lorde, A. (1980) *The cancer journals*. San Francisco, CA: Spinsters Ink.

Losco, J. and Epstein, S. (1975) Humor preferences as a subtle measure of attitudes toward the same and opposite sex. *Journal of Personality*, 43, 321–334.

Lott, B. (1981) A feminist critique of androgyny: toward the elimination of gender attributions for learned behavior. In C. Mayo and N. Henley (eds), *Gender and nonverbal behavior* (pp. 171–180). New York: Springer-Verlag.

Lott, B. (1985) The devaluation of women's competence. *Journal of Social Issues*, 41, 43–60.

Love, A. M. and Deckers, L. (1989) Humor appreciation as a function of sexual, aggressive, and sexist content. *Sex Roles*, 20, 649–654.

Lutfiyya, M. N. (1992) Critical street theorizing: a case study of Ladies Against Women, or, comedy as political policy development. *Women's Studies in Communication*, 15, 25–48.

Lykes, M. B. (1985) Gender and individualistic vs. collectivist bases for notions about the self. *Journal of Personality*, 53, 356–383.

MacDonald, M. L. (1982) Assertion training for women. In J. P. Curran and P. M. Monti (eds), *Social skills training: a practical handbook for assessment and treatment* (pp. 253–279). New York: Guilford.

Major, B. and Deaux, K. (1982) Individual differences in justice behavior. In J. Greenberg and R. L. Cohen (eds), *Equity and justice in social behavior*. New York: Academic Press.

Major, B., McFarlin, D. B., and Gagnon, D. (1984) Overworked and underpaid: on the nature of gender differences in personal entitlement. *Journal of Personality and Social Psychology*, 47, 1399–1412.

Maltz, D. N. and Borker, R. A. (1982) A cultural approach to male–female miscommunication. In J. Gumperz (ed.), *Language and social identity*. Cambridge: Cambridge University Press.

Mannell, R. and McMahon, L. (1982) Humor as play: its relationship to psychological well-being during the course of a day. *Leisure Sciences*, 5, 143–155.

Marecek, J. (1989) Introduction to special issue: theory and method in feminist psychology. *Psychology of Women Quarterly*, 13, 367–378.

Marlowe, L. (1989) A sense of humor. In R. K. Unger (ed.), *Representations: Social constructions of gender* (pp. 145–154). Amityville, NY: Baywood.

McCaulay, M., Mintz, L., and Glenn, A. (1988) Body image, self-esteem and depression-proneness: closing the gender gap. *Sex Roles*, 18, 381–391.

McCullough, M. (forthcoming) *Claiming the margins: women's friendships across cultures.* Cresskill, NJ: Hampton.

McGhee, P. (1979) The role of laughter and humor in growing up female. In C. B. Kopp (ed.), *Becoming female: perspectives on development* (pp. 183–206). New York: Plenum.

McGhee, P. and Goldstein, J. (1983a) *Handbook of humor research*, vol. 1. New York: Springer-Verlag.

McGhee, P. and Goldstein, J. (1983b) *Handbook of humor research*, vol. 2. New York: Springer-Verlag.

McGrath, E., Keita, G., Strickland, B., and Russo, N. (1990) *Women and depression: risk factors and treatment issues.* Washington, DC: American Psychological Association.

McIntosh, P. (1983) *Interactive phases of curricular revision: a feminist perspective.* Wellesley, MA: Wellesley College Center for Research on Women.

McMillan, J. R., Clifton, A. K., McGrath, D., and Gale, W. S. (1977) Women's language: uncertainty or interpersonal sensitivity and emotionality? *Sex Roles*, 3, 545–559.

Mednick, M. T. S. (1989) On the politics of psychological constructs: stop the bandwagon, I want to get off. *American Psychologist*, 44, 1118–1123.

Merrill, L. (1988) Feminist humor: rebellious and self-affirming. In R. Barreca (ed.), *Last laughs: perspectives on women and comedy* (pp. 271–280). New York: Gordon and Breach.

Middleton, R. and Moland, J. (1959) Humor in negro and white subcultures: a study of jokes among university students. *American Sociological Review*, 24, 61–69.

Miller, J. B. (1976/86) *Toward a new psychology of women.* Boston: Beacon Press.

Miller, J. B. (1984) *The development of women's sense of self.* Work in Progress Papers No. 84–01. Wellesley, MA: Wellesley College, The Stone Center.

Miller, J. G. (1984) Culture and the development of everyday social explanation. *Journal of Personality and Social Psychology*, 46, 961–978.

Mintz, L. (ed.) (1988) *Humor in America: A research guide to genres and topics.* New York: Greenwood.

Modleski, T. (1980) The disappearing act: a study of Harlequin romances. *Signs*, 5, 435–448.

Moriarty, T. (1975) A nation of willing victims. *Psychology Today*, 9, 43–50.

Mulac, A. and Lundell, T. (1986) Linguistic contributors to the gender-linked language effect. *Journal of Language and Social Psychology*, 5, 85–102.

Mulac, A., Lundell, T. L., and Bradac, J. J. (1986) Male/female language differences and attributional consequences in a public speaking situation: toward an explanation of the gender-linked language effect. *Communication Monographs*, 53, 115–129.

Mulac, A., Wiemann, J. M., Widenmann, S. J., and Gibson, T. W. (1988) Male/female language differences and effects in same-sex and mixed-sex dyads: the gender-linked language effect. *Communication Monographs*, 55, 215–335.

Mulkay, M. (1988) *On humor.* New York: Basil Blackwell.

Naifeh, J. and Smith, G. W. (1984) *Why can't men open up?* New York: Warner.

Neisser, U. (1976) *Cognition and reality.* San Francisco: Freeman.

Neitz, M. (1980) Humor, hierarchy, and the changing status of women. *Psychiatry*, 43, 211–223.

Nichols, P. C. (1980) Women in their speech communities. In S. McConnell-Ginet, R. Borker, and N. Furman (eds), *Women and language in literature and society* (pp. 140–149). New York: Praeger.

Nichols, P. C. (1983) Linguistic options and choices for black women in the rural south. In B. Thorne, C. Kramarae, and and N. Henley (eds), *Language, gender and society* (pp. 54–68). Rowley, MA: Newbury House.

Nochlin, L. (1971) Why are there no great women artists? In V. Gornick and B. Moran (eds), *Woman in sexist society* (pp. 480–510). New York: Basic Books.

Nofsinger, R. (1991) *Everyday conversation.* Newbury Park, CA: Sage.

Norwood, R. (1985) *Women who love too much.* New York: Pocket Books.

O'Barr, W. (1984) Asking the right questions about language and power. In C. Kramarae, M. Schulz, and W. O'Barr (eds), *Language and power* (pp. 243–259). London: Sage.

Ochs, E. (1992) Indexing gender. In A. Duranti and C. Goodwin (eds), *Rethinking context: language as an interactive phenomenon* (pp. 335–358). Cambridge: Cambridge University Press.

Ochs, E. and Schieffelin, B. (1984) Language acquisition and socialization: three developmental stories. In R. Schweder and R. Levine (eds), *Culture theory: Essays in mind, self and emotion.* Cambridge: Cambridge University Press.

Omi, M. and Philipson, I. (1983) Misterhood is powerful. *Socialist Review,* 68, 9–27.

Palmore, E. (1986) Attitudes toward aging as shown by humor: a review. In L. Nahemow, K. A. McCluskey-Fawcett, and P. McGhee (eds), *Humor and aging* (pp. 100–119). New York: Academic Press.

Pantony, K. L. and Caplan, P. (1991) Delusional Dominating Personality Disorder: a modest proposal for identifying some consequences of rigid masculine socialization. *Canadian Psychology,* 32, 120–135.

Parker, I. (1992) *Critical analysis for social and individual psychology.* New York: Routledge.

Parlee, M. B. (1975) Review essay: psychology. *Signs,* 1, 119–138.

Parlee, M. B. (1979) Psychology and women. *Signs,* 5, 121–133.

Parlee, M. B. (1991) Happy birth-day to *Feminism and Psychology. Feminism and Psychology,* 1, 39–48.

Pearson, J. C., Turner, L. H., and Todd-Mancillas, W. (1991) *Gender and communication.* Dubuque, IA: William C. Brown.

Peplau, L. A. and Conrad, E. (1989) Beyond nonsexist research: the perils of feminist methods in psychology. *Psychology of Women Quarterly,* 13, 379–400.

Percell, L. (1977) Assertive behavior training and the enhancement of self-esteem. In R. E. Alberti (ed.), *Assertiveness: innovations, applications, issues* (pp. 59–66). San Luis Obispo, CA: Impact.

Phelps, S. and Austin, N. (1975) *The assertive woman.* San Luis Obispo, CA: Impact.

Pizzini, F. (1991) Communication hierarchies in humour: gender differences in the obstetrical/gynaecological setting. *Discourse and Society,* 2, 477–488.

Porter, N. and Geis, F. (1981) Women and nonverbal leadership cues: when seeing is not believing. In C. Mayo and N. Henley (eds), *Gender and nonverbal behavior* (pp. 39–61). New York: Springer-Verlag.

Potter, J. and Wetherell, M. (1987) *Discourse and social psychology.* London: Sage.

Putnam, L. (1982) In search of gender: a critique of communication and sex-roles research. *Women's Studies in Communication,* 5, 1–9.

Radway, J. (1984) *Reading the romance: women, patriarchy, and popular literature.* Chapel Hill, NC: University of North Carolina Press.

Rakos, R. F. (1979) Content consideration in the distinction between assertive and aggressive behavior. *Psychological Reports,* 44, 767–773.

Rakow, L. (1986) Rethinking gender research in communication. *Journal of Communication,* 36, 11–26.

Reid, P. T. (1993) Poor women in psychological research: shut up and shut out. *Psychology of Women Quarterly*, 17, 133–150.

Reinharz, S. (1992) *Feminist methods in social research*. New York: Oxford University Press.

Rich, A. R. and Schroeder, H. E. (1976) Research issues in assertiveness training. *Psychological Bulletin*, 83, 1081–1096.

Rimm, D. C. and Masters, J. C. (1979) *Behavior therapy: techniques and empirical findings*, 2nd edn. New York: Academic Press.

Rix, S. (1991) *The American woman 1990–1991: a status report*. New York: Norton.

Rodriguez, R., Nietzel, M. T., and Berzins, J. I. (1980) Sex role orientation and assertiveness among female college students. *Behavior Therapy*, 11, 353–366.

Rosenberg, R. (1982) *Beyond separate spheres: the intellectual roots of modern feminism*. New Haven: Yale.

Rosenkrantz, P., Vogel, S., Bee, H., Broverman, I., and Broverman, D. M. (1968) Sex role stereotypes and self-concepts in college students. *Journal of Consulting and Clinical Psychology*, 32, 287–293.

Ross, E. (1980) 'The love crisis': Couples advice books of the late 1970s. *Signs*, 6, 109–122.

Ruben, D. (1985) *Progress in assertiveness, 1973–1983: an analytical bibliography*. Metuchen, NJ: Scarecrow Press.

Sacks, H. (1978) Some technical considerations of a dirty joke. In J. Schenkein (ed.), *Studies in the organization of conversational interaction*. New York: Academic Press.

Sadker, M. and Sadker, D. (1994) *Failing at fairness: how America's schools cheat girls*. New York: Scribners.

Salter, A. (1949) *Conditioned reflex therapy*. New York: Creative Age Press.

Sattel, J. W. (1983) Men, inexpressiveness, and power. In B. Thorne, C. Kramarae, and N. Henley (eds), *Language, gender and society* (pp. 119–124). Rowley, MA: Newbury House.

Sawin, P. (1993) Narratives of the supernatural told by Bessie Eldreth of Boone, NC. Paper presented at the University of South Carolina Women's Studies Series, Columbia, SC.

Sayre, A. (1975) *Rosalind Franklin and DNA: a vivid view of what it is like to be a gifted woman in an especially male profession*. New York: Norton.

Scarborough, E. and Furumoto, L. (1987) *Untold lives: the first generation of American women psychologists*. New York: Columbia University Press.

Schilling, K. M. and Fuehrer, A. (1993) The politics of women's self-help books. *Feminism and Psychology*, 3, 418–422.

Schur, E. (1976) *The awareness trap*. New York: Quadrangle/New York Times Book Co.

Scult, A. (1986) Coming to terms with women's language. *Quarterly Journal of Speech*, 72, 318–352.

Searle, J. R. (1969) *Speech acts: an essay in the philosophy of language*. Cambridge: Cambridge University Press.

Searle, J. R. (1979) *Expression and meaning: studies in the theory of speech acts*. Cambridge: Cambridge University Press.

Sears, D. O. (1986) College sophomores in the laboratory: influences of a narrow data base on social psychology's view of human nature. *Journal of Personality and Social Psychology*, 51, 515–530.

Seligman, M. (1975) *Helplessness: on depression, development and death*. San Francisco: Freeman.

Serber, M. (1977) Teaching the nonverbal components of assertive training. In R. E. Alberti (ed.), *Assertiveness: innovations, applications, issues* (pp. 67–74). San Luis Obispo, CA: Impact.

Sethna, C. (1992) Accepting 'total and complete responsibility'. *Feminism and Psychology*, 2, 113–118.

Sheffield, C. (1989) Sexual terrorism. In J. Freeman (ed.), *Women: A feminist perspective* (pp. 3–19). Mountain View, CA: Mayfield.

Sheppard, A. (1986) From Kate Sanborn to feminist psychology: the social context of women's humor, 1885–1985. *Psychology of Women Quarterly*, 10, 155–170.

Sherif, C. W. (1979) Bias in psychology. In J. A. Sherman and E. T. Beck (eds), *The prism of sex: essays in the sociology of knowledge* (pp. 93–133). Madison: University of Wisconsin Press.

Shields, S. A. (1975) Functionalism, Darwinism, and the psychology of women: a study in social myth. *American Psychologist*, 30, 739–754.

Shields, S. A. (1982) The variability hypothesis: the history of a biological model of sex differences in intelligence. *Signs*, 7, 769–797.

Shoemaker, M. and Satterfield, D. O. (1977) Assertion training: an identity crisis that's coming on strong. In R. E. Alberti (ed.), *Assertiveness: innovations, applications, issues* (pp. 49–58). San Luis Obispo, CA: Impact.

Shotter, J. and Gergen, K. J. (eds) (1989) *Texts of identity*. London: Sage.

Silverstein, L. (1991) Transforming the debate about child care and maternal employment. *American Psychologist*, 46, 1025–1032.

Simkins-Bullock, J. A. and Wildman, B. G. (1991) An investigation into the relationship between gender and language. *Sex Roles*, 24, 149–160.

Simonds, W. (1992) *Women and self-help culture*. New Brunswick, NJ: Rutgers University Press.

Skinner, B. F. (1957) *Verbal behavior*. New York: Appleton-Century-Crofts.

Smith, M. J. (1975) *When I say no, I feel guilty*. New York: Dial.

Snyder, M., Tanke, E. D., and Berscheid, E. (1977) Social perception and interpersonal behavior: on the self-fulfilling nature of social stereotypes. *Journal of Personality and Social Psychology*, 35, 656–666.

Spelman, E. V. (1988) *Inessential women: problems of exclusion in feminist thought*. Boston: Beacon.

Spender, D. (1980) *Man made language*. London: Routledge and Kegan Paul.

Spender, D. (1982) *Invisible women: the schooling scandal*. London: Writers' and Readers' Publishing.

Spender, D. (1989) *The writing or the sex*. New York: Pergamon Press.

Squire, C. (1989) *Significant differences: feminism in psychology*. London: Routledge.

Stanback, M. H. (1985) Language and black women's place: evidence from the black middle class. In P. A. Treichler, C. Kramarae, and B. Stafford (eds), *For alma mater: theory and practice in feminist scholarship*. Urbana, IL: University of Illinois Press.

Stanback, M. (1988–89) Feminist theory and black women's talk. *Howard Journal of Communications*, 1, 187–194.

Steil, J. M. and Weltman, K. (1991) Marital inequality: the importance of resources, personal attributes, and social norms on career valuing and the allocation of domestic responsibilities. *Sex Roles*, 24, 161–179.

Steinem, G. (1983) *Outrageous acts and everyday rebellions*. New York: New American Library.

Stere, L. K. (1985) Feminist assertiveness training: self-esteem groups as skill training for women. In L. B. Rosewater and L. E. A. Walker (eds), *Handbook of feminist therapy* (pp. 51–61). New York: Springer.

Sterling, B. S. and Owen, J. W. (1982) Perceptions of demanding versus reasoning male and female police officers. *Personality and Social Psychology Bulletin*, 8, 336–340.

Stillion, J. and White, H. (1987) Feminist humor: who appreciates it and why? *Psychology of Women Quarterly*, 11, 219–232.

Stillman, D. and Beatts, A. (1976) *Titters: the first collection of humor by women*. New York: Collier.

Tannen, D. (1984) *Conversational style: analyzing talk among friends*. Norwood, NJ: Ablex.

Tannen, D. (1990) *You just don't understand: women and men in conversation*. New York: Ballantine.

Tannen, D. (1992) Response to Senta Troemel-Ploetz's 'Selling the apolitical' (1991). *Discourse and Society*, 3, 249–254.

Tannen, D. (1994) *Talking from nine to five*. New York: William Morrow.

Teitelbaum, P. (1989) Feminist theory and standardized testing. In A. M. Jaggar and S. Bordo (eds), *Gender/body/knowledge* (pp. 324–335). New Brunswick: Rutgers University Press.

Thakerar, J., Giles, H., and Cheshire, J. (1982) Psychological and linguistic parameters of speech accommodation theory. In C. Fraser and K. Scherer (eds), *Advances in the social psychology of language* (pp. 205–256). New York: Cambridge University Press.

Thorne, B. and Henley, N. (eds) (1975) *Language and sex: differences and dominance*. Rowley, MA: Newbury House.

Thorne, B., Kramarae, C., and Henley, N. (eds) (1983) *Language, gender and society*. Rowley, MA: Newbury House.

Tiefer, L. (1991) A brief history of the Association for Women in Psychology: 1969–1991. *Psychology of Women Quarterly*, 15, 635–650.

Todd, A. and Fisher, S. (eds) (1988) *Gender and discourse: the power of talk*. Norwood, NJ: Ablex.

Torres, L. (1992) Women and language: from sex differences to power dynamics. In C. Kramarae and D. Spender (eds), *The knowledge explosion: generations of feminist scholarship*. New York: Teachers College Press.

Troemel-Ploetz, S. (1991) Review essay: selling the apolitical. *Discourse and Society*, 2, 489–502.

Unger, R. (1979) Toward a redefinition of sex and gender. *American Psychologist*, 34, 1085–1094.

Unger, R. (1981) Sex as a social reality: field and laboratory research. *Psychology of Women Quarterly*, 5, 645-653.

Unger, R. (1983) Through the looking glass: no wonderland yet! (The reciprocal relationship between methodology and models of reality). *Psychology of Women Quarterly*, 8, 9–32.

Unger, R. (1989) Explorations in feminist ideology: surprising consistencies and unexamined conflicts. In R. Unger (ed.), *Representations: social constructions of gender* (pp. 203–211). Amityville, NY: Baywood.

Unger, R. (1992) Will the real sex difference please stand up? *Feminism and Psychology*, 2, 231–238.

Unger, R. and Crawford, M. (1989) Methods and values in decisions about gender differences (review of *Sex differences in social behavior*). *Contemporary Psychology*, 34, 122–123.

Unger, R. and Crawford, M. (1992) *Women and gender: a feminist psychology*. New York and Philadelphia: McGraw-Hill and Temple University Press.[2nd edn in press]

Unger, R. and Crawford, M. (1993) Commentary: Sex and gender – the troubled relationship between terms and concepts. *Psychological Science*, 4, 122–124.

United Nations (1991) *The world's women 1970–1990: trends and statistics*. New York: United Nations Publications.

Unknown (1990) 'The rape' of Mr Smith. In S. Ruth (ed.), *Issues in feminism*, 3rd edn, (pp. 283–284). Mountain View, CA: Mayfield.

Walker, N. (1988) *A very serious thing: women's humor and American culture*. Minneapolis: University of Minnesota Press.

Walkerdine, V. (1988) *The mastery of reason*. New York: Routledge.

Wallston, B. and O'Leary, V. (1981) Sex makes a difference: differential perceptions of women and men. In L. Wheeler (ed.), *Review of personality and social psychology*, vol. 2 (pp. 9–41). Beverly Hills, CA: Sage.

Weisstein, N. (1968) *Kinder, Kirche, Küche as scientific law: psychology constructs the female*. Boston: New England Free Press.

Weisstein, N. (1973) *Laugh? I nearly died*. Pittsburgh, PA: Know, Inc.

West, C. (1984) When the doctor is a lady. *Symbolic Interaction*, 7, 87–106.

West, C. and Zimmerman, D. H. (1983) Small insults: a study of interruptions in cross-sex conversations between unacquainted persons. In B. Thorne, C. Kramarae, and N. Henley (eds), *Language, gender and society* (pp. 103–119). Rowley, MA: Newbury House.

West, C. and Zimmerman, D. H. (1985) Gender, language, and discourse. In T. A. van Dijk (ed.), *Handbook of discourse analysis*, vol. 4 (pp. 103–124). Orlando, FL: Academic.

West, C. and Zimmerman, D. H. (1987) Doing gender. *Gender and Society*, 1, 125–151.

White, C. (1988) Liberating laughter: an inquiry into the nature, content, and functions of feminist humor. In B. Bate and A. Taylor (eds), *Women communicating: studies of women's talk*. Norwood, NJ: Ablex Publishing Co.

Whiteley, J. M. and Flowers, J. V. (eds) (1978) *Approaches to assertion training*. Monterey, CA: Brooks/Cole.

Wiley, M. and Eskilson, A. (1982) Coping in the corporation: sex role constraints. *Journal of Applied Social Psychology*, 12, 1–11.

Wilkinson, S. (1990) Women's organizations in psychology: institutional constraints on disciplinary change. *Australian Psychologist*, 25, 256–269.

Wilkinson, S. and Burns, J. (1990) Women organizing within psychology: two accounts. In E. Burman (ed.), *Feminists and psychological practice* (pp. 140–162). London: Sage.

Wilkinson, S. and Kitzinger, C. (eds) (1993) *Heterosexism: a feminism and psychology reader*. London: Sage.

Wilkinson, S. and Kitzinger, C. (eds) (1995) *Feminism and discourse: psychological perspectives*. London: Sage.

Wine, J. D. and Smye, M. D. (eds) (1981) *Social competence*. New York: Guilford.

Wolf, N. (1991) *The beauty myth*. New York: Morrow and Co.

Wolfe, J. L. and Fodor, I. G. (1978) A cognitive/behavioral approach to modifying assertive behavior in women. In J. M. Whiteley and J. V. Flowers (eds), *Approaches to assertion training* (pp. 141–157). Monterey, CA: Brooks/Cole.

Wolpe, J. (1958) *Psychotherapy by reciprocal inhibition*. Stanford, CA: Stanford University Press.

Wolpe, J. and Lazarus, A. A. (1966) *Behavior therapy techniques: a guide to the treatment of neuroses*. Oxford: Pergamon.

Worell, J. (1988) Women's satisfaction in close relationships. *Clinical Psychology Review*, 8, 477–498.

Yarkin, K., Town, J., and Wallston, B. (1982) Blacks and women must try harder: stimulus persons' race and sex and attributions of causality. *Personality and Social Psychology Bulletin*, 8, 21–24.

Yoder, J. (1985) An academic woman as a token: a case study. *Journal of Social Issues*, 41, 61–72.

Yoder, J. and Kahn, A. (1992) Toward a feminist understanding of women and power. *Psychology of Women Quarterly*, 16, 381–388.

Zahn, C. J. (1989) The bases for differing evaluations of male and female speech: evidence from ratings of transcribed conversation. *Communication Monographs*, 56, 59–74.

Zimmerman, D. H. and West, C. (1975) Sex roles, interruptions, and silences in conversation. In B. Thorne and N. Henley (eds), *Language and sex: difference and dominance*. Rowley, MA: Newbury House.

Index